To Doctors
Earle & Webb –
with my regards –
(Please share this book.)

SPKaiser
rbkaiser @ justgoodcompany.com

D0807845

THE POLITICS OF SEX AND RELIGION

A Case History in the Development
of Doctrine, 1962-1984

Robert Blair Kaiser

Leaven Press

Copyright © 1985 by
Robert Blair Kaiser

All rights reserved. No part of this book may be reproduced or transmitted
in any form or by any means, electronic or mechanical, including photo-
copying, recording or by an information storage and retrieval system
without permission in writing from the Publisher.

Leaven Press is a service of National Catholic Reporter Publishing Inc.

Library of Congress Catalog Card Number: 84-82552
ISBN: 934134-16-2
Published by: Leaven Press
              P.O. Box 40292
              Kansas City, MO 64141
Printed and bound in the United States of America.

Dedication

To William Van Etten Casey, Jesuit, scholar, friend, who didn't think I should waste my time on this "because no one's interested in birth control any more." Stubborn, I suppose, I had to tell this most dear father that I was forging ahead. "I think this story is not so much about birth control," I told him. "It is a tale that could confirm the faith of millions who believe in a church that lives and grows—and thinks."

Acknowledgements

I wish to thank members of the Pontifical Commission for the Study of Population, the Family and Birth who granted me interviews and (in the case of some) access to their papers and correspondence: Alfons Auer of Tübingen, Thomas Burch of Toronto, Patty Crowley of Chicago, Bernard Häring of Rome, Pierre de Locht of Brussels, John Marshall of London, John T. Noonan of Berkeley, Giacomo Perico of Milan, Josef Maria Reuss of Mainz, West Germany, and Leo Josef Suenens, Cardinal-Archbishop of Malines-Brussels, Belgium.

I am also grateful to a number of other church scholars who gave me direction and guidance: to Jan Grootaers of Brussels, Arthur McCormack of London, Joseph Selling of the Catholic University of Louvain, and Warren Reich and Richard McCormick, both of the Kennedy Institute at Georgetown University.

My thanks also to Wendy Schlereth, for helping me with access to the Crowley Collection at the Archives of the University of Notre Dame.

Introduction

In the early 1960s, when I was a correspondent in Rome for *Time* magazine, I helped chronicle the most accelerated change in the history of the church. I watched two popes, more than 2,000 bishops and almost as many theologians begin to rethink everything that generations of Catholics had taken for granted, then work out, after four years of debate in the Second Vatican Ecumenical Council, a new chapter that would return the people of God to a more primitive Christianity and get them ready as well for the new kind of world that obviously lay ahead.[1]

Almost overnight, the church had a new view of what it could be: more democratic, more pluralistic, more free, more human, more humble in the face of history. And it all seemed to begin with Pope John XXIII, who asked the bishops to help him bring the church "up to date." That was a revolutionary idea in itself.

In the hundred years that preceded the council, the men who ran things in Rome had not worried much about being up to date. They had, rather, taken some radical steps to squelch those who wanted to keep pace with the times. In 1907, Pope Pius X condemned not only the heresy he called modernism, but also the men tainted with it, forcing one, an English Jesuit named George Tyrrell, out of the Society of Jesus and, at age 45, into an early grave.

Fifty-five years later, it appeared that Tyrrell had merely been a little ahead of his time. He had offended Rome by stating that formulations of the faith must change as the church moves through history. But Pope John XXIII opened his council in 1962 by announcing that he wanted to fashion a new kind of church in a new kind of world. He wanted to "meet the needs of the present day by demonstrating the validity of the church's teaching." Others could guard the faith like an ancient heirloom. He would take "a step forward toward a deeper penetration and developing realization of the faith . . . through modern research and scholarly disciplines." And then, a thought which might have come from George Tyrrell: "The substance of the faith is one thing. The way in which it is presented is quite another."

1

Those who held the highest posts in the Vatican may have blanched at this new expression, by a pope, of propositions condemned by a previous pope. One of these was the man who held the highest post of all, Alfredo Ottaviani, secretary of the Sacred Congregation of the Holy Office (later called the Congregation for the Doctrine of the Faith). Given the nature of his job, which was to guard something he called the deposit of faith, Cardinal Ottaviani could hardly cheer this call for change. Even his personal coat of arms was inscribed with the motto *Semper Idem*, "Always the Same." When I saw it in the waiting room of his office at the Pallazo Sant' Ufficio, I didn't have the temerity to ask the cardinal, "The same as what?" From my limited study of church history, I didn't know the church had had periods of flux as well as fixity. Nor did I realize how much the autumn of 1962 marked the beginning of a real revolution in the church.

At that time Pope John XXIII was leading the charge toward change, and some new Tyrrells were ready to help. They were thinkers who had been reevaluating the church's mission in the devastation of Europe after World War II, the very visionaries whose ideas had been suppressed by Pope Pius XII in the 1950s. Now, a dozen years later, they were being asked by John to help chart a reformist course.

What did they and the pope want? They would make the church less Roman and more catholic, less a church of laws, and more a church of love. The idea was to help people, not hurt them.

One example: for centuries, Catholics had abstained from flesh meat on Fridays as a penance in memory of Christ's crucifixion. That was one of the marks of being Catholic, maybe only a symbol, but an important one. Some time in the seventeenth century, however, the church's canon lawyers took over, and, as lawyers will, tried to codify the symbol. Perhaps they did this in order to tighten control of a Christendom then beginning to crumble. But the church lawyers not only described Catholics as "the folks who don't eat meat on Friday," they also decreed that any Catholic who did eat meat on Friday committed a mortal sin. They made it harder, not easier, for people to be good Christians, and in a matter that was morally indifferent.

Shortly after the council ended in 1965, the bishops went home and repealed that law, taking some pains to explain to their people: the old meatless Friday law was a church law, proscribing something that wasn't a sin in itself. If the church could make the law, the church could unmake it. Unmaking this law was part of the church's new style, called for by Pope John. But few asked what implications this repeal had for the authority of the pope and his bishops and their "power to bind consciences." Did the pope and the bishops really have that kind of power? A mischievous fellow who worked for *The New Yorker* spotlighted the arrogance of that claim with a drawing of an assistant devil asking the head devil, "What do we do with all the guys who ate meat on Friday?"

The point was: "The guys who ate meat on Friday" weren't in hell and the church hadn't sent anyone there. Leaders at Pope John's council said they had a new approach. They wanted to stop frightening people, or boring them, with "Thou-shalt-nots" and start emphasizing the Good News of Christ, a message they said would "give us joy as it calls upon us to bring forth fruit in charity for the life of the world." If people sin, the church need not condemn them, because sin depends on their free choice, not on compulsions over which they have little or no control. They condemn themselves.

This was an old idea. In the thirteenth century, Thomas Aquinas wrote that "God is not offended by us, except by reason of the fact that we act against our own good." But it sounded new to many Catholics who had grown up with the Roman Catechism. That teaching tool, and its various local translations, such as the U.S. Baltimore Catechism, preoccupied Catholics with the notion of sin, particularly sexual sins. They knew about mortal sins and venial sins and the difference between them. They knew they committed a mortal sin, one that would send them to hell if they died unrepentant: 1) when the matter was serious, 2) when they knew it was serious, and 3) when they did it anyway "with full consent of the will." Thus, stealing was a sin, and it was a "serious matter" during the 1950s if one stole more than 50 dollars. Anything less was not "serious matter," and, therefore, a venial sin.

So far, fair enough. Life would be terribly grim for most people unless the moral theologians and the confessors they trained gave them some elbow room. But in one important area the common sense broke down: sex. There, authorities said, everything was "serious matter." The expression was: *In re venerea, nulla est parvitas materiae,* "In the area of sex, there is no small matter."[2] It was a hard saying. Catholics who believed it either lived like angels or went around feeling a lot of guilt or just said, "The hell with even trying to be a good Catholic." Catholic sociologists have contended that this teaching, the Catch 22 of modern Catholicism, was the single most important factor involved in young people leaving the church.

According to church historians, this "no small matter" doctrine didn't emerge until the early part of the seventeenth century, when some Jesuits began to challenge the rigorism of contemporary Dominicans whose teachings reflected a fear of sex that has been common enough in many religious circles to this day. Soon the two orders locked in debate. Rather than let the debate help clarify things, however, the Jesuit general intervened. He told his men he knew how offensive their position was to the ears of the reigning pontiff, Pope Pius V, a Dominican. And he ordered them to keep their objections to themselves. The "no small matter" doctrine prevailed, and, for centuries, this rigorism tended to drive young people away from the church—until they married.

After marriage, however, when many of these young people who had fallen away came back, new rules faced them. Now sexual intercourse was suddenly not a sin, but part of a couple's God-given duty, for this insured the continuation of the human species. The church had been teaching this since the fourth century, when St. Augustine fought a group of heretics who were so "spiritual," at least in theory, that they didn't believe in sexual intercourse, didn't believe in having children. Then came Catch 23, although Catholic moralists didn't get specific about this until rather recently: sexual intercourse was not part of the divine plan if a couple did anything to "deliberately frustrate that act in its natural power to generate life."

These last words are from Pope Pius XI's encyclical *Casti Connubii*, promulgated in December 1930 as the church's immediate answer to a general conference of the Anglican church at Lambeth, England. The Anglicans hadn't said contraception was good, although they would, later, in 1958. They insisted that "the primary and obvious method [of limiting offspring] is complete abstinence (as far as may be necessary) in a life of discipline and self-control lived in the power of the Holy Spirit." But they allowed that contraception was permitted in special cases.

Pius XI's reaction to this was ponderous. He said he saw himself "standing in the midst of moral ruin" and compelled to condemn contraception as "an offense against the law of God and of nature" and to brand those who indulged in it "with the guilt of a grave sin." His successor, Pope Pius XII, referred to this pronouncement more than once, and ratified it, he thought, for all time: "This precept is as valid today as it was yesterday, and it will be the same always, because it does not imply a precept of human law, but is the expression of a law which is natural and divine."

And that is the way the doctrine remained, for three decades. Not even rhythm was acceptable to the rulemakers in Rome, until, after further reflection, Pope Pius XII allowed it: given good reasons, he said, such as a threat to mother's health, Catholics could practice periodic continence, that is, confine their lovemaking to times of the month when conception was impossible or, at least, unlikely. Not until 1960 did an English priest found the first Roman Catholic family planning clinic—and even that move brought him considerable grief from those who had been catechized all too well in the old notion that Catholics had a special call to have as many children as they could.

Until the fall of 1963, the method known as rhythm was the only form of birth control acceptable to "the magisterium"—a curious expression that came into vogue in the nineteenth century to describe the church's "teaching office."[3] (As we shall see, magisterium became a power word, and a fighting word as well.) Few, if any, Catholics challenged that magisterium on birth control. For three years before the council opened, Catholics from around the world were encouraged to write about their wishes for change in requests (or *postulata*) to the council. On the eve of the council, I studied these *postulata* and could not find any indications that a single Catholic bishop ever handed on a request that the church relax its strictures against contraception. This wasn't something the church could change. Most Catholics (and every bishop) knew that contraception was not wrong because the church condemned it. Rather, the church condemned it because it was wrong. And an overwhelming majority of Catholics believed that it was so gravely sinful that they could not even be forgiven for it in the confessional (unless they promised to give up this habitual crime against nature).

Not more than four years later, a papal commission would urge that the pope change the church's traditional teaching on birth control. But the pope, who had been saying that he alone would decide on this agonizing question, spurned his own commission, then had his final word in an encyclical called *Humanae Vitae*.

But it wasn't the final word. As John Carmel Heenan, cardinal-archbishop of Westminster, said then to John Todd, the British Catholic editor and publisher, "It's too late." He knew that Catholic couples the world over and their priests had already made their own decision, one diametrically opposed to the pope's. By July 1968, when *Humanae Vitae* was signed and promulgated, scientific polls showed that a preponderant majority of Catholic couples in western Europe, the United States and Canada were practicing contraception, and, by most accounts, doing so in good conscience. (Elsewhere, they didn't do much polling on these matters.)

Priests were starting to accent the positive, telling couples that marriage is a unique mystery of total self giving which finds its deepest expression in the sexual act, an embodiment of their desire to give life and children to each other. How many children? They said each couple should decide according to their own circumstances; particular birth control methods are a matter more of aesthetics than ethics, and, morally, motives are more important than methods. Couples saw the reasonability of that. They applauded those priests who did not preach against birth control, but only for "responsible parenthood."

Today, a large majority of Catholics still hold the same enlightened view, in spite of the Vatican's insistence on the old position, and the efforts of the current pope, John Paul II, and his lieutenants to make "orthodoxy" on birth control a touchstone of loyalty to Rome. Many Catholic pastors can only scratch their heads when they are asked how the pope can push a campaign against birth control with no regard for the changing belief and practice of Catholic couples over the past twenty years. Few informed priests or lay people agree with the pope's widely published position in 1984 (given during a series of 14 extraordinary discourses on birth control) that sex "ceases to be an act of love" whenever any kind of birth control is used. Catholic married couples simply yawned over this. What, they said, did the pope know? For those capable of such independent judgment, at least, birth control stopped being a moral problem. In practice, many Catholics changed their belief concerning a moral doctrine once thought unchangeable.

This book attempts to tell the story of how this happened. It is, perhaps, one of the most significant chapters in the history of the church—for the words and deeds recounted here have had an impact on far more than the birth control issue. Birth control was like a football, rather insignificant in itself, an inflated bladder covered by stitched cowhide to be kicked back and forth by two teams of sweating giants. Looking at the events 20 years later, many will see what was far more important: the playing field, the players, what they were playing for, and, significantly, the final outcome, which was toted up not by an official scorekeeper, but by the people in the stands.

That outcome threw new light on what has passed for "the church's teaching" on the meaning of sex. It also helped put in historic perspective the import of the church's authority on any moral question. In and through what came to be known as the birth control debate, many Catholics—possibly an 85 percent majority—found out that in matters of their own marital morals, the pope wasn't in charge. They were.

* * *

George A. Kelly, a New York priest who was a member of the papal birth control commission (though he appeared only briefly at commission meetings in March 1965), published an angry book in 1981 that told part of this story.[4] To Msgr. Kelly, it was a story of how the church "lost its people to contraception, and in a very few years."

I am trying to tell another version of the story. I focus mainly on the radical happenings behind the scenes in Rome, between April 1964 and June 1966, at meetings of the council's Mixed Commission on the family and of the Pontifical Commission for the Study of Population, the Family and Birth. These meetings signaled a curious, unusual moment in history. They accelerated discussion in an important inner circle of the church, and though the meetings were secret, newsleaks about them contributed to a worldwide debate and a general growth in understanding which might otherwise have taken decades.

The process helped those privy to it see how changes in church practice, almost imperceptible in ages past, could unfold much faster in a mass mediated world. This unfolding made many blink in wonder and surprise: what kind of church was this?

The new perspective made people see the church in new ways, much as the time lapse photography in movies such as Walt Disney's "Living Desert" made them see the natural world anew. In the Disney films, moviegoers watched cactus flowers bud and bloom in a few seconds. In the media, during the birth control debate, Christians observed a new kind of church blossom in three short years, to become more democratic, more pluralistic, more independent, more free—as the world itself had become during the twentieth century.

This church's tie to the world was in keeping with an old idea: the church was "incarnational," one founded, its followers believed, by God-become-flesh, by a God who chose to enter human history and start his pilgrim people on a march through that history.

In the middle of the birth control debate, churchmen and women realized some up-to-then-hidden corollaries of that idea: that men and women who are members of Christ continue to grow through time; and as extensions of the living Christ, continue to deepen understandings of their mission, but not necessarily at the same rate, and not always with the same clarity in New Zealand as in New York. Hence, in a church that was an extension in time of the Christ who had come to make men and women free, Catholics would realize that they could differ with one another, could even differ from their so-called leaders and still be good Catholics. They began to understand that there were graduations of truth and that their positions on specific moral questions could and would differ. Otherwise, they would be lost in fideism: reason could never prevail, only the fiat of a pope acting like an ayatollah who would brook no other opinion than his own.[5]

Hans Küng, the eminent Roman Catholic theologian now teaching in Tübingen and Ann Arbor, has described the general change in self-understanding as part of a "paradigm shift," a change in the way people all over the world, in the church and outside it, now see themselves in relation to old structures of power. After the council, many stopped thinking of the church as "the pope and the bishops." During the birth control debate, couples learned to stop asking, "When is the church going to do something about birth control?" Couples started doing something about it themselves. *They* were the church.

John Cogley, an American journalist covering the council, epitomized the new spirit with one of his "Poems on Postcards."

Who Is the Church?

Who?

You.

Leo Josef Suenens, the cardinal-archbishop of Malines-Brussels, put it in a slightly different way. The Belgian cardinal used a nautical metaphor. He said the church was like a ship, not one in dry dock, but one on the high seas of history.

> The church herself is the scene of great activity: crew and passengers are learning every day at what point their lot is identical and how life on board concerns all of them. . . . From a timeless church we have passed to the image of a church situated at the very heart of history. This change of imagery imposes a kind of mental revolution. We have to learn to see the church as the people of God sailing across the ages, passing from one culture to another and conditioned by history.[6]

In this story, the actors are indeed conditioned by history, by the history of the twentieth century, which, if it is about anything, is about the passing of power, from old elite institutions to the people. Many readers may recall that "Power to the People" was a rallying cry during the civil rights march on Selma, Alabama, in 1965. But this idea wasn't conceived by Martin Luther King. It was planted early in the century during the bloody struggles of the American labor movement, it germinated in the Bolshevik revolution, was watered in India by Mohandas Gandhi, and took root during World War II in the mind of a Lutheran minister named Dietrich Bonhoeffer who saw what the Nazis were doing to his country and told his people they had to resist, because they were part of "a world coming of age." When people come of age, they pass from one culture to another, from slavery where they have been the unthinking pawns of others, to freedom where they are acting persons in their own right.

This is a story about a group of loyal Catholics who became acting persons. In their deliberations and study, members of Pope Paul VI's birth control commission (and, coordinately, millions of Catholics around the world) learned that there was nothing particularly heaven sent about the ethics of marriage. They found they were not engaged in attaining truths about God, but about man and woman. If God had any messages for them on this subject, he was not communicating them via Western Union, or through the pope (who was asking *them* for their advice). They were looking out at the world around them at a particular point in time, and at their contemporaries who were trying to come to grips with their sexuality. And they were asking, "What helps people, what hurts them?"

They learned that the church's teaching on any moral matter depended on prudential judgments, as the Vatican would point out in 1983, apropos of the U.S. bishops' impending pastoral letter, "The Challenge of Peace." A Vatican memorandum said, "Bishops must not take sides when various moral choices are possible. This has to be taken into account when general moral principles are applied to concrete situations, facts, government policies, or strategies." In other words, the church is to use restraint where there are legitimate conflicting views. On the war and peace issue, it is easy for pastors to grant the notion that good Christians can agree on the ends and disagree on the means to get there.

In recent history, however, it has been more difficult for these same pastors to apply the same reasonability to any moral matter having to do with sex. Here, some continue to hammer out sets of rigid rules (nothing in this area being "small matter") and insist that people follow them, or be damned.

But the pope's commission could see these rules were not revealed on Mt. Sinai or chiseled in granite. The world was changing, people were changing. And most of the members of the papal commission felt that pastors who kept promulgating all the old rules ran the risk of giving bad guidance. When the U.S. bishops finally issued the final draft of their peace pastoral in 1984, they were not looking at a world that armed itself with bows and arrows, but with megaton nuclear warheads. New factors, new risks, new rules.

In the area of sex and marriage morality, the members of this papal birth control commission knew they were living in the midst of a revolution of rising expectations. Those in advanced western societies had rejected the idea of arranged marriages. For the first time, perhaps, love was seen to be "of the essence" of marriage. Women were beginning to see themselves as chattel no longer, to be used by their husbands as baby machines or cooks or homemakers, but as full human beings who had the same options men had, if they chose to take them.

The impact of such a new Zeitgeist on the birth control question was obvious. A woman tied to babymaking and homemaking duties could not easily work as a lawyer, or a research biologist or a television newswoman. If she wanted motherhood, she might have to schedule it in a ten-year plan.

Perhaps this is why the birth control debate came with the suddenness and force that it did. Until the people of God (half of whom are women) could resolve this moral problem, there would be no progress possible for the women of the world. Progress had to come on two fronts. Before the feminine revolution could really take hold, someone had to develop a relatively easy, safe, aesthetic form of birth control, like the pill. And then, others had to determine that it was an entirely moral act to actually use the pill in family planning. Only then could the movement move ahead to meet other challenges, not the least of them hurled down by Pope John Paul II himself, whose view of women is more than a century out of date.

At the synod of 1980, some bishops looked on the women's movement and saw that it was good. Robert Lebel, bishop of Valleyfield, Quebec, said, "The state of submission and oppression which women are subjected to in the world is a sinful situation. . . . The church ought to recognize as positive the modern feminist movement: It is a question, as a whole, of progress within civilization and it is one more step in the coming of the kingdom." He urged that the church start finding ways for women to play roles in the church as important as those of men.

But in the closing session of the synod on October 25, Pope John Paul II vetoed Bishop Lebel's sentiments by translating them this way:

In words both opportune and persuasive the synod has spoken of woman with reverence and a grateful spirit, especially of her dignity and vocation as a daughter of God, as a wife and as a mother. It is commendably asked that women should not be forced to engage in external work, proper to a certain role, or, as they say, profession, but rather so that the family might be able to live rightly, that the mother might devote herself fully to the family.[7]

In Poland, perhaps, a woman's place is in the home. To a Polish pope, this seems only proper. But a church that calls itself catholic, or universal, needs a pope with a wider vision. For all his charisma with crowds, for all his energy and zeal, this pope has the decided limitations of his own culture and of his own nation. They are understandable enough: had he spent his life in Cincinnati and Chicago instead of Krakow and Rome, he might think more like Phil Donahue than St. Stanislaus Kostka.

But the pope is a Pole. This may be a major problem for the church in the 1980s. But it is only temporary. This, too, shall pass. A bigger problem: those in the church who pay almost sacramental homage to any pope. According to Gabriel Daly, an Irish Augustinian who had made a study of modernism in the church:

The role of the papacy in all this has been, and remains, paramount. No question in contemporary Catholicism, however, is proving more intractable or more acutely sensitive. Room for constuctive maneuver is menacingly small. The collegial ideal which might have been the queen of Vatican II's achievements is now a sleeping princess.

The people of God will, of course survive, maybe even mature at a faster rate if they have to suffer this pope and his efforts to turn the church back to the way it was before the council. They know that the pope, after all, is not the church. They know that the synod of bishops which will meet in Rome in November 1985 cannot have the authority or the credibility of the Second Vatican Ecumenical Council. That council took three and a half years of preparation and four years of unfettered debate, all of it a spontaneous and democratic expression of a universal church that had shivered for too long under the chilly authoritarianism of previous ages. The 1985 synod will meet for two weeks, which is just about enough time for this pope to impose his singular views on the bishops who show up.

I suspect there are not many among the people of God who will accept such an approach. They will see it, I believe, as little more than an old papal power trip, and go on claiming the freedom of their own charisms, no matter what the pope tells them to think. Prelates and priests around the world who do not want to build up the battlements but share their goodness with others will draw their own maps for another kind of trip.

Andrew Greeley, priest and scholar and man of faith, has maintained that churchmen will still have a place in the new world. They will have "powers of persuasion and inspiration—not inconsiderable powers for religious leaders even if some leaders' skills in such powers have atrophied from infrequent exercise."

The church has resources (Greeley wrote) to provide illumination, motivation, direction, vision and reinforcement for the agonies and the ambiguities in the human search for growth and fulfillment in sexual intimacy. To the extent that church leaders are willing to turn their attentions to such tasks they will have a ready audience when they speak of sexual matters. When, however, church leaders issue rules, laws, orders, proclamations, prohibitions and denunciations on matters of human sexuality, no one will listen to them.

No one will listen until churchmen (and women) have something to say that is worth listening to and in ways that are not boring. Churchmen (and women) might consider leaving their old moralisms behind and learning the art their Lord knew so well, the art of storytelling. The new politics of persuasion demand that much. And if they have to moralize, they might consider doing so in something less than thunderous tones. Richard McCormick, the Jesuit moral theologian from Washington, D.C., cites the 1976 pastoral letter of Francis J. Mugavero, bishop of Brooklyn, "Sexuality —God's Gift."[8]

Bishop Mugavero wrote, "We do not fear sexuality, we embrace it. What we fear at times is our own inability to think as highly of the gift as does the God who made us sexual beings."

Commented Father McCormick:

Mugavero's language and tone meet people where they are. Tone, in moral matters, is not everything, but it is enormously important; for it reveals attitudes toward persons, norms, conflicts, God, the human condition. Because this is so, tone not only affects communicability; at some point it also cuts very close to the basic value judgments themselves.

* * *

Who might care about any of this?

Perhaps scholars of every stripe who are fascinated by the history of ideas.

Perhaps men and women of other religions who believe they, too, must grow and adapt to a new kind of world. I don't think they can read here about the church's agony, wrestling with the birth control debate and about the way people struck a *modus vivendi* after that struggle was over, without considering it a cautionary tale. They must realize that the most well educated members of their own churches are losing their parochialism in an increasingly mass mediated world. These church members may fall away from the faith of their fathers if they cannot reconcile that faith with everything else in their lives that they find good and rewarding.

Others might also care: teachers, social workers, doctors, nurses and others in the helping professions. It may be true, as some claim, that many Catholics now practice birth control "in good conscience." But, according to physicians who work in a new branch of medicine that goes under the general name of "psychosomatic," too many women who practice birth control are still afflicted with deep guilt about it. Often enough, say the doctors, they "embody" their guilt in cancers of the breast and ovaries. It is clear to me that these women need a kind of liberation. Perhaps that will come here in these pages, where they can read about a saintly band of papal advisors who thought long and hard about this question, and came to new understandings which they dared to assert even when they knew the assertion would pain the pope. I consider them heroes and heroines. Their example and the power of their reason (not the power of power) should help others think new, unguilty thoughts, and act upon them, freely and with mature understanding.

Men and women in public life, especially those with Catholic constituencies, might also be pleased to get an inside, demythologizing glimpse into the politics of sex and religion. Once they see how the church has gone through the throes of working out new ecclesiologies and new ethics, maybe they will feel freer than they do now to seize active leadership on questions of population control, and, therefore, on other matters dealing with world hunger and, ultimately, with world peace.

* * *

I disagree with Monsignor Kelly's view that the church has "lost its people to contraception."

In the first place, the church, by common agreement of the Second Vatican Ecumenical Council, *is* the people, priests and non-priests alike. Only Monsignor Kelly's clerical view of the church puts the priest-people on one side and the people-people on the other.

In the second place, few of the people of God in the postconciliar church are "lost." I rather think they feel good about being part of a church that is trying, at last, to understand that God didn't make a mistake when he gave them a gift that could find such an easy and satisfying expression in the act that is called "making love." Otherwise, how explain that these days, in contrast to the days before Vatican II, 95 percent of the people in the pews will approach the communion rail week after week without going to confession first? Have they lost their sense of sin or only freed themselves from the notion that sin was what priests and nuns *told* them was sinful?

But that may be the most important point of all. I call this tale *The Politics of Sex and Religion* because it is a story of how churchmen tried to use old anathemas on birth control (and, by extension, on all the so-called sexual sins) in order to maintain a power that was under assault. Churchmen had established the power relationship centuries before (in the thirteenth, to be exact) by instituting the practice of confession. Confession put men and women under their subjection. Michel Foucault, the French philosopher, explains:

> Confession is a ritual that unfolds within a power relationship, for one does not confess without the presence (or virtual presence) of a partner who is not simply the interlocutor but the authority who requires the confession, prescribes and appreciates it, and intervenes in order to judge, punish, forgive, console, and reconcile. . . .[9]

Those who understand what the battle over birth control really meant have escaped this kind of slavery. When the battle was over, the balance of power had shifted, away from priest (and pope) and toward the people. For them, it was not a question of seizing power, but opting for something which liberationists of all stripes call "empowerment," a fashionable word that means nothing more than what we used to call growing up.

This is really a story of how the people of God grew up, and in a very few years.

Del Mar, California
January 1985

Chapter One

The first open break in the dike started, appropriately enough, in The Netherlands. On March 21, 1963, Willem Bekkers, bishop of 's-Hertogen-bosch, went on KRO, the Catholic broadcasting station in Holland, and questioned the traditional teaching on several counts. He talked of "birth regulation" rather than "birth control" and called it "an integral part of the total task entrusted to married people." And what did birth regulation mean? Said Bekkers: ". . . man has got to project the number of his offspring against the whole, kaleidoscopic background of his married life; there is no particular merit in having a large or a small family. . . . The couple, and they alone, decide what the size of their family should be and what span of time there should be between the births of their children. Their human love and sense of responsibility may encourage them to create a large or a small family, to expand or to limit. This is a matter for their own consciences, with which nobody must interfere."

Bekkers warned against every technique of birth control, even rhythm, because each was a possible threat to "mutual love and faithfulness," and insisted that not even rhythm presented a definitive answer for many couples. "There may be certain situations," he said, "in which it is impossible to be mindful of all and every Christian and human value at the same time." He called for a discussion of this question and expressed the hope that an exchange of ideas could help his people "arrive at often unexpected views and pointers for our own lives."[10]

Birth control was not on the Vatican Council's agenda, but on August 10, partly to deflect some criticism from Rome that had rained down on the Dutch church for Bekkers' remarks, the bishops of Holland proposed that the council, already a year along in its work, take up the question. By the time the second council session began in the fall of 1963, there was talk around Rome of Bekkers' forthright statement and of the Dutch hierarchy's proposal. In the open climate created by the council, that was enough to start some theologians talking about Bekkers' challenge.

More and more frequently during the extra-conciliar gatherings of October and November 1963, I would hear, or overhear, some theologians

15

saying that, whether birth control was on the docket or not, the council had to take up the question. They weren't saying this was the most important issue before the church, but one problem that needed a new look.

World leaders were then engaged in serious discussions about "the population explosion." And some church demographers informed and reflected that concern. Many Catholic social scientists accepted predictions that the world's population would double in 35 years, and they also agreed that the church ought to try to help the human race by approving, in certain parts of the world, at least, the production of fewer babies and more food.

This wasn't a radical view, not even in Rome. The official church had already helped promote this shift. There had been a time, not so very many years before, when "good Catholic families" were "large Catholic families." Churchmen found ingenious ways of getting that idea across. In the 1940s, Thomas A. Connolly, archbishop of Seattle, Washington, took over the baptismal ceremonies when a couple produced their twelfth child, and the people of Seattle would generally find a picture in Monday's *Post-Intelligencer* of the squalling baby, the proud mother and a smiling Archbishop Connolly.

That attitude was changing. As far back as 1954, Pope Pius XII told delegates to the World Population Conference in Rome that the church was not ignorant of population problems and was trying to do something about them. He referred to his statement in 1951, when he gave the church's first official approval to the rhythm method and expressed the hope that scientists "would succeed in giving to this method a sufficiently sure basis" because the church "looks with sympathy and understanding on the real difficulties of married life in our times."

Pope John XXIII made pertinent references to population problems in his major encyclicals, *Mater et Magistra* and *Pacem in Terris*, insisting there is no single population problem but varied population problems in different areas of the world that cannot be answered simplistically, as by sterilization in India, but require thorough readjustments in three general areas: economic, demographic and cultural.

In 1953, when Pope Paul VI was an undersecretary of state in the Vatican, he sent a letter to the Twenty Sixth Italian Catholic Social Week, attempting to answer those who said the church was "preventing" solutions to the population problem. He made five points: 1) population problems are of extreme importance, 2) they are not merely economic, but also have a moral and religious character, 3) they have a vital bearing on world peace, 4) they can have no solution which does not have a due regard for the sacred and inviolable value of human life, and, 5) goods created by God for all people should reach all people.

No real problem, then, about the end. Population and fertility control were becoming more and more acceptable. The only question lay in the means. But the means available to Catholics were narrow: any intervention other than the rhythm method was immoral.

Then, in the spring of 1963, John Rock of Boston challenged the church to reevaluate this position with publication of *The Time Has Come: A Catholic Doctor's Proposals to End the Battle Over Birth Control*. Dr. Rock was a professor at Harvard, and one of the men who helped develop the birth control pill. He was a Catholic (his own bishop, Richard Cushing, resisted pressures to make Rock an ex-Catholic) and he was saying this pill didn't have to violate the norms of Pope Pius XII. To him, the pill was a "morally permissible variant of the rhythm method."

He didn't get far with co-religionists in his own country. Catholic moralists, in particular, were scathing in their criticism. Rock was not a theologian. What did he know? Pope Pius XII had already condemned Rock's pill five years before. There was no need for further discussion. Informed U.S. Catholics seemed to agree with the American moralists. They regarded Rock as a good physician and a bad ethician.

In Rome, other theologians were saying those priests may have been too quick to condemn. Pope Paul VI's own private theologian, Bernard Häring, a German Redemptorist teaching in Rome, was somewhat open to Rock's suggestion. In an interview during the last week of January 1964, Father Häring told me, concerning the pill, "We have a right to help nature." He said he saw no reason women couldn't take the pill to help "obtain a normal cycle." He didn't know whether the Rock pill could be considered temporary sterilization, but noted that advances made in pharmaceuticals and synthetic production of estrogen and progesteron were proceeding apace. He expressed the hope that scientists would soon find "a Catholic pill" that would "perfect natural functions"—that is, not inhibit ovulation completely, but rather make it possible for a woman to ovulate every month, when she wanted to. He thought a pill called "Duphaston" might be the answer.

And then, Häring changed the ground of our discussion. He said it was important for him that the church not persist in asking Catholic couples to take "a moralistic, sin-centered approach" to this question. He wanted to see couples give themselves to each other in meaningful acts of true love. The church ought to be most concerned with helping couples see and correct the things that hurt them most: selfishness, childish behavior, exploitation of each other. Parenthood should be "responsible"—governed by wisdom and justice to all—husband, wife, children, even society. But, to Häring, how people achieved responsible parenthood was secondary.

Father Häring was a lean, almost cadaverous fellow with cool blue eyes, but his manner was warm, enthusiastic. He took the initiative, and suggested other theologians in the church were trying to reevaluate church teachings on marriage as he was. He listed their names: a dozen theologians in Europe, who, he believed, might open up to me, especially if they could speak candidly without being identified. Reporters call this protocol "not-for-attribution"—a newsgathering mode used in Washington and elsewhere to protect sources who might get in trouble with their superiors for their candor with the press.

And so, in February 1964, I set out on an unusual special assignment for *Time*. I went to The Netherlands first, to see Leo Alting von Geusau, a priest from Groningen who directed the Dutch Documentation Center in conciliar Rome. He had been one of the regulars who gathered at my Roman apartment every Sunday night during the first two council sessions, a friend, and my best source on the church in Holland. I had never asked him about birth control.[11]

But now, as we were driving into Amsterdam from the airport, he told me that they'd been discussing this issue here for some time. Years before, the Dutch bishops had ordered staff members of Dutch Catholic Action to organize an opinion survey on seven aspects of marriage as it was lived in The Netherlands. The staff made a second poll of doctors and priests to find out how they dealt with particular marriage problems they encountered in their daily work. And finally, the staff asked twenty of the country's best theologians what they thought about Catholics using birth control pills.

Father von Geusau said the study took two years. On December 7, 1962, the bishops got a 470-page report which "opened their eyes." A high percentage of Catholics found official church teaching and preaching on marriage totally inadequate. The bishops also learned that of the twenty theologians giving opinions on the pill, eighteen believed that contraception by means of the pill most widely used in The Netherlands was "tolerable" or "good." Only two said it was illicit.

With such a report in their hands, the Dutch bishops could hardly help but open up a bit. Some opened up more than others and Willem Bekkers of 's-Hertogenbosch perhaps more than most. Von Geusau said, "Bishop Bekkers is a courageous man. He is not a theologian himself. He was a parish priest before he became a bishop. Like Pope John, he is intuitive. When he doesn't know what to do, but feels as a pastor what is right, he does it. He is a courageous man."

"Do all the Dutch bishops agree with Bishop Bekkers?" I asked von Geusau.

"Many do," he said. "In August, they issued a private instruction on the pill to all their priests. They said they didn't have clear cut answers. They said that new opinions about men and women and human sexuality have raised new questions and that theologians are divided on the answers to these questions. They said they hoped the council would deal with this question (so the whole church could be involved, not just the church of Holland)."

"And what advice," I asked, "are priests supposed to give their people?"

"In general," he said, "they are supposed to say that anti-conception is not good, but that birth control pills are licit in particular instances because theologians are divided on the matter."

I whistled. If that were so, and Catholics around the world were to know it, then I could see a possible solution to the question. If theologians were divided, the church's strictures against birth control pills were in the category of "doubtful law." My Jesuits had taught me that "a doubtful law does not oblige." And why not? Because life would be too grim if, in doubtful matters, a person always had to opt for the safer, stricter course. A matter was said to be "in doubt" if reputable authorities were divided.

But *were* the authorities divided? It seemed to be a question best answered by a reporter. I would soon see.

* * *

Von Geusau wasn't about to let me see only one side of the pill question. We visited Hendrik Rottinghuis, director of obstetrics and gynecology at Amsterdam's largest Catholic hospital, who said that if there were no moral question about the pill, there might be a medical one. Dr. Rottinghuis said he had many medical reservations about its continued use. The pill was "contra-indicated" in patients with an abnormal liver, in patients suffering from hypertension, in patients with a history of diabetes, heart, liver or kidney trouble. "The side effects of this pill are so deep that a doctor must have very good reasons to prescribe them. You can't hand these things out like peppermints." He said he felt all right about recommending the pill on a short term basis, especially when he was helping a woman regularize her period. "But with young women who have ten or fifteen fertile years ahead, I can't take a chance. I really can't imagine there's a right way to suppress a woman's fertility for any great span of her life."

Rottinghuis said he and his staff preferred prescribing the rhythm method to patients seeking help on spacing their children, "even though it is easier and less time consuming to hand our patients the pill. For the first months, we have to give a couple close guidance in rhythm. It's a method that is easier for more experienced couples. For younger couples, it is harder, and so we have to lead them, they have to grow to that method." He implied that in these cases, he did prescribe the pill or even a condom or diaphragm. "We try to go to the perfect. We don't get there right away, but we keep trying. There is so much more stress in this culture we live in today, and so, if the same control insisted on in past ages is not possible, we have to find new solutions. Pope Pius XII called for that. So did Cardinal Suenens."

I nodded at the reference to Leo Josef Suenens, archbishop of Malines-Brussels. Since 1958, the cardinal had been holding conferences in Belgium to consider the problem of population control, presiding over a group of demographers and sociologists, physicians and theologians, most of them Catholic, to see what, if anything, the church could contribute to the solution of something they all agreed needed attention. Many in the church were saying openly that the church wasn't against population control, only that it didn't want to see people use methods that would hurt them.

Less than a year before this in Rome, Igino Cardinale, an undersecretary of state at the Vatican, had received Donald Straus, president of the International Planned Parenthood Federation, and assured him the church was as concerned as he was about the population explosion. Straus phoned me when he was in Rome, at the suggestion of Monsignor Cardinale. The monsignor had told him, "Mr. Kaiser has some good insights on this question." I was somewhat embarrassed by this: I didn't have any special insights, and suspected that Monsignor Cardinale wanted *Time* magazine to know that Planned Parenthood was in town and the Vatican was not un friendly to the goals of Planned Parenthood. Cardinale was American-born but possessed of a fine Italian hand. More important, he was part of an inner guard close to Pope John.

If I had had better instincts at the time, I might have pursued this line with Cardinale, might even have discovered that Pope John XXIII had appointed a six-man commission to advise him on the birth control question. Pope John died before that group met, but he had established a precedent for his successor, Paul VI. The six members of that group, all regulars at Cardinal Suenens' yearly conferences, were: Stanislaus de Lestapis, a French Jesuit specializing in the sociology of the family; John Marshall, a British physician who had pioneered the temperature rhythm method in a successful experiment on the Isle of Mauritius; Clement Mertens, a Belgian Jesuit and demographer; Henri de Riedmatten, a Swiss Dominican who worked as a Vatican observer at the United Nations in Geneva; Pierre Van Rossum, a Brussels physician; and Jaques Mertens de Wilmars, a professor at Louvain in Belgium.

But at this point, I knew nothing of that commission. It had met only once—on October 12 and 13, 1963—in Louvain (during the second session of the council). I only knew that The Netherlands seemed to be where the most avant-garde thinking was going on. And now I was interviewing a Dutch Catholic physician who still believed firmly in rhythm.

Dr. Rottinghuis was proud to report that 87 percent of his patients were on rhythm. "It's psychologically better and helps a couple mature together in their love. The opposite, or contraceptive, mentality makes women feel frustrated and exploited. Some of them complain, 'Why is it that you doctors always make us the guinea pigs? Why don't you find some pills for men to take?' " He smiled at the common sense logic of this. "So far, we've had more luck tempering the woman's fertility. But if we do live in such a stressful civilization, maybe we have to find some drugs to suppress the libido of the husband. Oh, there are such drugs. But they have disastrous side effects. Men grow breasts. Their eyeballs turn red. Or green."

* * *

Bishop Bekkers was to receive me and Father von Geusau at ten in the morning, in his home across the street from the fifteenth century Gothic cathedral of St. Jan in the middle of 's-Hertogenbosch (which means "the duke's woods"), then a town of 85,000 about 50 miles southeast of Amsterdam. The bishop's auxiliary, Jan Bluyssen, appeared in the parlor first, all smiles. He explained that Bekkers had been sick with the flu for three days, but definitely wanted to see me. Bishop Bluyssen poured coffee and said he had heard that the Dutch bishops were no longer alone on the frontiers of this question.

"Bishop Josef Reuss, he is the rector of the seminary in Mainz, has just published a provocative article on the birth control question in the *Tübinger Theologische Quartalschrift,*" said Bluyssen. "And I hear that the auxiliary bishop of Strasbourg has finished a new book on marriage called *Mysterium Magnum.*"

He told me there had been a quiet, scholarly effort for some time in the church to create a whole new anthropology of marriage. "We're trying," he said, "to break down the static ideas about man according to the medieval notions of natural law."

"Static?"

"As opposed to dynamic or changing," he said. He explained that theologians had been accustomed to thinking about man "as an abstraction, apart from the concrete and changing circumstances of his daily life." Traditional theologians, he said, had taken an entirely biological definition of the word "natural" applied to sexual intercourse. "They looked at the coital act itself outside of its larger context, that is, as a part of love and marriage. You can't build a whole system of morals on that."

Then Bekkers entered the parlor, his eyes puffy, whether from sleep or from the effects of the flu, I could not tell. He was a man of little more than medium height, with the solidity of a linebacker in the National Football League. He had heavy eyebrows and straight dark hair starting to thin on top. We exchanged some pleasantries. He recalled when we had first met, at a reception in October at the Rome Hilton.

In English, I asked Bekkers his reasons for asserting that the lawfulness of the pill was still an "open question."

Bekkers turned to Father von Geusau and said, in Dutch, "He's going to see Father Schillebeeckx later, isn't he?" Von Geusau nodded, told him we had an appointment with Schillebeeckx that very evening. Schillebeeckx was one of the world's most distinguished Roman Catholic theologians. Bekkers told me he was glad I was seeing Schillebeeckx. He then settled back and said the church would have to reevaluate its prime document on this question. He was referring to *Casti Connubii*, the encyclical Pope Pius XI promulgated in 1930.

Bekkers said reevaluation would have to come, "no matter whether one takes it as a disciplinary document or a doctrinal statement. In the first place, an encyclical is not infallible. Some may object and say, " 'Yes, but when a teaching gets the consensus of all the bishops, then you have to regard it as authentic teaching.' " Bekkers said he wasn't quite sure there had ever been, or was now, a real consensus of the bishops: "What may seem like a consensus may be a mere slavish and subservient parroting of the pope's words."

Bekkers explained the difference between a consensus of the bishops and the consensus of the church. Only a consensus of the entire church, all the faithful, determined "Catholic" positions on faith and morals. Perhaps because he was a pastor first and an administrator second, Bekkers seemed to put great weight into his argument based on the "concensus of the faithful." I asked whether we were going to determine right and wrong by putting things to a ballot, with a "moral"choice going to the side that had the most votes.

"Not at all," he said. "The people of God have the Holy Spirit among them." It was a simple statement, but not even the great John Henry Newman, who had written a seminal work in 1878 called "On Consulting the Faithful on Matters of Doctrine," had put it any better. Bishop Bekkers went on: "The people have troubles. They are inquiring. And so I argue this way: if I see people in the church not going to communion, because they feel guilty in violating the ban on contraception, and I know they are the kind of people who would otherwise be going to communion, then I say this is a reason for reconsidering the entire question."

Bekkers warned that it would be wrong for me to write my report as if I were telling Catholics whether or not they could use the pill. The story, he said, goes much deeper. He kept insisting and Bishop Bluyssen chimed in in agreement, that everything within a marriage, including the biological elements, "must serve the highest value of marriage."

But what *was* the highest value of marriage? Ever since *Casti Connubii*, Roman authorities had come down hard on any theologian who dared assert that the primary end of marriage was not "the procreation and education of children." Now Bekkers and Bluyssen were saying that wasn't primary, but rather "the mutual love between husband and wife." They felt comfortable with this assertion, no matter what Rome had said in 1944. But I knew I was not going to hear the end of this argument soon, especially when Bekkers added that the church had to interpret *Casti Connubii* within the context of the time it was written, and that progressive movements within the church would lead to "a development in the church, even of dogma. The context of a dogma can change. And we are now in a new context."

He referred to the special report (or *relatio*) of Emile Josef DeSmedt, bishop of Bruges, Belgium, a stirring speech that had introduced the text on religious liberty to the council fathers the previous November. This address had drawn the loudest, most prolonged applause in the council thus far—a significant event, because Bishop DeSmedt had eloquently argued for the necessity of both continuity and change in doctrinal matters. Bekkers said he believed the church was in an evolutionary stage in the marriage question. "The pill itself is in evolution," he said, "and our team here of moralists are all in evolution."

I asked him what he meant by the pill being "in evolution."

"I hear they are refining it," he said. "Perhaps not so much of an estrogen count?" Laughingly, he recalled hearing about a case where a doctor prescribed the pill for a mother of five. Whether for psychological or physical reasons, no one knew, but, Bekkers said, the pill made the woman's libido soar. "She was so wild. She wanted her husband five times a day, and he couldn't deliver. In this case, the pill was a bad thing. It was ruining the marriage."

* * *

From Bishop Bekkers' residence, Father von Geusau drove me to a town called Oss, in the middle of Bekkers' diocese. Oss was the home of The Netherlands' largest pharmaceutical house, Organon. Organon manufactured Lyndiol, a pill very much like the American Enovid, made by Lederle. Cost: $1.20 for twenty pills, a month's supply. Dutch physicians were prescribing Lyndiol to women who were having trouble regulating their monthly cycles or needed to space their babies (or avoid any more children at all). In this predominantly Catholic part of The Netherlands, 90 percent of Organon's 2,000 employees were Catholic, but most of these worked in the plant's factory. Among the executives, there was only one Catholic, a young, rosy-cheeked research physician named Hendrik van Kaap.

Dr. van Kaap was Organon's ad director. As such, he had to be able to talk to the company chemists, understand what they were doing, then formulate Organon's approach to the public, write ad copy, tell detailmen what to say and what not to say. He was responsible for Organon's public image. As we drove up to the modernistic brick, aluminum and glass headquarters that dominated Oss, I wondered how van Kaap could reconcile his professional position with his faith.

"It wasn't easy for me at first," he confessed in his office over the omnipresent Dutch cup of coffee. "I went through some kind of crisis before I was able to take this job." Instead of saying to himself, "My faith is one thing and my job is another" (as I suspected some American Catholics must have been doing at that moment in history), van Kaap talked to Bishop Bekkers and to Dutch theologians to learn their opinion about the pill.

After a series of long, earnest and sometimes technical conversations, their verdict came in: take the job. "Since that time," he said, "the climate has changed a lot. At first, we didn't even talk about Lyndiol as a contraceptive, we just said it was for menstrual disorders. We didn't want to make trouble. But things change fast here. I lectured on this subject on a panel with some theologians last June. The talk I'm going to give tonight"—he waved some notes in front of me—"will be very different." By different, I supposed he meant more frank.

"When I talk to theologians," he said, "I must clarify my words and my descriptions of the key processes [that occur when a woman takes the pill] as much as possible, then leave it to the theologians to make the moral judgments. Then I have to listen to their explanations to see if they have understood me correctly."

I asked van Kaap about the possible side effects of the pill. He reported that the U.S. Federal Drug Administration's original report that the pill could cause thrombophlebitis (blood clotting) was a simple arithmetical error. Where a figure should have read "200," it falsely read "2,000," and that, explained van Kaap, accounted for the original FDA report, then, shortly afterward, its hurried retraction. Van Kaap told me Gregory Pincus, the inventor, with John Rock, of the birth control pill, had ruled out the possibility that the pill could cause cancer. He did allow that the medical profession would have to do continual research in this area, but he took an airy view of the fears expressed by Hendrik Rottinghuis in Amsterdam.

"The use of tranquilizers probably kills some brain cells every time you take one," he observed. "But nobody says anything about that. The trouble is that the pill is connected with sex, and that creates all kinds of fears that somehow we are offending the gods.

"You find so many people worrying about those poor shrinking ovaries," he said, referring to another invariable side effect: a woman on the pill soon found that her ovaries had shrunk to a third their normal size; they seemed to resemble the ovaries of a woman who had gone through menopause. "But," he added, "we see the rebound phenomenon and we see that nature takes care." Physicians were finding that the pill could help a woman *have* babies. These doctors would put a woman on the pill for a few months, then take her off. Result: the hitherto barren patient would not only conceive, she might even have twins or triplets. Experts called this "ovulation rebound."

I asked van Kaap whether pill use was on the rise. He apologized for not being able to reveal his company's sales figures. I learned later that Organon's pill business was growing at a rate of 40 percent a year in The Netherlands, the United Kingdom and Egypt, Organon's principal markets, but he allowed that the pill was becoming common in The Netherlands. He said that he had heard that boys out on a first serious date with a girl were starting to ask, "Are you on the pill?"

Boys? Girls? Dates? Up to this point my inquiries had focused on the efforts of certain liberal churchmen to reevaluate the church's teachings on the pill within marriage. I began to realize that, whatever the church taught or didn't teach about the pill, that pill was going to bring on profound changes in society, and that moralists could well ask what effect the pill would have on the sex life of the unmarried.

On that score alone, I could foresee shaking of heads and wagging of fingers among members of the old guard. To these, sex had only one justification: begetting children. Once you started allowing couples the pleasures of sex without the concomitant duty of procreation, weren't you setting up a new kind of sex-oriented culture, a new heaven on earth which would compete with the church's classic reward system? In fact, several characters in John Updike's novel, *Couples*, would soon be overheard to say before some extracurricular and impromptu lovemaking, "Welcome to the post-pill paradise."

*　*　*

As a large grandfather clock was chiming 8 p.m., Edward Schillebeeckx, Willem van der Marck and David LeFort received me and von Geusau in Father Schillebeeckx's beautiful, book-lined study at the Collegium Albertinum in Nijmegen. The three of them, garbed in immaculate white Dominican habits, stood around a low table set with coffee cups, murmuring welcomes and inviting us to join them in after-dinner drinks and cigars.

Schillebeeckx, his hair prematurely white, opened his palm to the table, indicating at least seven cigar boxes, each filled with a different brand. The Dutch, I was learning, were great smokers, but the evening became so intellectually absorbing that I could not recall whether any of us touched a cigar or even a cigarette. I vaguely remember gulping one cup of coffee.

Father van der Marck, tall, fair and in his mid-thirties, had joined us at the insistence of von Geusau and of Schillebeeckx, because he had just published a revisionist view of the pill in *Tijdschrift voor Theologie*, a learned journal edited in Nijmegen. I had seen an English abstract of the piece, which had van der Marck stating, "Fertility control is not only licit and approved by the church, it is a Christian responsibility. As for the means to be employed in fertility control, the rhythm method has until now received exclusive approval, not, indeed, because it is so 'natural' (human nature obviously includes technique), but, as the history of this question reveals, because it does not interfere with the marital act itself. In this respect, the pill offers no difficulty. The question of its actual goodness or badness must thus be answered from other perspectives: health, growth in mutual love or alienation, etc., more or less as in the case of the rhythm method. Good reasons must exist for its use and thus everything depends upon the personal attitude and mentality of the married couple."

Father LeFort, an American member of the Dominican order who had been studying under Schillebeeckx for two and a half years, was there as a translator. Schillebeeckx spoke English and a half dozen other languages, and never needed LeFort to interpret for me. But he preferred the precision of his Dutch and LeFort's careful translation from Dutch to English so his thought could come through exactly. "This," he said, "is the kernel of what I wrote for the Dutch bishops' pastoral letter on marriage in 1960. I've incorporated it into a book which we're waiting to publish."

I turned a questioning look in the direction of von Geusau. He explained later that publication of the Dutch bishops' pastoral in Italy had caused some little furor in the Vatican. The Dutch bishops quickly withdrew the Italian translation from circulation, and they even tried to keep Schillebeeckx out of circulation for awhile. They did that by not naming him as an official expert, or *peritus*, at the council, so he would not have to go through the Vatican equivalent of a security clearance.

I understood. The American bishops had done the same in the case of John Courtney Murray, a New York Jesuit stationed at Woodstock, Maryland, whose writings on chuch-state relations had incurred the wrath of Cardinal Ottaviani in Rome. The then-usual results: Murray was forbidden by his Jesuit superiors to publish anything on church-state questions. During the council's second session, Francis Spellman, cardinal-archbishop of New York, brought Father Murray to Rome as his personal theologian, then had him named as *peritus* when the tide started to turn in favor of the council's declaration on religious liberty.

Schillebeeckx said he saw a ladder of values in marriage, with love at the top and biology at the bottom. "Since the biological value is secondary, or lower," he said, "its exclusion can be justified by reason of the highest value. As this exclusion is taken up into the interpersonal relationship, then the damage to the integrity is removed. If there can be no more children in marriage, then use of the pill can be justified by reason of its being taken up into the higher value. In this case, the love removes the element which would secondarily damage the integrity of the whole. If the use of the pill, however, is not taken up into the higher level, then the integrity of the relationship is damaged."

"Taken up?" I said I didn't understand.

Schillebeeckx explained. "If a couple uses the pill in a seeking for mere erotic play, then they remain on the biological level. On the other hand, if the erotic play leads to greater love . . ."

I nodded.

"In any single act within marriage," continued Schillebeeckx, "it is not necessary that all values be present, but it is always necessary that the first, or highest, value be there even though, in the concrete, the self-giving may be lacking, man being what he is, never perfectly unselfish in this life."

What impact would this thinking have on current questions concerning the pill? Schillebeeckx said mechanical contraceptives "*may* disturb the number one value as it is expressed in the corporality." It was a celibate's guess, stated in carefully abstract language, that a couple at play couldn't stop to insert a diaphragm or roll on a rubber without in some way damaging the beauty of their lovemaking (which may be true for some couples and not for others, depending on contingent factors, including their sense of humor). In that sense, Schillebeeckx said he favored the pill "because taking the pill is outside the personal act," which, I supposed, would be true if a woman were to take the pill every morning when, and as automatically as, she brushes her teeth.

To me, that seemed an aesthetic judgment rather than an ethical one, and I would later discover that the earliest Greeks made no distinction between aesthetics and ethics. I wondered if this judgment wouldn't lead Schillebeeckx to favor rhythm over any other birth control method.

He surprised me. "Not necessarily," he said. "If a couple cannot have any more children, the couple are morally obliged to choose the more efficacious means." He said this without hesitation, as if he had already been asked the question more than once. It was the first time I heard a Catholic theologian call contraception "a moral obligation."

I asked the Dominicans if contraception is "according to nature" or "against nature."

Schillebeeckx said, "It is necessary to put the stress, not on the concept of 'nature' but on 'the person.' 'Nature' *is* based on some absolute, but we are only coming to a gradual understanding of this idea." Moreover, added Schillebeeckx, "man's nature is itself in evolution. Nature is essentially dynamic. For example, there was a time when love did not belong to the essence of marriage. Now it does." He cited as an example the bigamy of

Abraham, "which was not a sin, not even a material sin, because the objective norm of morality is the essence of man as we see it at the time." Van der Marck and LeFort nodded in agreement.

We spoke for some time about the classic divisions of "primary and secondary ends of marriage." Some progressive theologians, I had read, were making a distinction between the ontological and the psychological ends of the act, in which case, they said, the church's traditional division is in "the objective order" but not "the subjective order." Schillebeeckx said he didn't go along with that. "The interpersonal, gift-giving, love aspect is not on the so-called subjective side. It really *is* the objective norm."

Schillebeeckx observed that "in the Middle Ages, coitus was only ethically responsible if there was a chance of conception. Since then, there's been some development of a doctrine." He and van der Marck agreed that this medieval concept tended to depersonalize marriage. And they threw up their hands in mock horror at the old teaching that marriage was somehow designed as "a remedy for man's concupiscence."

I asked the group what effect this new approach would have on the church during the next ten years. All were sure that the news of it would have an immediate impact. Somewhat anxiously, van der Marck asked, "Will the Americans think this is heresy?"

I assured him that some certainly would. For myself, I was satisfied that one major theologian (besides Father Häring) had a view on contraception decidedly different from that of the Holy Office. And that if Schillebeeckx had come to this conclusion, then so had others. I wondered if there were enough dissenting theologians to lead a prudent person to the opinion that the church's classic prohibition was in the category of "doubtful law."

* * *

The next morning, back in Amsterdam, von Geusau and I found ourselves in the offices of Cornelius Trimbos, a psychiatrist in his late forties and medical director of the Dutch National Catholic Bureau of Mental Health. Dr. Trimbos was one of the country's leading Catholic laymen, invariably included in the private symposia on marital ethics then being conducted by the Dutch bishops.

Trimbos was giving us his view of the rhythm method: "I have no grounds for saying that rhythm is always the best from a psychiatrist's point of view. Rhythm is good in good marriages. But in a marriage that is going through troubles, the pill may be better. And in some lower social levels, I would rather say that rhythm is not the answer because some people act on a more instinctual level."

He thought that if the church were to begin teaching that the pill is acceptable in cases where, up to now, rhythm had been acceptable, "it would have a good effect. It would mean that many Catholic couples would have less anxiety and better mental health. But I wonder what older couples will feel about it? The ones who have already been indoctrinated? I got a letter today from a mother of eleven children saying, 'Can't you help us? We who have large families feel we are now on trial.'" Dr. Trimbos smiled and turned his palms upward, as if to say, "When will we grow up?"

He scored the old Catholic handbook mentality. "It was easier to live, maybe, under a lot of rules. But it didn't make people more mature." He admitted it was going to be more difficult to explain "the love vision" of the newer theologians to lay people. Perhaps even more difficult: explaining it to priests whose bias against sex was built into their early seminary training.

Von Geusau agreed. In his seminary, girls and women were always referred to as "sharks." He said, "And when a professor had to teach anything connected with the sixth commandment, he would set up a picture of the Virgin Mary and light two candles."

* * *

But that was old school. When I got off the train to visit the Catholic University of Louvain, I found the American College full of high achievers from all over the United States being educated for the priesthood in a different view. I met three of them on the street, introduced myself as a reporter for *Time* and was greeted with friendly smiles and then the question, "How did you hear so soon?"

"Hear what?" I asked.

"About Canon Janssens' article."

I told them Canon Janssens was on my list of people to see. But what article were they speaking of? They told me I was in luck: yesterday, Louis Janssens had published a 30-page essay in *Ephemerides Theologicae Lovanienses*, the Louvain theological quarterly, that came out unequivocally for the pill. One of my American informants said, all agog, "In class, Louis Janssens talks all around the subject. But here, in this article, he sums up everything."

I was eager to meet Janssens. He was not so eager to meet me. He didn't show up for an eleven o'clock appointment at the university. I finally found him at his home on 95 Avenue Cardinal Mercier, Heverlee, Louvain. He turned out to be a charming little old man, smoking a little Dutch cigar in his little book-lined study. He reminded me of no one so much as Edmund Gwenn, the fellow who played Kris Kringle in the movie *Miracle on 34th Street*.

To most of my early questions, he said, "Well, you'll find the answer to that in my article." His article, "Conjugal Morality and Progesterons," was a masterpiece of casuistry, applying old rules to a new situation. The pill, he claimed, was much like rhythm. "Rhythm positively excludes procreation: it creates an obstacle of a temporal sort by exclusively choosing the time for sexual relations during periods of sterility." Mechanical means of birth control, on the other hand, "constitute a barrier between the organs of the husband and wife of a spatial sort. Mechanical means of contraception tend to destroy the meaning of conjugal love. But the use of certain pharmaceuticals, *c'est une autre chose.* It doesn't destroy anything. The pill works more like rhythm."

I pointed out that Pope Pius XII had condemned a birth control pill in 1958, on the grounds that it created a "temporary sterilization." Janssens denied that the new pill did anything of the sort. He said he was relying on the testimony of a medical colleague, Jacques Férin, whose article on medical aspects of the pill joined his in the same issue of the Louvain quarterly. And on the word of John Rock. He insisted that all the pill did was put a woman's ovaries into a state of temporary repose. Instead of having any sterilizing effect, the pill made a woman even more fertile. He cited the phenomenon known as "ovulation rebound."

His conclusion: conscientious and responsible use of the pill can be a good act, possibly even better than the rhythm method.

Janssens had a twinkle in his eye as he summed up his argument, and I had the impression he was playing a little game, almost as if he were beating Pope Pius XII at ping pong, and with the pope's own brand of sandpaper paddle. He seemed more interested in what he termed "a more important question," the history of the church's evolving attitudes on sex.

He was very hard on St. Augustine who, he said, had a pessimistic view of desire and sexual pleasure. According to Augustine, the only excuses for a married couple's making love were "the exigencies of procreation and the need to prevent adulterous acts in marriage." Conjugal love was (or ought to be) purely spiritual. Carnal desire could only sully it. This is why St. Augustine wished Christian couples could find a way to practice complete continence in order to be united, "not by the bonds of the flesh, but by those of the heart."

Janssens found this fantastic. "And now, understand this." Janssens lit another little Dutch cigar, then waved it like a baton. "St. Augustine himself concluded that if a way could be found to continue the human race without using human intercourse, intercourse would be illicit. Now, when modern scientists made this dream possible through artificial insemination, Pope Pius XII instinctively condemned it. Yes, he condemned it!"

Janssens shook his head and smiled. "It does not appear that Pope Pius XII took into consideration all the implications of the principle invoked to condemn artificial insemination." He meant, I gathered, that Pope Pius

XII could have spoken more clearly in that context about sexual inter-course as a good in itself but chose not to do so. Janssens proceeded to do it for me: "The conjugal act, in its natural structure, is a personal function-ing, an immediate and simultaneous cooperation between the husband and wife, a functioning which, by the very nature of the two acting powers and the singular character of the act itself, is the expression of a reciprocal gift which, according to the Scriptures, brings about a union in one body, one flesh."

He applied this theory to birth control, which he chose to call "voluntary procreation." He mentioned "the duty of fecundity" but said that could be tempered by conditions. "A couple can practice voluntary procreation for good reasons: medical, social, economic, demographic. . . ."

* * *

What did the Americans studying at Louvain think of Janssens? After my interview with him, I spoke in a large classroom (or a small audito-rium) to more than a hundred students, many destined to be bishops, who cheered my presence on this story. Afterward, I sat around with a handful of men who wanted to chat. No one seemed to have any objections to Jansens' arguments. But some were concerned about the effect his argu-ment would have on American Catholics, especially if they read about it first in *Time* magazine. One young theologian said *Time* was not an apt messenger for such news. He said the Janssens article had appeared in a scientific theological review, and theologians should come to it that way first, not by reading about it in *Time*. *Time* would sensationalize the story.

I shrugged. "*Time* has been reporting news about the council that no one else has reported," I said. "If it's true, what difference where a reader reads it?" A look of dismay came over some faces. "Look," I said, "this is news. You shouldn't try to manage it."

* * *

I had lunch in the town of Louvain the next day with Clement Mertens, a Jesuit and a demographer, who told me quickly, "There is no single population problem. There are population problems. In India, one situa-tion. In Belgium another. Here, in Belgium, responsible parenthood would seem to require larger rather than smaller families."

Father Mertens, who was seeing me because another Jesuit, a mutual friend, had asked him to, seemed nervous in my presence. I did not know it at the time, but he was one of the six original members of the papal birth control commission appointed by Pope John, and news of that commission was one of the Vatican's closely guarded secrets. Perhaps he was afraid I would ask about his membership on that commission.

I told him I had seen Father Schillebeeckx and Canon Janssens. Mertens said he had some reservations about Janssens' article, "especially about the pill." Why? "Because the pill is not the solution to the population problems in the Third World countries." And he seemed to have some theological objections to all this emphasis by such as Schillebeeckx and Janssens on "the interpersonal, gift-giving aspect" of the marriage relationship. "This giving of self," said Mertens, "is *for* something else, both ontologically and psychologically." He quoted the French story teller, Antoine de Saint Exupery: "To love each other, it is not enough to look at each other, but the couple must look out to something else."

He said that "for years now, progressive theologians have been giving the act of coitus great transcendence. Do they want to say now that it is merely biological?" I told him I didn't think Schillebeeckx was saying that. He shook his head. He wasn't so worried about Schillebeeckx. He was worried about *Time*'s poking into this story. He said, "I admit there should be a dialogue on this question among the theologians. But this is not the time to have the dialogue on the open market."

In my briefcase, I had a copy of an article by Mertens published a few weeks before in *Nouvelle Revue Theologique*:

> An immense effort is needed in probing deeply into these (population) questions and in spreading information, and in this everyone, priests and laymen, must take part. The need for it is urgent. In a world that has been taken by surprise by a sudden and powerful surge of the life force, Christians cannot fail in their duty to be the light of the world, the salt of the earth. We must act quickly, for tomorrow may be too late . . . There must be the boldness to preach a planned parenthood, to show the Christian values it brings with it. We hardly know of any important moves that have been made in this direction.

He concluded that the Vatican and the bishops should take the lead here. "Otherwise, the timorous or the lazy will invoke what they claim will be the will of authority that a problem so delicate should not be broached."

* * *

In Paris, I found another Jesuit as cautious as Mertens, Stanislaus De Lestapis, another of the original six appointed to Pope John XXIII's birth control commission. His demographic writings had already been hailed around the world, particularly a thoughtful chapter on "the contraceptive civilization" in his book, *Family Planning and Modern Problems*. I was surprised when this lean, wall-eyed intellectual arrived at the restaurant for lunch driving a motorcycle, wearing a red and white crash helmet. (My American Jesuit guide explained that the French Jesuits, once so identified with the nation's elite, were now making a concerted effort to be part of the proletariat.)

He, too, disagreed with Canon Janssens. He had seen the disciplinary value of the rhythm method and couldn't approve any way but rhythm.

I asked, "You know what they call folks in the United States who practice rhythm?" He did not. "Parents," I said with a grin.

He did not grin. He told me that the rhythm method had worked very well in controlled, church-backed experiments in Nantes, on the Isle of Reunion in the Indian Ocean and on the Isle of Mauritius. Still, he conceded that even rhythm had dangers. "It can lead to Pharisaism," he said, "and that's where we are the most vulnerable."

Father de Lestapis was off on the morrow for Rome, to teach a course at the Gregorian University. He said he would teach that the pill is okay, "to regulate, but not inhibit ovulation." He insisted, through lunch, that men (he did not mention women) "grow more mature, leave adolescent selfish levels, by mastering themselves on the psychological level." He believed a pill culture would make things too easy. In such a culture, men would not learn to master themselves.

Finally, he mused about the tendency of both Catholics and Protestants to take static approaches. "Catholics have taken a moralistic approach. Protestants have taken a philanthropic approach. But both groups are leaving their fixed positions, becoming more dynamic in dialogue." I asked him what Protestants must do. He refrained from responding to that. But he said Catholics "should give up the old moralistic approach and ask what is better for men, humanly speaking."

* * *

I talked to many others, priests and lay people, on my trip to The Netherlands, Belgium and France. Though I had heard endorsements of the pill from some of the best theologians in the Lowlands, I hadn't recorded any general approval of the pill as ethically or aesthetically better than other methods. On the contrary, I still found almost everyone praising the rhythm method as "a more perfect way," at least for those who could make it work.

And some almost made rhythm into an ideology. One of these was Jan Holt, a Dutch physician who had achieved worldwide renown for his successful "Holt temperature method." Dr. Holt's book, *Marriage and Periodic Abstinence*, went through seven Dutch editions and had been translated into seven languages. Largely for this reason, Pope Pius XII had made him a Knight of St. Gregory. Rhythm was his business, so I was not surprised to hear him say that "even if the church approves other methods, I would not go along with the church." To Dr. Holt, rhythm was "natural" and therefore good in itself, like eating whole grain cereals. Holt's rhythm was only "natural" if you forgot that his rhythm didn't work unless people used thermometers, which was part art and part science.

* * *

I had dinner in Paris with Charles Rendu and his wife in their home on the Rue de Regard. Like Dr. Holt, Monsieur and Madame Rendu had invested much of their Catholic zeal in rhythm as a cause. They taught classes in rhythm at the *Equipe de Notre Dame* in Paris, a rough equivalent to the Christian Family Movement in the United States and analogous to the *Movimento Familia Cattolica* in Latin America. They tried to show other couples that the self-control needed to practice rhythm actually helped them love one another more, not less. I applauded this. But I was startled to learn, later, that the Rendus' children were adopted. The practice of rhythm was not a personal problem for the Rendus.

* * *

I knew my New York editors would have a hard time believing that "the church," which had been so adamant on this question, could possibly change. I reminded them that a different kind of church was evolving out of the council, a church which had achieved new freedom, one that could now speak with many voices. Furthermore, I had to convince them that the voices I was recording were important voices that added up to more than a whisper in the church. I tried, also, to guess about the echoes this story would have in ensuing months. I wrote: "The undercurrent has suddenly broken to the surface and, unless I miss my guess, will become a tidal wave."

In Rome, in all of Holland, in Belgium, in France (where I have taken my soundings), in Germany (where I understand the same depths are being reached), the theologians are daring to talk about their new insights. Their bishops are adding up the insights and some have already given their private assent to the revisionist thinking. Some have even succeeded in getting the new insights incorporated into the latest draft of the council's *Schema* 17 [later 13]. If the council gets into open debate on that *schema*, there will be fireworks such as never seen before. The same open-door closed-door groups will do battle. But their past battles such as the ones over mass in the vernacular or the two fonts of revelation or the nature of the church will be as the Battle of Lexington to the Third World War.

I predicted *Time*'s story would create an uproar because, I told my editors, it "hits at an aspect of the so-called population explosion, a problem that involves governmental policy (eugenic, social and public health policies), the improvement of the status of women, the education of the young, even peace and war."

Chapter Two

For weeks *Time* sat on my story, though it was written by John Elson and edited by Bill Forbis and ready to go to press on February 15. Otto Fuerbringer, my managing editor in New York, held it up because he decided *Time*'s readers should have a good medical account of the pill. That ought to come before a theological reflection about it.

And so *Time* (which finally published its report of new stirrings in the church in its April 10 issue) could hardly be accused of rushing into print with this story. *Time*'s hesitation gave the men at the American College in Louvain what they had wanted: a chance to get the first word about Janssens' revisionist views of the pill into the Catholic press first.

Years later, I learned what had happened. A seminarian airmailed a copy of Janssens' article to S.J. Adamo, editor of the *Camden Star Herald*, a diocesan weekly in New Jersey, together with a letter explaining why Monsignor Adamo should try to scoop *Time*: an article in *Time* would confuse the faithful.

There was some justification for that view. Catholics, particularly many American Catholics, had been accustomed to marching in lock step, preferably on direct orders from Rome, or, if that were not possible, from their own bishops. Many would not believe *Time*'s report, particularly if the news tended to contradict what they'd been told for decades about the immutability of the church's teaching on birth control.

And so, with a news story about Janssens dated February 28, 1964, Monsignor Adamo scored his newsbeat on *Time*. His piece in the *Camden Star Herald* was syndicated for the U.S. Catholic press, though suppressed by many official diocesan weeklies. Even so, the story taxed the credulity of many, especially when the American moralists got out their long knives to cut up Canon Janssens.

Francis J. Connell, a Redemptorist and a former dean of the School of Theology at the Catholic University of America, said it would be impossible ever to reconcile Janssens' position with church teaching. To do so, he said, "we would have to throw out the last 400 years of theological development." John J. Lynch, professor of moral theology at the Jesuit scholasticate in Weston, Massachusetts, said Janssens' views were "totally invalid and impossible to reconcile with present theological principles." Father Lynch predicted that it might take "a statement from the Holy See to straighten out the whole thing."

Two other New England Jesuits weighed in with attacks on Janssens. John C. Ford told National Catholic News Service (the U.S. bishops' press agency) that the pill distributed under the brand name Enovid was exactly the one Pope Pius XII condemned in 1958, a condemnation still in force. "Consequently, unless and until the Holy See gives its approval to some other teaching (a highly unlikely eventuality), no lesser authority in the church, and least of all a private theologian, is at liberty to teach a different doctrine or to free Catholics from their obligation to accept papal teaching." And Edward Duff, a noted Jesuit journalist, wrote of Janssens, ". . . . no established Catholic theologian is on record as agreeing with him."

Father Duff should have said no *American* theologian was on record. Even as Duff's article was published March 6, at least two other established Catholic theologians were agreeing publicly with Janssens: Willem van der Marck and Bishop J.M. Reuss of Mainz, West Germany. Obviously, the American moralists weren't keeping in touch with their European conferees. Neither were the editors from some U.S. Catholic weeklies, who allowed uninformed, almost hysterical attacks on Janssens.

A columnist at the *Register*, a national Catholic weekly, classed him as a dangerous heretic who should be placed alongside Arius, Nestorius, Luther and Loisy, but charitably allowed that this "young Belgian professor" probably didn't know any better. In fact, this young Belgian professor was an old-looking 56, a doctor of sacred theology, a priest in excellent standing with his archbishop, Cardinal Suenens, and a professor of 22 years standing at Louvain, one of the best Catholic universities in the world.

One problem was that U.S. Catholics had been trained to think "official" statements from the pope or the Holy Office determined what was moral or immoral. Until the pope changed his tune, everyone in the church was supposed to go along with the old melody. In the week my story appeared in *Time*, John V. Sheridan, director of public information for the Archdiocese of Los Angeles, voiced this approach with a column in his archdiocesan weekly, *The Tidings*:

> . . . the richest source of confusion [wrote Monsignor Sheridan about Canon Janssens' position] is the oversimplified and thus misleading treatments which it is bound to get in popular journals like *Time*. The church's position on contraception has not changed, is not changing and gives no indications that it will change. The authorities engaged in discussions on the use of the pill as a contraceptive are not . . . claiming to do so as official teachers or theolo-

gians; they have generally confined their views to theological
journals . . . [these are] personal considerations and cannot be
used as a basis for forming a Catholic conscience until they are—a
very remote possibility—approved by the church, which they are
most definitely not at this time.[12]

Monsignor Sheridan was giving his readers the party line, taught
mainly in Rome: birth control is a sin until the pope says it isn't. But this
was part of the old legalism which the council was rejecting, fashioned as it
was after a secular model which many bishops believed had outlived its
usefulness to the church.

Some American bishops reacted even more negatively than Monsignor
Sheridan to the *Time* story. Like the old Persian kings, they were ready to
kill the messenger bearing the bad news. I learned that one, Albert
Zuroweste, bishop of Belleville, Illinois, phoned Henry R. Luce, my
editor-in-chief, to demand I be fired, on the grounds that I had concocted
the whole story. As gently as he could, Mr. Luce assured him, fingering my
file, that Mr. Kaiser had concocted nothing.

* * *

Both Luce and Zuroweste would have been surprised to learn that, even
as they were speaking, papal advisers were meeting secretly in Rome, on
April 3, 4, and 5, to deal, mainly, with the question of the pill. The birth
control commission had already met six months earlier in Louvain, in
October 1963, to consider proper stances for the church to take when its
representatives would attend a forthcoming conference on population at
New Delhi, the March 1964 World Health Congress meeting in Geneva,
and the World Population Congress in 1965.

Many believe this was the only reason Pope Paul VI had for bringing
together this commission, composed as it was of four social scientists and
two physicians. But Pope Paul did not appoint these men. Pope John
XXIII did, several months before his death. And what motivated Pope
John? The demographic question? Probably not. There is some reason to
believe Pope John was more interested in the birth control question as it
impinged on the daily lives of good Catholics.

My source on this is Igino Cardinale, the Vatican diplomat who was part
of Pope John's inner circle during the years I was covering Rome for *Time*.
One night in May 1981, when I was having dinner with Archbishop Cardi-
nale at the nunciature in Brussels, he told me Loris Capovilla got John
XXIII thinking about new approaches. Cardinale quoted Monsignor
Capovilla, Pope John's personal secretary, speaking to the pope in 1963:
"You know, Holiness, we have to do something about birth control. You
go around here asking the young men who work in the Vatican how many

children they have. They always say, one. Or maybe two. Hardly ever three. Or more. Have you ever stopped to wonder why? I think it is because these men cannot afford to have more children. They're good Catholics. They want to be good Catholics. But if they listen to us, they have to live with their wives as brothers and sisters. We can't ask that. It's too hard. It's unreasonable."

As Cardinale told it, Capovilla said the pope thought he would appoint a commission to advise him. Whom should he appoint? He would ask Cardinal Suenens, who had been having these conferences in Belgium, for names. He got the names, made the appointments, then soon became very ill, and died before the commission could meet. "John's intent," Cardinale said, "wasn't only demography. He wanted to see how solid the doctrine really was."

Loris Capovilla, who was appointed bishop of Loreto after the death of Pope John, did not remember it quite this way. In a personal letter to me, postmarked October 6, 1981, Bishop Capovilla denied bringing up the matter with the pope, and said he let the Secretariat of State and the Holy Office deal with such matters. As far as he knew, Cardinal Suenens came to the pope with the idea.

I think Cardinale remembered more of the truth than Capovilla wanted to, for Capovilla was always sensitive to the charge that he went outside his competence as the pope's secretary to fill the pope's head with crazy ideas.

But the point is this: the commission's beginnings had to do with more than demography. In December 1965, Cardinal Suenens told me at his residence in Malines that he had urged a commission on Pope John (and, later, on Pope Paul) in an effort to see if the church could take an intelligent position on responsible parenthood, and at least try to reform the old idea, "the more children the better." Suenens added with a smile, "The commission couldn't stop there. It went on to consider every aspect of the problem."

Furthermore, the records show that the commission went beyond the demographic question, even in its first meeting, in October 1963, when the commission attempted to determine which particular methods of birth control the church could approve from a moral standpoint and which ones it could not. Pope Paul obviously wanted some guidance on the pill. As it turned out, the commission's members had not been able to give him much help here: no one knew enough about the precise workings of the pill to make a recommendation.

The pill itself, a synthetic form of progesteron which suppressed ovulation, was something new. It wasn't developed until 1953. It didn't undergo extensive testing until 1956. And it wasn't approved by the U.S. Federal Drug Administration until 1960. Doctors had documented the pill's short term side effects (nausea, vomiting, vertigo, headaches, tenderness of the

breasts, increased weight, upset nerves), but no one knew what its long
term effects would be. Researchers in 1963 hadn't yet determined how
women could tolerate the pill for, say, a decade or more. Was the church to
approve something that might be a medical disaster?

In his 22-page report of that 1963 meeting, Henri de Riedmatten, the
Dominican secretary of the commission, made more than one mention of
Thalidomide, a tranquilizing drug that had its sad side effects: women who
took it during the first trimester of pregnancy gave birth to children with
little stumps instead of arms.

As for morality, if the pill made the womb unfit for "nesting" of the
fertilized egg, the pill was out: it was "a veritable abortifacient" and would
fall under the church's condemnation of abortion, a sin against the fifth
commandment. On the other hand, if the pill merely suppressed ovulation, it was possible a woman could use it in various therapeutic ways, say,
to correct a condition such as endometriosis or dysmenorrhea, even
though the pill would make a woman sterile for a time. Here, the long-
standing principle of the double effect would come into play, according to a
rule Pope Pius XII had established in 1958.

And if a woman took the pill with a directly contraceptive intent? The
group said Pius XII had dealt with this, too, called it "temporary sterilization," and said it was not permitted. But some of the group questioned that
judgment. They pointed out that the pill didn't destroy any organs, didn't
erase the ovaries or cut off the tubes, and therefore it didn't cause the
"mutilating" sterilization condemned by the pope. Here, the group
members recommended caution until research studies could tell them
more about the way the pill put ovaries into "a state of repose." The report
said it would be "preferable on the part of the Authority [meaning the
pope] not to take a definitive position on the morality of using the pill."

At this point, members of the pope's commission were being cautious,
not radical. They certainly weren't challenging Pius XII's teaching. Quite
the contrary, they felt bound by no less than six papal statements in the
1950s dealing with birth control. With great deference, de Riedmatten
cited each of them in his report, and called them "luminous teachings."

Because of those teachings, the church should take a stand as soon as
possible, said de Riedmatten, against governments that threatened to take
more and more drastic measures in face of their runaway population
growth. If the church didn't squelch these moves, de Riedmatten noted,
the church had already done so successfully in many places, it would not be
fulfilling its role as "the defender of the natural moral law." The church
should also be concerned about certain groups that were not only engaged
in an intensive propaganda campaign, but also helping make contraceptives easily available almost everywhere.

At this point during the 1963 meeting, the commission gave no indication that it had any reformist ideas, except to note that the church lacked clarity in its teaching on responsible parenthood, and perhaps had problems with its approach to sexuality in general.

Should the church work toward a conciliar statement, perhaps clear up the confusion of some pastors who were promoting "the most adventuresome methods?"

No. The group said the pope should not wait for the council. He should bring some "light and order" to those in doubt, and the sooner the better. Perhaps he should think of giving "a discourse," something along the lines of Pius XII's famous address in 1951 to the Italian midwives.

In that 1951 discourse, which would assume high importance at a critical point in deliberations of the commission, Pius XII conceded that couples could, without sinning, make love during the so-called safe period, if they had good reasons for limiting the number of their children. Pius XII made this concession after twenty years of quiet theological debate, triggered in 1930 when two physicians working independently in different parts of the world, Kyusaku Ogino and Herman Knaus, learned to calculate the incidence and length of a woman's sterile period.

But if Pope Paul VI were to give a solemn discourse in the manner of Pius XII's to the midwives, the commission felt he should not limit himself to a narrow statement on conjugal morality. He should take a large view, speak about the responsibilities of being a member of the human race in the latter half of the twentieth century. No matter what the church had taught about the ends of marriage and the instrinsic evil of contraception, these men of the church knew that overpopulation threatened the race: it helped create world hunger, which led to unrest, even wars.

They hoped modern science might show the way, might come up with birth control methods "that could be harmonized with the needs of human love and human morality." At least, de Riedmatten wrote, science should come up with some way to make the rhythm method more secure.

De Riedmatten devoted several pages of his report to rhythm, both the temperature method and the calendar method. At least one commission member, John Marshall, a neurologist and psychiatrist at Queen's Hospital in London, had a personal stake in rhythm. Dr. Marshall was a devout Catholic. He had studied with the Salesians in Boultway, Lancashire, and, in 1950, answered a plea for help from the Catholic Marriage Advisory Council in London. The priests running the council asked Marshall to apply his medical expertise to the problem of natural family planning.

Marshall found the calendar method wasn't working well and started looking into the temperature method. He took a trip to The Netherlands to see Jan Holt, caught him on the run from Amsterdam to Indonesia, and learned all about the temperature method in the Amsterdam airport as Dr. Holt spread his charts over the floor, oblivious of the dozens of folk gathered around to kibbitz. Marshall brought Holt's temperature method to Britain, and England's whole Catholic apparatus started preaching Holt.

Hearing of this campaign, government officials from the Island of Mauritius, off the southeastern coast of Africa, called on Marshall for help. Their island had licked malaria, their population was booming and their people had few opportunities to go elsewhere. Could Marshall help them promote population control that would be acceptable to their Catholic majority? Marshall agreed. If he could make rhythm work among the underdeveloped peoples of Mauritius, he could make it work anywhere.

At this point, most commission members felt as Marshall did about rhythm. It was the Catholic method of birth control. De Riedmatten went even further. In fact, he told the commission, rhythm was "the Christian position."

It seems curious now, after all that has happened in Christendom since 1963, to find de Riedmatten referring to rhythm as "the Christian position." But 1963 was the first year of a new era of understanding among Christians, all of whom the fathers of the Second Vatican Council would soon decree as part of "the church." As a result, many Catholics were beginning to see that Rome's stand on anything was not necessarily the only Christian position. At the council, bishops sought out "the separated brethren," they didn't call them Protestants, for insights on almost everything. The Anglicans, for instance, were represented at the council, and their view on birth control differed from Rome's. Wasn't the Anglican position also "a Christian position"? In 1963, few in the Roman church would have gone so far as that.

But many in the church were ready to take a much more active role in building a better world. Some commission members felt that if international organizations were promoting sterilization and abortion as solutions to the population explosion, maybe that was because Catholics had let these organizations take shape without their presence. Aloofness had been an official Roman policy, but there was no reason this attitude should continue. In fact, two members of this papal commission had actually attended the conference on population in New Delhi to represent the church. So did a dozen other Catholics, all with the Vatican's blessing, though that permission came very late and not without a fight between the open-door, closed-door factions in Rome.

Since the 1963 meeting of Paul VI's birth control commission produced so little, the pope wanted its members to meet again. Now, in April 1964, they were doing so, and the group had grown. There were seven new members, many no doubt suggested by Cardinal Suenens, and this team would provide the pope with a good deal more theological reflection than he had received so far. No theologians had been on the first panel. De

Lestapis and Clement Mertens were Jesuits, but their advanced training was in sociology, not theology. Mertens de Wilmars was a layman and a sociologist. De Riedmatten was a Dominican priest, but not a professional theologian; he was a Vatican diplomat working as an observer at the United Nations in Geneva. The other two, Marshall and Pierre Van Rossum, were laymen and physicians.

And so, Pope Paul suggested adding two more sociologists, Bernard Colombo of Venice, Italy, and Thomas K. Burch of Washington, D.C., and five theologians: Josef Fuchs, Bernard Häring, Jan Visser, Marcelino Zalba* and Pierre de Locht. Fuchs, from West Germany, and Zalba, from Spain, were Jesuit priests who taught moral theology at the Gregorian University in Rome. Visser and Häring, both German Redemptorists, taught moral theology at the Pontifical Lateran University. De Locht was a canon of the Archdiocese of Malines-Brussels and an adviser to Cardinal Suenens.

Häring and de Locht saw themselves as a liberal minority on the commission, and they knew that the pope knew this. De Riedmatten told them as much when he wrote to them of their appointments: "It is the Authority [which is how de Riedmatten most frequently referred to the pope] who has wanted diverse currents of opinion to be represented in the group." And he added: "Yours are well known."

The pope knew Häring's views because Häring was one of the pope's personal theologians in Rome, and he knew de Locht's, according to de Locht's surmise, because the Holy Office had called him to account for something he had said in Belgium several years before concerning birth control. Nevertheless, the pope wanted these men on the commission. Why? This, to some of the pope's most conservative advisers, was Paul VI's fatal flaw: He had a scientific bent, he had to look at every side of every question. Even before he was elected pope, even before he had been appointed archbishop of Milan, even when he was working in the Vatican's secretariat of state, Giovanni Battista Montini was known as a Hamlet, "sicklied o'er with the pale cast of thought." But de Riedmatten cautioned de Locht and Häring: "The Authority demands that the group be surrounded with the greatest reserve and the greatest discretion. You should consider your participation in the group highly confidential." Members kept that confidence. Many are still keeping it today, more than 20 years later.

---

*Father Zalba was the first theologian to propose that the Vatican allow nuns in the war-torn Congo to use the pill as a precaution in case of rape. The Holy Office bought his suggestion, even though it was predicated on an argument the Holy Office was not willing to extend any further, that children were not "the end" of rape, but of marriage.

They gathered for their second meeting at the Domus Mariae, an un-heated private residence in Rome secured by Father Mertens, and no news of the meeting would break for another year. In this April 1964 session, the group had the same items on its agenda, both suggested by the pope: 1) how the church should deal with the morality of birth control—and there are strong indications that the pope was still thinking mainly of the pill, and 2) how the church should deal with various governments and the UN on the demographic problem.

But these 13 came no closer to a solution on either item than did the first group of six. In fact, anyone studying the 19-page core of the commission's April 1964 report could see clues that the group was, rather, beginning to move away from "a solution."

De Riedmatten reported that members could agree on many principles but were given some pause, especially by the suggestions of Canon de Locht and Father Häring that the church take a somewhat longer view of the birth control question. The church's teachings on the natural law were a late development in history. Shouldn't the church go back to the Bible and look at the sacramentality of marriage, at marriage as a community of salvation? Marriage was supposed to help people, not hurt them, yet the church was making things more difficult.

One conservative in the group had argued with this. Pastors, he said, were always merciful and patient with human weakness. But de Locht op-posed this line of argument. Pastors were merciful and patient, he said, not because of human weakness but because they were much more in touch with real life, where people of good will found genuine conflicts that chal-lenged the validity of the abstract laws being handed down. De Locht's view would become common in the upcoming birth control debate: the idea that the real order of things might have some sway over the ideal.

At this point, someone on the commission startled everyone by crying, "But now, Canon de Locht, aren't you raising questions of fundamental theology?" The unspoken premise was clear: "We are not supposed to be raising fundamental questions, are we?"

De Locht's reply: "Yes. Why not?"

Everyone sat back, thought that over for a few moments and asked themselves the same question: "Indeed, why not?"

"No one actually said this out loud," Marshall told me in a June 1981 interview, "but I think everyone said to himself at that moment that it ob-viously *was* appropriate for this commission to raise questions of funda-mental theology." It was a turning point. Many commission members had started out to prepare the church's traditional arguments against birth control so that international organizations then promoting population planning around the world could appreciate the Holy See's point of view. Then commission members discovered that at least one of the theologians brought in by the pope to help them prepare those arguments was proposing they reevaluate the church's whole approach and that many of the others were inclined to agree this was a good idea.

The members solemnized the moment by taking a coffee break. "We were out on this large terrace," said Marshall, "and I can recall that a few of us were standing in a small group together, not really saying very much, and thinking hard about what de Locht had said, and looking down to the other end of the terrace. There was Canon de Locht pacing back and forth, saying his rosary. Whether he was experiencing a crisis of his own at this moment, I cannot say. But that's what I imagined." Marshall guessed de Locht was praying for special guidance, because now he knew, as he had not known before, that this commission was ready to plunge into deeper waters.

When the meeting resumed, Dr. Van Rossum indicated he was ready to take that plunge, too. Obviously, Van Rossum had been thinking about this for some time. He first apologized for his lack of expertise in theology, then gulped and said that if married couples had a duty to love one another as married folks do, "carnally," he failed to see the difference between a couple's making love when they knew they couldn't make a baby and their taking more positive steps not to make a baby when they still had a duty to love each other.

One priest pointed out the difference: in practicing rhythm, a couple didn't do anything "to frustrate nature" but did "go against the finality of the act" when they took positive steps to avoid conception.

Van Rossum countered that the celibates were trying to impose their spirituality on married people. "You think of sex as something you must avoid in order to be faithful to your vocation. That is all right for you. But our vocation is to love one another." They all knew what he meant by "love."

That shocked the celibates. Several said they could see his point. But how primary was this duty, for a couple to make love, uh, carnally? Now they were getting into a more radical question, one Rome had been squelching theologians for raising since 1937. It was church doctrine, affirmed by the Holy Office most definitively in 1944, that the primary end of marriage was "the procreation and education of children" and the secondary end was "the mutual love of husband and wife." Did the pope's commission want to challenge this?

Not openly. Not yet. De Riedmatten's report said the commission knew it could not change the church's traditional teaching on the primary end of marriage. Reason: pronouncements of the magisterium on this matter were "too recent to be questioned." But perhaps the church could reformulate that teaching and develop its implications. For example, the church often spoke of the *bonum prolis* (the good of the offspring) when it was thinking of procreation. But didn't the good of the offspring imply not only "bringing children into the world" but "bringing them up" as well, and making a home where conditions would be psychologically and materially conducive to that upbringing?

Suggesting a reformulation, not a change, owed something, perhaps, to Pope John and his words at the opening of the council, "the substance of the ancient doctrine is one thing, the way in which it is presented is another." It was a cunning proposal, one that might allow the church to save face and still help reform its teaching on the primary ends of marriage, something much needed, according to some members. Why? Because the old teaching gave many moderns "the impression that love is only secondary," which couples saw as false. And the commission members weren't talking about a couple's subjective feelings, because the physical and objective fact was that they made love much more often than they made babies. How, then, could procreation be "primary"?

"The group unanimously affirms," wrote de Riedmatten, "that love is at the heart of marriage, and a majority of the members agree that the love of husband and wife should not, in any way, be ranked among the secondary ends of marriage."

Was this the dose of "theological reflection" the pope had asked for? It was a beginning.

For the rest, judging from de Riedmatten's report, the commission members did not find much more agreement. They were in apparent accord on rhythm: it was still "the most desirable means of exercising responsible parenthood." But many were reluctant to condemn the pill. The pill wasn't sterilization. Sometimes, a woman's ovaries were "at rest" naturally. Why couldn't a woman recreate a natural situation?

But then, the members started asking one another, "What do we mean by natural?" Here, they encountered wide disagreement, especially when they tied the concept "natural" to marriage. Famine and disease were also "natural," but men and women of science had done something about these, which was one reason for the current world population crisis. They concluded that "natural law alone cannot provide a good answer to this question." They felt they had to go beyond natural law, look to revelation and the witness of Christian couples. For this, they needed more time. They agreed they would meet again at Louvain in early September. Then they adjourned.

* * *

But the commission hadn't helped the pope deal with the problems of the moment. The situation was getting out of hand. Janssens and van der Marck and Reuss had expressed opinions in theological journals intended for private circulation. Now the pope was reading about them, that first week in April, in *Time* magazine. Now he knew; debate in the church could no longer be a quiet one, nor confined to theologians.

No pope had ever faced a situation like this. None of the historic theological disputes, such as the controversy concerning the human nature of Christ, had had quite the popular interest this one had. This question of birth control touched the most intimate part of people's lives, every day. Besides, during most of the old disputes, nothing like the mass media existed. Now, the modern mass media were not only able to report the pros and cons of this question, they also had a new wish to do so. For much of the twentieth century, news of the church was sectarian, published if at all on the Saturday church page, broadcast on Sunday mornings. Now, the media had become fascinated by the drama of this ancient institution trying to change itself. The church was hot news. And not even an obscure article in *Ephemerides Theologicae Lovanienses* could escape media attention.

As a result, Catholics who had been silent on this question all their lives suddenly had something to say about the church's classic stand against birth control. Now that Canon Janssens and Father van der Marck and Bishop Reuss had dared to disagree openly with the old teaching, many others felt they could disagree, too, and maybe add something to the mix of opinion.

This was a lesson in group dynamics, something like what had happened at the council in 1962. One of my friends, an archbishop, had told me then, "I was prepared to come to the council and approve all the Roman documents I'd been sent in the mail. But when I heard some of the church's most venerable cardinals criticizing those documents as out of date, I realized that I'd been thinking the same secret thoughts all my life. I just didn't have the sense of freedom that allowed me to express them. Soon, of course, I could express them."

That man was Thomas d'Esterre Roberts, the Jesuit archbishop of Bombay, native of Liverpool, who had abdicated his archdiocese in favor of an Indian, Valerian Gracias, long before it was fashionable for the church to give much authority or status to indigenous clergy in Africa and Asia. He didn't have much to say at the council, except for one important intervention on peace and war. But he used his newly found freedom to speak his mind to the press. And, partly because of the liberating influence of the council's first two sessions, he would do so most tellingly in April 1964 on birth control.

On April 19, *The Times* of London carried a page one story under the headline, "A Vatican dissident on birth control." It reported the views of Archbishop Roberts, then living at the Jesuits' Farm Street Mission in Mayfair. Roberts' full views had appeared in the April issue of *Search*, a monthly newsletter edited by Michael de la Bedoyere, former editor of *The*

Catholic Herald, England's leading Catholic newspaper. "If I were an Anglican," Archbishop Roberts was quoted as saying, "I would accept the position taken by the Lambeth Conference. How you can destroy that position by reason alone is not clear to me."

I was familiar with Roberts' opinions, having heard them expressed in various ways when he was my houseguest in Rome during the first two sessions of the council. Now he was going public with a favorite theme; he was testing the weakest link in the church's traditional teaching on birth control, the notion that reason alone could demonstrate that contraception was intrinsically evil. "Intrinsically evil" meant always wrong in itself, never moral under any circumstances, which made it more clearly evil than taking another's life, an act justified in self defense, for example. Both Pius XI and Pius XII had said contraception violated natural and divine law. But they also said this was a conclusion from reason, not revelation. Roberts' implicit challenge to the magisterium: either prove this prohibition from reason or drop it. Anything else would be an abuse of authority.

The reporter for *The Times* said Roberts would return to the council in the fall, when he was "expected to raise the issue." In that same page one story, *The Times* quoted John Ryan, a Roman Catholic gynecologist with a West End practice, who said he agreed with the archbishop and was "sure his words will be welcomed by the Catholic medical profession." *The Times* also quoted Thomas Corbishley, the Jesuit superior at Farm Street, who said Roberts' remarks were "interesting as perhaps the first British statement of this question. It is too early to say whether one agrees with him, but it is certainly true that the church's position on birth control will have to be reconsidered."

Roberts was a maverick, a pacifist who had marched with Bertrand Russell to demonstrate against "the bomb," and, because of that eccentricity, looked upon with some suspicion by most of the English hierarchy. He spent much of his time during the council sessions sipping coffee and schnapps at the Bar Jonah behind the main altar of St. Peter's, trading gossip, asking impertinent questions. He had bushy white eyebrows, a prominent forehead much like the one Phidias gave Plato, and the slightly raffish look of Alec Guinness playing Gulley Jimson in *The Horse's Mouth*.

But he was an archbishop, holy, courageous and humble, humble enough to tell me, the day we first met in Rome, that his elevation to the episcopacy in 1937 was a mistake, a clerical error. He had been minding his own business, rector of a small Jesuit college in Liverpool, when he got the news about Bombay. Not until he'd received the holy oils did some Vatican functionary discover he'd tabbed the wrong English Jesuit. By then, it was too late.

I thought, *O felix culpa*, oh, happy blunder! Perhaps the Holy Spirit

knew what She was doing. In teeming, turbulent, overpopulated, super-
stitious Bombay, where Catholics totaled no more than 0.02 percent of the
population, T.D. Roberts became a pastoral, compassionate shepherd who
had free time to think deeply about the church's mission in the world. If he
hadn't been in Bombay, he never could have told de la Bedoyere (as he did),
"The whole end of marriage is not to have as many children as possible,
but as many as can be brought up to lead happy and useful lives. An Indian
lives in a mud hut with his wife and several children, too poor to be able to
afford any light, and forced to be with his wife every night for twelve hours
in the dark, and having nothing else at all but her love.

"The Protestant missionary offers a contraceptive not as an ideal solution but as a lesser evil than sterilization, than abortion, than the hunger
of his children, than the death of his wife or the death of their married
love."

Roberts was not only the first episcopal voice raised in Great Britain. He
also stepped up the level of the debate. He was not arguing for the pill, as
van der Marck, Janssens and Reuss had done. He was doing something far
more radical: questioning the intrinsic evil of contraception itself, no
matter what the means, and also challenging church teaching, which many
Catholics then believed to be "infallible" on a matter of marital morals.

Roberts' statement galvanized John Carmel Heenan, archbishop of
Westminster, into action. He immediately drafted a statement for public
consumption, checked it out with other English bishops, and had it printed
in *The Catholic Herald* May 7 "in the name of the hierarchy of England
and Wales." It said, in part:

The church knows well that her children are undergoing a period
of great strain. Their difficulties are only increased when it is
irresponsibly suggested that the council may produce a new moral
code for married people.

It has even been suggested that the council could approve the
practice of contraception. But the church, while free to revise her
own positive laws, has no power of any kind to alter the laws of God.

Archbishop Heenan quoted Pius XI, Pius XII and St. Augustine's
opinion that "intercourse is unlawful and wicked where the conception of
the offspring is prevented." He expressed fatherly compassion for couples
who find themselves faced with an "agonizing choice between natural
instincts and the law of God." But he said he couldn't change God's law.

That very evening, the BBC asked for a comment from Norman St. John
Stevas, a Catholic legal scholar and a member of Parliament. Mr. St. John
Stevas said Heenan's statement was so unequivocal that it would silence
the debate. "I was swiftly proved wrong," St. John Stevas later recalled.
"Archbishop Roberts himself defended his attitude in an article published
in *The Evening Standard* on 19 May. Catholics wrote to *The Times*, the

Guardian and *The Daily Telegraph,* expressing different points of view. A lively correspondence emerged in the columns of *The Spectator.* The controversy also raged in Catholic papers, such as *The Tablet* and *The Catholic Herald.*"[13]

To St. John Stevas, "This represented a new development in Catholic life in England. Hitherto public controversy among Catholics had been minimal and confined to the Catholic papers. For the first time, Catholics in England were using the secular news media as a means of expressing their views."

Some of these views were telling. In the letters column of *The Times,* for example, A.E.P. Duffy, a Labor member of Parliament, asked a pointed historical question: "Is the archbishop saying that the natural law is incapable of a changed interpretation in the light of changed circumstances, and that this has never been reflected in traditional teaching?"

And then Henry Bettenson, an Anglican clergyman, caught Dr. Heenan in a misquotation of St. Augustine which exactly proved Mr. Duffy's point. In a letter to *The Times,* Mr. Bettenson wrote that the archbishop's statement had St. Augustine condemning intercourse within marriage "where the conception of offspring is *prevented.*" St. Augustine said "where the conception of offspring is *avoided.*" Bettenson concluded: "The change is significant, for Augustine's word would include in the condemnation the use of the 'rhythm' method of birth control, which the Roman church allows." In other words, Pius XII, the first pope to approve rhythm, had gone beyond St. Augustine. Pius XII himself had already re-interpreted natural law.

Being caught on that one was bad enough for Heenan. But then, a further insult: George Armstrong, Rome correspondent for *The Guardian,* took Heenan's statement to Bernard Häring and asked what he thought of it. According to the headline on Armstrong's page one story in *The Guardian,* Archbishop Heenan's view was "outdated."

Rome, May 8

An eminent Vatican theologian takes issue with Dr. Heenan, archbishop of Westminster and the English and Welsh hierarchy on their statement yesterday, which warns Roman Catholics against the use of pills which grant them temporary sterilization.

According to this authority, most theologians would consider use of the pill, in certain circumstances, as tolerable and the lesser of the evils. A clear distinction is needed now between the new pill and the familiar, mechanical means of contraception.

Who was this eminent Vatican theologian? Armstrong described him as having impeccable credentials:

Father Bernard Häring, aged 51, is a German professor of moral and social theology at the Alfonsian Academy and the Lateran

University in Rome. He has been invited to sit with the ecumenical council as an expert, and he is secretary of the commission which is preparing the council's crucial *schema*, "The Church and the Modern World." Most significantly, Father Häring was chosen to deliver 28 sermons to Pope Paul and the Curia during the recent papal Lenten retreat.

According to Häring, the pills, "unlike [other] contraceptives, do not interfere with the act of conjugal intercourse. They affect the functions of nature, an altogether different thing." Häring said he thought the church would distinguish between these pills and other contraceptives. "I am sure there will be developments along that line in Catholic doctrine. I think the British bishops erred in this in their statement."

One of the world's top theologians, expressing an opinion in his own specialty, moral theology, was contradicting the British bishops. The stunning force of this story was a bit blunted after Derek Worlock, Dr. Heenan's secretary, phoned Häring in Rome and demanded to know if he had said the British bishops "erred." Häring hadn't said that and had to deny it. *The Guardian* printed Armstrong's correction, minor in itself, but one that threw enough dust in the air to save some of Heenan's face:

Father Häring did not use the word "erred" in the interview. I now have played the tape of the interview for a German colleague, for a professor of English at the Rome Catholic University, and for the rector of the English College, Monsignor Allan Clark. One thought that the verb, in the Father's thick German accent, was "roared." Painstakingly, we have now puzzled it out.

What Father Häring said was this: "One thing is clear, I think that the statement of the British bishops was lawed especially out on this." What Father Häring meant by this was that the British bishops had "outlawed" the *arbitrary* use of all contraceptives, including the pill.

The word "erred" has a stronger meaning to ecclesiastics than "wrong," and it must be clear that Father Häring considers the bishops wrong in condemning the pill. He argues that "the question is quite a new one" and that "the question is still an open one."

The point was clear enough: the British bishops were holding back important information: there was a diversity of opinion within the church on birth control. This created an even bigger credibility gap for Archbishop Heenan, who was only trying to give his people the benefit of the moral theology he had learned in the seminary.

But, proverbially, all good things and bad come in threes. Heenan would be buffeted once more, this time, it seemed at first, by Cardinal Ottaviani. The secretary of the Holy Office gave a four-question interview to *Vita*, an Italian version of *Time*. Lamberto Furno, *Vita*'s crack religion reporter, specifically asked Ottaviani about Archbishop Heenan's May 7 statement on "the Catholic pill" and about Cardinal Suenens' remark at a Boston news conference, also on May 7, that, "Naturally, we cannot accept sterilization, but I am told that a pill will soon be available that avoids this."

Ottaviani said the Vatican "doesn't like this or that local authority to express doctrinal views on debated questions which call rather for a central directive: differences of opinion can arise, and, especially in doctrinal matters, it is necessary to preserve unity of thought and policy. The supreme magisterium [a phrase much favored by Ottaviani] must speak in grave and debatable questions, which should not be left to a single opinion, whether that of a bishop or a cardinal."

In *The Guardian*, George Armstong reported this as a rebuke to Archbishop Heenan, neglecting to add that Ottaviani's words could be applied easily to Archbishop Roberts as well. This forced Heenan's secretary to phone Rome, again, to seek a clarification from Ottaviani.

The cardinal promptly wrote Heenan a note saying he was on Heenan's side. He had intended only "to warn those who launch new theories on questions which must still await the guidance of the supreme magisterium of the church."

In the *Vita* interview, Ottaviani made a doctrinal statement against the use of the pill. Pills were different from rhythm, he said, since "pills act directly to impede the course of the conjugal act." But he saw no inconsistency in making his own pronouncement: he was not an ordinary bishop, he was secretary of the Holy Office and, therefore, a principal determining force behind pronouncements of the "supreme magisterium."

In December 1962, I interviewed the cardinal. In an incautious moment, and by implication, he had admitted he was above all the church's other bishops, even when they were in an ecumenical council. I was asking him about a reform of the Holy Office proposed on the council floor. He nodded and told me that the council could certainly draft a plan for reform. "When the council is finished with it," he said, "then we will consider it." He spoke as if he had veto power over a general council.

Ottaviani's primary objections to the pill were tied to an old natural law argument based on the biological integrity of the act of intercourse. He had for Reporter Furno other, perhaps sociological, arguments as well. Furno suggested to Ottaviani that the church's strictures on birth control were one of the principal reasons keeping people away from the sacraments. (This was the view of Bishop Bekkers and of many other pastors in 1964.) Asked Furno: "Would adoption of the pill with the church's consent favor a revival of religious life?"

Ottaviani's reply confirmed the suspicions of many lay people, that some clerics' fevered imaginings about married life as a kind of uninterrupted sexual whoopee clouded their thinking. Said the cardinal: "It might instead favor hedonism."

Would the pill alone make Catholic couples, especially those good people who had been trying to live up to church teachings, into devotees of this old abstraction? I discussed this notion with Michael Novak, an old friend. "I don't know what the cardinal thinks married folks do all the time," said Michael, with some exasperation. "But Karen and I are busy people. We both work hard all day long. At night we're tired. I wish we could devote more time than we do to each other. Yes, to giving each other more pleasure. Maybe we'd have a better marriage if we did." Would couples like the Novaks, given the pill, become hedonists? That, apparently, was one of Cardinal Ottaviani's fears.

Cardinal Ottaviani gave his interview to *Vita* at the end of May. But his efforts to dampen the fires of debate hardly seemed to work. On the contrary, the cardinal's informants in the U.S., guardians of faith and morals as he was, told him the American publishing industry was cranking out books on this hot new subject. Michael Novak had just finished *The Experience of Marriage*, a moving account by a dozen lay people largely intended to educate the clergy about things they never learned in the seminary. Louis Dupré was expanding a philosophic reevaluation of church teaching on birth control, originally published in the Catholic quarterly *Cross Currents*, into a book called *Contraception and Catholics*. In both England and the U.S., Leo Pyle brought together arguments on both sides of the question in *The Pill and Birth Regulation*. William Birmingham was editing an anthology, *What Modern Catholics Think About Birth Control.** And Archbishop Roberts had agreed to write the first chapter of a book edited by Gregory Baum, an Augustinian priest from Toronto, who worked at the Secretariat for Promoting Christian Unity, which would be called oxymoronically, *Contraception and Holiness.*

Even the University of Notre Dame, a bastion of American Catholicism, had had two conferences on the Problem of Population featuring leading U.S. Catholic philosophers, moral theologians, physicians and social

---

*The most shocking contribution in this book was Daniel Sullivan's history of Catholic thinking about women, marriage, love and sexuality. This thinking, wrote Sullivan, has been based, in part, on views expressed by some of the most eminent fathers and doctors of the church: of St. Jerome, that a woman is "the devil's gateway, a dangerous species, a scorpion's dart." Of St. John Damascene that she is a "sicked she-ass, a hideous tapeworm, the advanced post of hell." Of St. Clement of Alexandria that it "is shameful for her to think about what nature she has." Of St. Francis de Sales that married couples should not think about the act they might have to perform at night. Of St. Thomas Aquinas that "woman is misbegotten and defective." Of Pope St. Gregory the Great that woman's "use" is twofold: harlotry or maternity.

scientists. The second, in March 1964, had ended up endorsing the concept of responsible parenthood, reinterpreting natural law concerning birth control and suggesting that Catholics not participate in legal attempts to ban the sale of contraceptives "for reasons implicit in the character of a pluralistic society."[14]

It is not known whether at this juncture Ottaviani suggested to Pope Paul VI that perhaps the pope could do what the secretary of the Holy Office had been unable to do: try to tell Catholics everywhere, the Robertses and the Janssens and the van der Marcks and the Reusses, perhaps also the lay people who were now getting into the act, to hold up their pronouncements on the pill. It is likely that Ottaviani did so. It would have been natural for him to remind the pope that the supreme pontiff, not the council, as some were suggesting, would solve this disputed question.

At any rate, in the first week of June, Canon de Locht and the other dozen members of the birth control commission received a telegram from Amleto Cicognani, the Vatican's secretary of state, asking them to come to Rome for an urgent meeting on June 14. Canon de Locht said the telegram didn't say why. "We would find out when we got there," de Locht wrote in his diary.

The telegram did tell him this: that Cardinal Cicognani was concerned about public controversy stimulated by the reports of these new thinkers, whose opinions were "disturbing the children of the church."

This phrase in Cicognani's message, *l'inquietude de ses enfants*, probably reflected the paternalism of not only Cicognani, but the pope, too. The faithful were "children" not to be "disturbed." But the faithful most concerned about this question, de Locht would note, were not children, but adults, married couples, who, if they were disturbed, had every reason to be disturbed, and much to gain if their disturbance led them to think things through for themselves, instead of doing what they were told.

The commission members were informed they were to help the pope make "a pronouncement" about the birth control controversy on June 24, the feast of the pope's namesake, John the Baptist, and the first anniversary of his coronation as pope. That word "pronouncement" serves now as a clue to the then prevailing mind set of the pope's advisers. "Pronouncements" alone do not teach. In many parts of our society, pronouncements provoke quite the opposite response intended by the one making them.

When the commission members convened, they found their number had grown again. Now they were fifteen. The two new members, both intimates of the pope, were Tullo Goffi, a priest from the pope's hometown of Brescia, and Ferdinando Lambruschini, a theologian from the Lateran University in Rome. According to Canon de Locht, this group was urged to come to some conclusions with dispatch, because the pope wanted to say something, soon, about three items: 1) The basic question: the relationship between love and children, the primary end of marriage, 2) The call to life, one of the major responsibilities of a married couple, 3) The ways in which couples can exercise responsible parenthood, rhythm, the pill.

Members soon concluded they had to help the pope articulate the relationship "between fecundity and love," and they could not put love in any kind of second place. But the group was far from united, even in this. Some members expressed this fear: "If love is in the first place, then anything goes." Some of the same members bogged the commission down in peripheral matters, such as a discussion on the conditions required for a valid marriage. And then, when the members turned to yet another discussion of the pill, they didn't zero in on the root of the question at all, but wandered off into a debate on "the official doctrine of the church" and the need for maintaining continuity of doctrine.

Altogether, an unsatisfying session. Despite this, toward the end, they voted. De Riedmatten asked how the group felt about 1) the pill, and 2) the advisability of a papal pronouncement at this time.

Fourteen members voted. (Father Häring didn't attend this meeting.) Nine said they believed any contraceptive use of the pill should be forbidden. Five said they didn't know whether it should be, though two of the five, Van Rossum and de Locht, said they were leaning in its favor. None believed a papal statement approving the pill was possible or desirable now. Nevertheless, all wanted the pope to say something. But what? Their suggestion was vagueness itself: "To recall fundamental principles of morality, to stimulate research, and sustain pastoral action."

The only place the commission report was clear was too clear to suit de Locht. The report gave unconditional approval to rhythm, an approval which hardly reflected the questions and hesitations of some in the group. The report spoke of rhythm as a Christian ideal, an appeal for couples to transcend a "carnal" expression of their love and embark on a "progressive spiritualization" of it, modeling their marriages on the life of Mary and Joseph, who, tradition says, never made love, uh, carnally.

After these ambiguous cues from the commission, de Locht noted in his diary that he expected the pope to speak on birth control, come down hard in favor of rhythm, avoid saying anything about the pill, and remind confessors the old doctrine was still in force.

He was mostly right. On June 23, before the assembled college of cardinals, the pope made his celebrated reference to the complex and delicate birth control problem and said the norms given by Pope Pius XII "must be considered valid, at least until we feel obliged in conscience to change them. In matters of such gravity, it seems well that Catholics should wish to follow one law, that which the church authoritatively puts forward. And it therefore seems opportune to recommend that no one, for the present, take it upon himself to make pronouncements in terms different from the prevailing norm."

That sounded like a door slamming. But no. The pope was equivocal enough to leave the door open—a bit. He said the church would have to "proclaim the law of God in light of the scientific, social and psychological truths which in these times have undergone new and very ample study and documentation." And that it would be "necessary to face attentively this development, both theoretical and practical, of the question. And this, in fact, is what the church is doing."

At this point he revealed, for the first time, though somewhat obliquely, the existence of a papal commission: "The question is being subjected to study, as wide and profound as possible, as grave and honest as it must be on a subject of such importance. It is under study which, we may say, we hope will soon be concluded with the cooperation of many and outstanding experts. We will therefore soon give the conclusions of it in the form which will be considered most adapted to the subject and to the aim to be achieved."

* * *

To many of the Vatican's old guard, the pope's words could have been less Hamletic—to be or not to be and all that—but they were precisely what some Vatican officials needed to justify their ordering that the world's bishops shut up about birth control. June 25, two days after Paul's talk to the cardinals, Konrad Bafile, apostolic nuncio in Bad Godesberg, wrote the German hierarchy under the seal of Holy Office secrecy, which would lead one to conclude that this order was coming from the Holy Office. He warned about public declarations, opinions and theories on birth control that had been coming from Catholic scholars, even members of the episcopate, "which do not always conform to the traditional doctrine of the church."

The nuncio observed that this talk had "produced the impression that differences of opinion exist concerning this most important and delicate of questions. This has caused much insecurity, indeed, even confusion among the faithful." For this reason, he told the bishops to refrain from public declarations and to keep an eye on their theologians and scholars.

In Mainz, Josef Maria Reuss read the letter carefully, set it on top of a pile of papers on his desk, and sighed. Bishop Reuss had helped give the impression that differences of opinion did exist in the church. But it was true! There *were* differences of opinion. Would Cardinal Ottaviani deny the truth? Ah, well, he said to one of his priests, "I will stop writing on this, for a time." It is possible that he dreamed of being appointed to a place on the pope's commission.

* * *

Now the issue was closed, for the time being. Or was it? Some believed the tail end of the pope's June 23 statement conceded that the teaching of the church could change. Others said that the pope had simply expressed his willingness to let experts put that teaching to a test. In fact, if anyone had been privy to the papal commission's debates, they would have had more than enough reason to conclude that the pope's experts, though leaning to the traditional teaching, were far from certain on the question.

De Locht wrote a long note to de Riedmatten protesting de Riedmatten's report to the pope of the commission's June 14 meeting. "The Holy Father ought to know that our group labored under a certain working hypothesis [that this pope was bound by the pronouncements of past popes]. But there are other hypotheses which are not to be condemned out of hand."

De Locht said he could understand how a majority of the group could condemn the pill by leaning on Pius XII's view that the pill amounted to a direct sterilization. But he didn't see how the group could reduce all discussion of the pill to sterilization. And he added that a commission such as this one should be able to go to the heart of the question and not have its hands tied.

The commission, he said, had far too narrow a focus. It hadn't yet embraced the insights of married couples* or of some of the church's best

---

*Canon de Locht would take no chances that the church would continue to labor over this question without strong input from married couples. He suggested to a Belgian couple he knew well, Herman and Lena Buelens, that they draft an appeal to the pope and the bishops of the council reflecting the feelings of lay men and women. The Buelenses did so, and persuaded more than 120 Catholic intellectuals from many scientific fields to sign it, including 55 physicians, 30 university professors, and some who signed as parents. The statement pointed out the entirely new situation in world population, a situation brought about by mankind's intelligent intervention in what previously appeared to be natural laws regulating population growth, and now calling for control of the situation mankind has created. It urged extreme caution in applying natural law doctrine here. Men and women would seem to have norms in the overall good of the individual and of mankind, to which the natural law must likewise be directed. This is by no means conceived as a denial of God's absolute sovereignty, but as recognition of the responsible role that God has entrusted to human intelligence in the creative process. In various surgical and other fields, it is recognized and obvious that humans can intervene in the biological order for the sake of a greater good. The claims of the

theologians, hadn't even given them a hearing. It hadn't taken a broad perspective on marriage and its values. And it hadn't gone into the basic question: what is marriage for?

Father Häring wrote de Riedmatten a similar note. Perhaps others on the commission did the same. It is likely their observations were relayed to the pope and gave him pause, if only because everything gave this pope pause. But now the third session of the council was coming up fast. Perhaps the council itself would give the pope and the commission some guidance.

greater well-being of the individual and of humanity could demand active intervention in the field of human fertility. If the majority of sexual acts are neither potentially nor actually fertile, it is difficult to see that fertility can be considered the end of each individual act: it would appear to belong to the whole of married life.

In October, the Buelenses made sure their statement was delivered to every council father in Rome.[15]

Chapter Three

Guidance to the commission from the council would come, principally, in and through the council's *Pastoral Constitution on the Church in the Modern World*, which was being worked out in the fall of 1964 under the code words "*Schema* 13."

That *schema* (the Greek word means nothing more than "plan" or "draft") signalized the strange and original wish of Pope John to help the people of God see themselves "in the world" in a new way. For centuries, many in the church had been readier to judge and condemn the world than to help save it. John XXIII had presented a new vision. In his encyclical *Pacem in Terris*, he indicated that the time had come for the church to share in humanity's mysterious providential movements toward human unity. He wanted to help the entire body of Christians go along with these movements, to take a place in the modern world, to cooperate with people of every race and religion and contribute "to the building up of a community of peoples based on truth, justice, love and freedom," to become "a spark of light, a center of love" among peoples.

Commentators on the council can give a careful exegesis of John's words and actions during the fall of 1962 to demonstrate what he wanted. He did not want the council fathers to look on the church as a juridical entity, for such an abstraction would inevitably put "the church" as an institution in opposition to another abstaction, "the world." Rather, he wanted them to see the church as "the people of God" marching together in some mysterious journey through time, historical beings subject to the conditions of their places and their times, real people who happened to be citizens of the U.S.A. or the U.S.S.R. or the U.A.R. or the U.K., charged to witness in a world dying for lack of love.

It took the council fathers some time to get the idea, though Pope John had tried to make this clear on several occasions. In a remarkable address to humanity which he wrote through much of the night of September 9, 1962, and delivered on Vatican Radio September 11, he said, "The world indeed has need of Christ, and it is the church which must bring Christ to the world." He then listed the principal problems of this world in crisis.

The family. Their daily bread. Poverty. Social injustice. Underdeveloped nations. Religious liberty. And the greatest problem of all: peace.

Vatican bureaucrats, however, had their own narrower agenda; in several years of laborious preparation, members of the curia and some others had produced 70 conciliar projects. But not one of them dealt with any of these issues. How could Pope John cut through them all and get on with more important questions? Fortunately, Pope John's council had bright bishops, possessing extraordinary political skills, including the ability to turn a good phrase. Dom Helder Camara, then an auxiliary bishop of Rio de Janeiro, kept appearing at little discussion groups around Rome, a tiny man with sad eyes and delicate hands, asking, "Are we to spend our whole time discussing internal church problems while two-thirds of mankind is dying of hunger?" He was secretary of the Brazilian bishops' conference (more than 300 strong, the biggest such group at the council), and he called together the secretaries of other bishops' conferences: France, The Netherlands, Germany, Canada, Japan, India, Africa, to see how they could move things outward.

Someone suggested they talk to Leo Josef Suenens and they did. Cardinal Suenens invited Helder Camara and the secretaries of the bishops' conferences to speak to an international group at the Belgian College in Rome December 1. Suenens and the rest concluded they needed a new project on the church in the world.

Toward the end of the council's first session, on December 4, 1962, Cardinal Suenens rose in the conciliar hall of St. Peter's, a tall, impressive man, lean, graying at the temples, dark eyes flashing, and called upon the council to engage in a discussion with other Christians and with the whole world, move into the broader, more engrossing problems of life and death that faced the world there and then. "We must say something about the very life of the human person, the inviolability of that life, its procreation, its extension in what is called the population explosion. The church must speak on social justice. What is the theological and practical duty of rich nations toward the Third World or the nations that suffer from hunger? The church must speak about bringing the Gospel to the poor and some of the conditions the church must meet to make that Gospel relevant to them. The church must speak about international peace and war in a way that can help enlighten the world."

The next day, Giovanni Battista Montini, archbishop of Milan, took the council floor to express his agreement with this. Only one thing was wrong with the plan, though Cardinal Montini did not express his reservations about it there and then. He would take steps to correct the deficiency shortly after he became Pope Paul VI in June 1963. The problem was this: if the council was to speak for "the people of God" and engage in "a dialogue with the world," it had to bring in lay men and women, who had a conversance with the world that most bishops lacked. The council had to go beyond the strict canonical definition of a council: bishops advised by theologians. And so Pope Paul VI brought lay people into the commission charged with drafting *Schema* 13. This, he said, would give Vatican II "its own true character."

Inevitably, some bishops opposed this novelty, this entering into a dialogue with the world. At the beginning of the council's third session, in the fall of 1964, some even tried to scuttle *Schema* 13 so they could close the council in November. Some in the church never wanted a council in the first place; these, and possibly a few others upset by all the changes being mandated in an institution once seen as somehow above history, wanted to wrap things up, before the council could do any more damage. One way of doing that was to remove *Schema* 13 from the agenda altogether.

For a time, during the autumn of 1964, it looked as if those in charge might do exactly that. There were so many things wrong with the *schema*. Objections came from all sides; it was too general, it was too concrete, it was too modern, it was too traditional. It was too short. It was too long (it had four chapters and five lengthy appendices, called *adnexa*, containing, in part, earlier versions of the *schema* that had been discarded from earlier drafts but retained as explanatory matter). It was too ambitious. It didn't say enough.

But the real problem was this: the people behind it were the council's progressive elite* who were making every effort to speak not in old scholastic propositions that could be applied in unequivocal fashion to any problem, but in language that people from all walks of life (except, perhaps, the council's old line conservatives) could understand. One of the council fathers who praised this "heuristic approach": Karol Wojtyla, archbishop of Krakow, Poland.

For several days in the fall of 1964, the fathers deliberated about the *schema*, whether to accept it as a good starting point, or, as Archbishop Heenan of Westminster suggested, toss it into a postconciliar hopper and give it to specialists and priests with pastoral experience. They might produce a satisfactory text, he said, in three or four years.

---

*Bernard Häring lists the names of this elite group in a series of footnotes that follow his account in *Concilium* of the intense writing and rewriting of the *schema*, which went through at least seven rewrites before it got to the council in the fall of 1964. The list represents a kind of honor roll of the council's leading lights: Cardinals Suenens and Koenig, Bishops Ancel, Blomjous, Charue, Dearden, Garrone, Glorieux, Guano, Hengsbach, McGrath, Menager, Roy, Schroffer, Wright, Canons Delhaye, Dondeyne, Haubtmann, Heylen, Fathers Calvez, Congar, Danielou, de Lubac, de Riedmatten, Häring, Hirschmann, Houtart, Laurentin, Pavan, Philips, Rahner, Schillebeeckx, Sigmond, Tucci.[16]

Heenan was still smarting over the beating he had taken in the spring over birth control from Father Häring, one of the principal experts working on the marriage chapter and secretary of the Mixed Central Commission charged with producing the *schema*. Heenan zeroed in on the likes of Häring who had arranged for the bishops to debate the *schema* but leave the *adnexa* alone, a course Heenan said would be fatal, because it would leave interpretation of the council to the *periti*.

Timeo peritos adnexa ferentes, said Heenan, warning of the *periti* and their interpretations. As much as anyone, Heenan enjoyed a well-turned phrase, a play here on Virgil's line, "I fear the Greeks bearing gifts." Heenan went on:

Between sessions of this council, the church of God has suffered a great deal from the writings and speeches of some of the *periti*. They are few in number but their sound has gone forth to the ends of the earth. These few specialists care nothing for the ordinary teaching authority of the bishops, nor, I regret to say, for that of the pope.

It is idle to show them a papal encyclical in which a point of Catholic doctrine is clearly laid down. They will immediately reply that a pope is not infallible when writing an encyclical. It really does not seem worthwhile for the pope to write any more encyclical letters, since they can apparently no longer be quoted in support of the faith.

We must protect the authority of the teaching church. It is of no avail to talk about a college of bishops if, in articles, books and speeches, specialists contradict and pour scorn on what a body of bishops teaches. Until now it has not been a doctrine of the church that the theologians admitted to the council are infallible. The theories of one or two must not be mistaken for a general agreement among theologians, which has, of course, special authority.

Heenan singled out the section of the *schema* dealing with marriage, which, he said, prophesied that a special kind of pill, "a panacea to solve all sexual problems between husbands and wives," was just around the corner. He criticized the *schema* for suggesting that "married couples and they alone must decide what is right and wrong."

Francis X. Murphy, the American Redemptorist historian who helped produce a four-volume work on the council under the pen name Xavier Rynne, wrote, "The majority was obviously stunned by the vehemence and unexpected nature of Archbishop Heenan's attack. The speech, of course, evoked a round of applause for its display of rhetorical skill. Cardinal Ruffini was seen to grasp the hand of the archbishop, who looked somewhat embarrassed and uneasy over support from this (conservative) quarter."

Would the attacks of Heenan and others carry the day? The prospect worried many council leaders, who felt that if the council addressed only internal problems of the church, it would betray Pope John's unique new vision. The problem was no one yet knew whether this third session would be the last. If the council were to fold this fall, not enough time remained to produce a *schema* on the church in the world. That alone would seem to dictate another session.

But did the pope want one? No one knew, until late October, when it seemed Paul VI decided there would have to be, if only and especially to provide sufficient time to complete *Schema* 13. On October 23, Pericle Felici, the council's secretary-general, announced the pope's commitment to another session.

With that, reported Xavier Rynne, "There was a notable relaxation of tension. . . . The mood of the council seemed to change from pessimism to one of cautious optimism. . . ." For the next two weeks, the fathers expressed their opinions about the *schema*. And they voted a preliminary acceptance of it, 1,579 votes to 296. This last move put the *schema* firmly into the conciliar hopper. The interventions, oral and written, would enable the commission to redraft the document after the council adjourned and prepare for a final vote in the fall of 1965.

The most sensitive chapter of this *schema* was the section on marriage. The council presidents made it clear to the council fathers they were to stay away from the birth control question, because the pope was reserving the solution of that to himself and probably because the pope and some of his advisers were uncomfortable with the subject itself.

For the most part, the bishops did avoid direct discussion of birth control, the morality of the pill, or the casuistry of contraception. Many thought it was better that they were forced to deal with more basic questions, the very questions which Canon de Locht had said the papal birth control commission was avoiding.

On October 29 and 30, the bishops dealt with basics, but startled many council fathers into thinking new thoughts. The old group dynamics were working again.

Henri Fesquet, the penetrating correspondent from *Le Monde*, the French daily, wrote, "One might have thought this discussion would be veiled, timid, and circumlocutory. But it wasn't. Once more, the pessimists were wrong. The council of the twentieth century is plowing into the thick of things. . . . We can no longer say that the church is afraid to admit her narrowness, her shortcomings, or even her Manicheanism. To recognize one's errors is to grow: thus, the church grew on Thursday at Vatican II. She exorcised her own demons forcefully. . . . Christianity, the religion of love, carried the day over that Catholicism which catalogued prohibitions like a counting machine."

The council fathers knew something special was about to happen. The day before, they had jammed the council's coffee bars throughout the morning. This morning, the bishops were in their seats listening hard. One, Mark Hurley of Santa Rosa, California, called the atmosphere "electric."

Ernesto Ruffini, cardinal-archbishop of Palermo, was the first to speak. It was almost as if the fathers needed someone to remind them what the church of yesterday still wanted to say today: "Let us imitate St. Augustine, who did not hesitate to say that if parents do not use marriage in a Christian way, they fall into debauchery and prostitution. Let us not fear to speak the truth. We need not go far to find it. Catholic doctrine is very clearly defined in Pius XI's encyclical *Casti Connubii* and Pius XII's address to the midwives. Let us therefore redraft the *schema* accordingly."

Three of the council's most respected leaders promptly rebutted Ruffini. Paul Emile Léger, cardinal-archbishop of Montreal, responded: "Many theologians think that our present difficulties derive from an inadequate presentation of the goals of marriage. We have had a pessimistic, negative attitude toward love. This *schema* is intended to amend these conceptions and clarify love and its purposes: the goal of procreation and the goal of personal fulfillment." Cardinal Léger said he wanted to see the *schema* go even further: to "present the manifestations of love as a goal of love itself. Love is good in itself. It makes its own demands and has its own laws. The *schema* is too hesitant. Let us be clear. Otherwise the fear of conjugal love that has so long paralyzed our theology will persist. We must affirm that the intimate union of the couple finds its legitimate end in itself, even when it is not directed toward procreation."

This was plain talk. If the council fathers would go along with Léger's assertion that, for married couples, love in its carnal expression is good in itself, old understandings of the church's birth control prohibitions were passe. The next man to use the microphone, Cardinal Suenens, would speak just as plainly. Suenens immediately proposed that a conciliar commission work closely with the pope's own birth control commission and, a dig at the secrecy surrounding the pope's group, he suggested their names be made public so that others could feed them information.

Suenens said he wondered "whether up to now we have given sufficient emphasis to all aspects of the teaching of the church on marriage, whether we have opened our hearts completely to the Spirit in order to understand the divine truth. The Bible is always the same. But hasn't there been too much emphasis on the passage from Genesis, 'Increase and multiply,' and not enough on another phrase which says, 'And they shall be two in one flesh'? These two truths are central and both are scriptural."

The cardinal said it was for the pope's commission to say whether the church had been stressing procreation at the expense of another equally important end of marriage, growth in conjugal unity. And he added:

In the same way, it is up to this commission to deal with the immense problem arising from the population explosion and over-population in many parts of the world. For the first time, we must proceed with such a study in the light of the faith. It is difficult, but the world, whether consciously or not, waits for the church to express her thought and to be a "light for the nations." Let no one say that in this way we open the way to moral laxity. The problem confronts us not because the faithful try to satisfy their passions and their egotism, but because thousands of them try with anguish to live in double fidelity, to the doctrine of the church and to the demands of conjugal and parental love.

Cardinal Suenens noted that the church had much to learn about the man-woman relationship. He wondered whether classical church doctrine took sufficient account of the new knowledge achieved by modern science, for example, with respect to "the complexity with which the real or the biological interferes with the psychological, the conscious with the subcon-cious. New possibilities are constantly being discovered in man of his power to direct nature. This gives rise to a deeper understanding of the unity of man. We have made progress since Aristotle (and even since St. Augustine). Let us have done with Manichean pessimism. In this way we will understand better what is against love and what is not against love. I beg you, my brother bishops, let us avoid a new Galileo affair. One is enough for the church."

While the applause was dying on that intervention, the Melkite patriarch of Antioch, Maximos IV Saigh, came to the dais. Tall, bearded, lithe for his 87 years, he had the reputation of being one of the most outspoken men in the council. He didn't care for the rule that all should use Latin. He spoke French. And this time, he spoke of one of the church's greatest scandals: what he called the disparity between official church doctrine and "the con-trary practice of the immense majority" of Christian couples. "The faith-ful," he said, "find themselves forced to live in conflict with the law of the church, far from the sacraments, in constant anguish, unable to find a via-ble solution between two contradictory imperatives: conscience and nor-mal married life. The council must find a practical solution. This is a pas-toral duty. We must say if God really wishes this enfeebling and unnatural impasse."

Maximos said, "In marriage, the development of personality and its in-tegration into the creative plan of God are all one. Thus, the end of mar-riage should not be divided into 'primary and secondary.' " Then he asked the most embarassing question:

And are we not entitled to ask if certain positions are not the out-come of outmoded ideas and, perhaps, a celibate psychosis on the part of those unacquainted with this sector of life? Are we not, perhaps unwittingly, setting up a Manichean conception of man and the world, in which the work of the flesh, vitiated in itself, is tolerated only in view of children? Is the external biological rectitude of an act the only criterion of morality, independent of family life, of its moral, conjugal and family climate, and of the grave imperatives of prudence which must be the basic rule of all our human activity?

According to reliable reports, many in the aula were astonished, agape. Maximos went on:

> Far from me to minimize the delicacy and the gravity of the subject, or of eventual abuses: but here, as elsewhere, isn't it the duty of the church to educate the moral sense of her children, to form them in moral responsibility, personal and communitarian, profoundly rooted in Christ, rather than to envelop it in a net of prescriptions and commandments, and to demand that they purely and simply conform to these with their eyes closed?

Maximos concluded that the council fathers should open their own eyes and be practical. "Let us see things as they are and not as we would like them to be. Otherwise we risk speaking in a desert. What is at stake is the future of the mission of the church in the world." He finished with a thought that might have come from Pope John:

> Let the world know this: the church looks upon the world with profound understanding, with a sincere admiration, with a sincere intention not to subjugate but to serve it, not to despise it but to appreciate it, not to condemn it but to support and save it.

The quote, not from John XXIII but from Paul VI, uttered at the opening of the council's second session, couldn't have been a more appropriate reminder to this council and the pope what kind of commitment had already been made to the people of God, who were living in a world God loved.

For the third time that day, applause followed the speaker. This time, the cardinal moderator cut it short by calling for the next speech. But the council fathers had already clapped their vote for a new direction. And then, hundreds of them trooped out to the coffee bars behind the main altar of St. Peter's, to gossip about this turning in time.

The gossip continued that afternoon, when members of the U.S. bishops' press panel tried to summarize the significance of the day's developments. Frederick McManus, a *peritus* from Boston, said, "It takes an occasion like a council to bring forth such an event. . . . It is now evident what sentiment does exist." George Higgins, a *peritus* from Washington, D.C., noted that not too long ago Catholics who wrote what Léger, Suenens and Maximos said on this day suffered for their courage. And Charles Davis, a leading theological adviser to the English hierarchy, said, "I am very conscious of the fact that the change in my position as a theologian today can hardly be overestimated. After this morning, it can be said that the state of the question has changed."

But Cardinal Ottaviani, who had listened to the speeches of Léger and Suenens and Maximos with astonishment, did not think anything had changed. "I am not pleased with the statement of the text that married couples can determine the number of children they are to have," Ottaviani told the council next day. "This is unheard of, from previous centuries up to our own times. The priest who speaks to you is the eleventh of twelve children, whose father was a laborer in a bakery, a laborer, not the owner of a bakery, a laborer. He never doubted Providence, never thought about limiting his family, even though there were difficulties."

Ottaviani said he would hand over the microphone to Michael Browne, a curial cardinal attached to the Holy Office, who would give the church's solid doctrine on this subject. But first, he hoped no one would think, from what had been said the previous day in the aula, that the church might have erred on this question. That, he said, would be an enormity.

Cardinal Browne reminded everyone about the certain teaching of the popes, of classical theology: "The primary end of marriage, the end of the work, is the procreation and the education of children. The secondary end is, on the one hand, the mutual aid of the spouses, and on the other, a remedy for concupiscence." Browne gave the best citations he could find: Pope Leo XIII's *Arcanum*, Pope Pius XI's *Casti Connubii* and Pope Pius XII's addresses to the Italian midwives and to "the doctors," meaning, probably, the pope's 1958 statement on the pill to the International Congress of Hematology.

But if Cardinals Ottaviani and Browne could settle the question by merely quoting three popes, why did the argument continue? It did, and would for another year, in and out of the council. No one would really know how the council fathers felt unless and until the final votes were taken in the fall of 1965.

In the meantime, reporters could only guess at "the mind of the council" by counting speeches on the "liberal" and "conservative" sides. Xavier Rynne tried this. He pointed out that of six speakers who followed Browne October 30, two agreed with Browne and four sided with Maximos IV and Cardinals Léger, Suenens and Bernard Jan Alfrink, the cardinal-archbishop of Utrecht, The Netherlands. Alfrink gave a detailed account earlier that day on the ends of marriage, which might have been, and probably was, written for him by Father Schillebeeckx.

Among the four speaking for something other than what the Holy Office had taught with certainty for years: Josef Maria Reuss, auxiliary bishop and rector of the seminary in Mainz, whose intervention was countersigned by 145 bishops from Hyderabad to Helsinki. His list of co-signers included three from the U.S.: Paul Schulte of Indianapolis, Ernest

Primeau of Manchester, Vermont, and Philip Hannan of Washington, D.C., and at least 50 bishops from Latin America.

Reuss, too, spoke on the primacy of love that ought to extend to all of marriage, and then added: "Without doubt couples should have the attitude that says yes to children. Couples should know they have a mandate from God, that they are called to have children, and that it is not permitted to neglect this charge for egoistic and arbitrary reasons. But couples themselves should make the responsible decision how many children they should have. As for all the other problems connected with this question, our *schema* does not say more than can be said today. Let no one claim that study is superfluous. In this question, not everything is so clear as some say it is. We must make a more profound inquiry: what really are God's commandments here and what kind of help can be given to couples in trouble?" He pleaded with the council to endorse further work of the pope's birth control commission.

I was not surprised to learn that Bishop Reuss was taking some leadership. I had seen his combative spirit during the council's second session in 1963, when he had been offended by a jejune *schema* on the mass communication media. The council presidents had rammed that *schema* through to a vote because they wanted to get it out of the way. It was on the agenda but hardly considered important enough, even by council liberals, to merit much discussion. On the day scheduled for final passage, November 25, 1963, Reuss lobbied against it. He had his objections mimeographed, rounded up aides, and, on the steps of St. Peter's, started distributing his thoughts to the bishops arriving for the morning session.

Other bishops, other *periti*, had lobbied for or against one project or another. But this time, Pericle Felici, secretary general of the council, heard what Reuss was doing on the steps of St. Peter's, called Vatican police and led them to Reuss and his men. The police confiscated some sheets, but Reuss, believing he was doing nothing wrong and that his conciliar freedom was under attack, refused to hand his over. With that, Archbishop Felici seized Reuss's papers and retreated into the conciliar aula where he supervised a vote that approved the mass media project. The lobbying of Reuss and others had some effect: 503 of the council fathers voted no, the largest negative vote on any of the council's projects.

John Cogley and Michael Novak and I, journalists at the council, had also lobbied against the mass media project; it reflected a hopelessly abstract view of the relationship between the church and modern culture. So, when rumors flew around Rome about the confrontation between Reuss and Felici, I visited Reuss at his pensione, the Villa Stuart, to get a first hand account.

I expected Reuss to be disappointed by the outcome of the vote and he was. But he was simultaneously exhilarated and outraged at the actions of

Felici. He was outraged because, as he told me in Latin (he did not speak English and I did not speak German), *Vi eripuit, a manibus meis, vi eripuit.* "With force, he tore [the papers] from my hands, with force."

Reuss's cool blue eyes twinkled and he lit himself a long cigar. He was delighted to have something on Archbishop Felici, a handsome barrel-chested man who had alienated council liberals by his efforts to keep everyone in line. Felici was an administrator whose job was to move things along, sometimes too quickly to suit the growing majority of bishops, who didn't think a serious council could rubber stamp the *schemata* prepared by the curia, then go home and leave the running of the church to the Roman dicasteries. Reuss said, "Felici was clearly wrong here."

"What will you do?" I asked.

"I don't know. But I will think of something."

He did. He sued Felici for damages in an ecclesiastical court. Both Felici and Pope Paul tried to dissuade Reuss. But Reuss was adamant. He'd been offended. He wanted satisfaction.

The last thing the pope wanted was a legal squabble between a leading member of the Roman curia and a German bishop. But, for a year, Reuss went ahead with the legal filings. Finally, on November 3, 1964, Reuss saw the pope in a private audience and, when the pope asked him once more about the lawsuit, Reuss finally relented. He told Paul VI he would drop the suit. Paul thanked him. He wondered whether he, the pope, could do anything for Reuss. Reuss said he wanted the pope to read an article in his briefcase. It was in German, but. . . .

He pulled out a piece he had written for a German quarterly, *Theologie der Gegenwart*, a thoughtful instruction for priests, suggesting how they should deal with people in confession regarding birth control. The pope took the article.*

On December 6, Reuss wrote the pope a note from Mainz, remembering his audience with thanks and enclosing a French translation of his article in *Gegenwart* and another called "The Mutual Gift of Husband and Wife and Procreation." He intended the latter to help advance the study already launched by the pope's birth control commission.

* * *

*In it, Reuss never mentioned the pill, but he seemed to be trying out an argument in favor of something like the pill in circumstances when a couple faces a "conflict situation." 1) They have a duty to make love to each other, and 2) they also have a duty not to have children. In that case, "the only solution in such a conflict is the performance of marital intercourse which cannot lead to conception. If rhythm is not possible as a solution to this dilemma, then a couple has a correspondingly grave reason to justify some interference with the biological-physiological processes." He then rules out (or leaves aside) one kind of interference, in the actual performance of the act, but justifies another kind of interference, in anticipation of a future act.

The commission? Henri de Riedmatten and his "executive board" were then in Brussels preparing an agenda for a commission meeting at Rome in late March 1965. Through Cardinal Cicognani, the pope had already suggested to de Riedmatten that he might appoint some more commission members, doctors, perhaps, and some psychologists, too. What about including some married couples on the commission? Some people from the Third World? Could de Riedmatten or others on the commission suggest names?

My guess, based on knowing how things work in the Vatican, is that de Riedmatten and others who had the pope's ear offered names of those who could make genuine contributions to the commission's studies. Cardinal Cicognani and the pope weighed the qualifications of the nominees and chose those who came recommended, first and foremost, as loyal sons and daughters of the church.

But it was loyalty first, professional credentials second. No one knew more about the pill than John Rock of Boston. No priest had amassed as much learning on demographic questions as Arthur McCormack of the Mill Hill Fathers. But both Dr. Rock and Father McCormack had already taken positions that seemed to clash with traditional Catholic teaching. No one asked them to be on the Pontifical Commission for the Study of Population, the Family and Birth.

Who then? It was a strange, mixed bag. De Riedmatten's list on December 1, 1964 (see Appendix A) included 34 lay men and women, nine members of the secular clergy, 12 members of religious orders. Many were professors at the great universities, most of them Catholic institutions: The Gregorian and the Lateran in Rome; Louvain in Belgium; Georgetown, Notre Dame in the U.S.; the Catholic University of Chile. Some came from the University of Paris, one, Colin Clark, from Oxford, one, André Hellegers, from the medical school at Johns Hopkins in Baltimore. Two were practicing psychiatrists: Jean Raymond Bertolus of Paris and John Cavanagh, an American then living in Rome who had been Cardinal Cicognani's personal physician during Cicognani's 25 years as apostolic delegate in the United States. Dr. Cavanagh had probably published more than any other American layman on sex and marriage.

Most members were from western Europe and the U.S. There were eight each from Belgium and France, seven from the United States, five Germans, five Italians, three Spaniards. A small representation came from the Third World, all men and women who had already represented the church at the population conference in New Delhi in 1963. And there were three married couples. The Laurent Potvins of Ottawa and the Charles Rendus of Paris ran clinics on the rhythm method. The Patrick Crowleys of Chicago, who were the lead couple in an international organization called the Christian Family Movement. By the beginning of December 1964, de Riedmatten's commission had grown from 15 to 55.

Many had no inkling they would be chosen. The Crowleys may have been typical. On December 3, the Crowleys received a letter from Albert Meyer, cardinal-archbishop of Chicago, containing several enclosures, each of them a surprise. Cardinal Meyer's note congratulated the Crowleys on their appointment. He added, "While nothing was indicated about keeping this appointment secret, for the time being, I would suggest that no publicity be given to the appointment until you have further word about the same from Cardinal Cicognani."

Appointment? Appointment to what? Another note in the same packet explained, a letter in English from Cardinal Cicognani, dated November 20. It had gone through channels, from Cicognani's office to the office of the Vatican's apostolic delegate in Washington, then to Cardinal Meyer, then to the Crowleys:

I have the pleasure of informing you that the Holy Father has deigned to appoint you members of the special committee for studies on problems of population and birth control.

The committee, formed at the beginning by a small group of experts, has been subsequently enlarged and at present it includes 55 Catholic scientists, members of the clergy and laity, of different nationalities. . . .

Cardinal Cicognani's note said the group would work under supervision of the Holy Office and that Henri de Riedmatten was commission secretary.

The Crowleys were thrilled, mainly because they had devoted much of their lives to the church. Pat had gone to Notre Dame, he was well known around Chicago as a good Catholic lawyer, and the Crowleys had one daughter who had become a Benedictine nun. Now they were on a papal commission, one important to Catholic families everywhere.

Patty Crowley recalls they soon got a note from de Riedmatten, telling them he expected them in Rome in late March. The Vatican would pay their expenses, unless they felt they could pay themselves.

Though the Crowleys were appointed because, presumably, they represented thousands of couples in the Christian Family Movement, their first move was not toward the couples but to clerics. They were nothing if not loyal to the church. And, for them, the church meant the institutional church: they first conferred with their own bishop, Cardinal Meyer, and their spiritual adviser, Reynold Hillenbrand, then they had lunch at the Mid-American Club in Chicago with a Jesuit Biblical scholar, John McKenzie.

"We'd never challenged the church's teaching on birth control," recalled Patty. "We believed whatever the pope said. And what he said wasn't a problem for us." Patty had had six pregnancies, four children. During the last birth, she almost died. She said necessary surgery at that time, performed to save her life, precluded her ever having any more children.

In a 1981 interview, Patty Crowley recalled how strange she and Pat felt about keeping their membership on the commission a secret. "We were on the commission, we thought, to speak for all the folk in the Christian Family Movement. To do that, we needed to know what they were thinking. But, at first, we couldn't even ask them. We were advised not to tell members of the CFM what we were up to." Why not? Patty suspects some churchmen could see, more clearly, perhaps, than the pope himself, how the birth control debate of 1964 was undermining old notions of church authority.[17]

For years, Catholics had been told on the highest authority that any form of birth control except rhythm was simply wrong. Now, informed Catholics knew there was some doubt about that, and their doubts tended to upset old assumptions. In English-speaking countries, particularly, Catholics had prided themselves in being different, even superior, to their Protestant cousins because they didn't practice birth control. To protect these people, and maintain their own credibility on matters of faith and morals, some bishops preferred their people didn't know too much about those doubts or about the commission the pope was assembling to deal with those doubts.

Some took extraordinary efforts to keep their people uninformed. Some U.S. bishops told editors of their diocesan newspapers not to print these stories coming across the Atlantic, these interviews with the likes of Father Häring. Result: the American church's most faithful couples didn't understand a theological dispute which had real relevance to their lives. They got a glimmer from *Time* and *Newsweek*. But how many people read *Time?*

Richard J. Walsh, a young American television producer who directed the broadcast division of the National Council of Catholic Men, believed he had a duty to tell American Catholics what was going on. What better mass medium than television? With the encouragement of his board, he got John Leo, then an editor of *Commonweal*, to write a four-part series on "The Church and Marriage." For a narrator, he hired Phil Scharper, editor-in-chief of Sheed & Ward, then the most prestigious Catholic publishing house in the U.S. He taped the series at the studios of the National Broadcasting Company in Rockefeller Center and scheduled it to run four consecutive Sundays in January on NBC's Catholic Hour.

Terence Cooke, chancellor of the Archdiocese of New York, learned of the shows. Though New York held no sway over the National Council of Catholic Men, Monsignor Cooke got on the phone to a man who did, Patrick O'Boyle, archbishop of Washington, D.C., and the chairman of the

U.S. bishops' conference. Archbishop O'Boyle, in turn, called Leo Binz, archbishop of Minneapolis-St. Paul, the man in charge of the NCCM, who importuned Martin H. Work, executive director of the NCCM, to cancel the series.

Work did. In a letter to NBC dated December 31, Work was candid. He said a number of bishops didn't want to sponsor a series airing "some of the delicate moral and theological issues contained in the scripts." He said the subject was still under discussion at the Vatican Council, that the Holy Father himself had instituted a study commission on the subject, and had recommended limiting public discussion on it.

Walsh was upset and puzzled. For years, the U.S. bishops had given the NCCM a free hand. It had produced a highly successful show for Fulton Sheen on both radio and television. Never in 35 years had the organization had to do anything like this. "The pope didn't ban all discussion of the question," he told Donald Quinn of the *St. Louis Review*, one of the nation's better diocesan papers. "We quoted the pope's statement several times in the series. He said that no one should make official pronouncements while the matter was under discussion." The programs were not "pronouncements," official or otherwise.

"There wasn't anything in our scripts that hadn't also appeared in the press," Walsh told me in March 1983. "We just felt we wanted to inform those American Catholics who may not have been reading the newspaper and magazine accounts of the debate. Those people were in no man's land."

They would stay there as far as the U.S. bishops were concerned. Said Walsh: "Binz hadn't seen any of the shows, but his answer was no. He didn't want any public discussion at all."

John Leo's script was hardly the problem. A matter-of-fact narrative, it told how the subject of marriage and the family had undergone a centuries-long development in the church, ending with the pope's seeming to re-open the question. Privately, some American bishops said they felt that reopening the question was the pope's first mistake. His second was telling the world about it. That only riled people up and involved them in discussions that were beyond their competence. But the bishops wouldn't compound that mistake by announcing it on American television, no matter how much Dick Walsh felt that couples needed to know. Years later, Martin Work summed up in behalf of the bishops: "They saw this series as a challenge to papal authority. The pope told them to be quiet and now they were going to make a big deal of it on national TV?"

Louis Arand, a theologian from the Catholic University of America who had been checking NCCM scripts for 35 years, may have articulated the standard clerical objections when he wrote this note to Walsh after he saw an early draft of the John Leo script:

I do not believe it is possible to discuss these issues before millions of people who are unable to make the distinctions and qualifications demanded by these talks. If there is no authoritative guidance and teaching, then everyone will and must feel free to come to his own conclusions. And mere private judgment in matters of morals will be at least as pernicious as private judgment in matters of dogma.[18]

Father Arand's view reflected the long-standing paternalism of churchmen who honestly felt they were serving their people by producing instant responses to every moral question without troubling the conscience of anyone. Council leaders were saying quite the opposite: that the teaching church should trouble the consciences of everyone. If the people of God were to get more involved in the world (as *Schema* 13 was urging them to do), they could only avoid the dangers of clericalism by not continuing to look upon the church as an "answer machine," especially on moral matters. Moral judgments were applications of the principles of practical reason by those who had to act. This was one reason Pope Paul wanted couples on a birth control commission. For the first time in history, the church was seeking qualified opinions not only from members of the celibate clergy, but also from married couples, like the Crowleys.

* * *

No one could have predicted then what a radical move this would be, certainly not the Crowleys, who didn't have a radical thought in their heads when they began, except one. As they made plans to jet for Rome in March, they wondered: would they go over empty handed and empty headed? What would they tell the commission? They weren't sure. But maybe some of their members had ideas. "Secrecy or no," they told each other, "we ought to be able to talk to our own CFM members, at least."

In phone calls, they discussed this with another commission member, André Hellegers, also married and a gynecologist from the medical school at Johns Hopkins. (Dr. Hellegers' young son would tell his classmates in Baltimore that his dad was "the pope's gynecologist.") Together they agreed on one plan. Hellegers would help them put together a questionnaire, and the Crowleys would send it to members of the Christian Family Movement. Hellegers felt that CFM people would repond to the Crowleys in a way they would not respond to him, or to any doctors, about their practice of rhythm. He felt such a study would prove not that rhythm did not work, but that it hadn't really been tried. Such a result, he said, "could take some of the pressure off the priests if they knew that their people really hadn't practiced rhythm, but only thought they had. They might then see the need for real expert rhythm advisers."

The Crowleys were eager to help. They said they would also be pleased to go to Baltimore (Hellegers' idea) for a preliminary meeting with other commission members, and did so, January 20, 1965. Others there: Donald Barrett of Notre Dame; John Macisco, a colleague of Thomas Burch at Georgetown, substituting for Burch, ill at the time; John C. Ford, the Jesuit moralist from New England; Dr. and Mme. Potvin from Ottawa and Dr. Hellegers. Purpose: to organize themselves (and perhaps the commission, too).

Someday historians will find a record of this meeting in the files of the commission. That report, sent to Rome by Donald Barrett, reflected some strong feelings. The North Americans were impatient with the inefficiency and fumbling of the commission thus far. And some of them could not understand why the pope didn't settle things beforehand.

Professor Burch had already told them most of the meetings he'd attended had been conducted in French. That scared some. They weren't frightened by the prospect of swimming in deep, new theological waters. At this time, they had no idea they'd be doing that. But they didn't see how they could handle the French. They passed a resolution asking the pope to provide simultaneous translations of everything said in commission meetings. They had other ideas for the pope: he ought to have all the meetings recorded and transcriptions for everyone, and have all the documents relating to the commission's work available to each member, and, a typically American solution, they proposed a bigger staff, and an adequate budget for the commission secretary. "A study of this importance thus conducted will approximate the sum of one million dollars," the Americans wrote.

They offered to raise the money, if that were a problem. "Hellegers had sources," recalled Thomas Burch. "He knew the Kennedys. Pat Crowley could have helped, too. But we never had to come up with it. The Vatican found the money elsewhere."

The Americans were as bold in setting forth their preconciliar ecclesiology as they were about money matters and logistics. They were actually going to tell the pope—they were almost cross with him for not having exercised sufficiently strong leadership to keep people in line—that in spite of his June 23 statement, "confusion among the faithful has not diminished, but has, if anything, increased." Too many supposed experts were giving speeches on birth control and there was considerable danger the church was "following the practice of the faithful, rather than determining it."

Somehow, this didn't have the right ring. The Crowleys were among those who said they'd rather not send this letter. This group seemed to be putting "the church" on one side and "the faithful" on the other, and ignoring the respected view of Cardinal Newman and others that anyone wishing to know Catholic doctrine, particularly on marriage, must "consult the faithful." The Crowleys objected to another recommendation in this draft that the pope first resolve confusion on contraception by giving an allocution to reaffirm church teaching authority through the magisterium. Then, the commission could go on to its "exhaustive study of the entire problem of birth control and population." Not mentioned: how the pope was supposed to resolve "confusion" before his commission had done its "exhaustive study."

In the end, the North Americans didn't send their letter to the pope. The Crowleys went home to Chicago and, with the encouragement and help of Hellegers and Barrett, drafted a survey for members of the Christian Family Movement, couples known as good Catholics in the 1950s and 1960s because they had big families. Most families they surveyed in the winter of 1965 had at least six children; some had 13. And what did they ask in their survey? Only a few questions aimed at finding out how successful these couples were in practicing rhythm, whether rhythm helped them regulate the size of their families, and why; and whether rhythm helped or hurt their marriages. The Crowleys started sending out their questionnaires in late January. By the time they were ready for their trip to Rome in late March, they would have a sheaf of surprising replies that would give everyone pause.

* * *

In mid-January, Bishop Reuss wrote Pope Paul another letter. He was sure the pope must be thinking about pastoral implications of a change on the birth control question:

In my humble opinion, it seems that the commission brought together by Your Holiness should ask whether it is certain that every anti-conceptive act, once one grants the liceity of rhythm, should be declared absolutely illicit. The church has not always taught the same things about what is licit in marriage.

Reuss anticipated an argument against this new view, the notion that a changing church would lose all credibility:

If the commission could come to some new understanding of the problem, there would be no harm to the authority of the magisterium. The faithful know how to distinguish between infallible doctrines and other doctrinal decisions which may be reformable. On the contrary, the faithful would be filled with more confidence in the magisterium because they would see that the magisterium is imbued with concern for the truth and for the good of souls.

In early February, Reuss got a response to this letter from Angelo Dell'Acqua, the top undersecretary of state in the Vatican. In curial Latin, Archbishop Dell'Acqua said the pope had read Reuss's note and was not wholly persuaded by Reuss's reasoning. Nevertheless, reported

Dell'Acqua, the vicar of Christ had ordered that Reuss's material be given to the papal commission.

Perhaps the pope was more impressed with Reuss's arguments than this note from Dell'Acqua revealed. In any event, two weeks later, Cardinal Cicognani informed Reuss the pope had appointed him to the Pontifical Commission for the Study of Population, the Family and Birth. Twenty years later, Reuss would tell me that the pope was giving him a payoff for dropping his lawsuit against Archbishop Felici. But now Reuss, too, would be at the March meeting.

So, too, would Leo Binz, archbishop of Minneapolis-St. Paul. The pope appointed him at the same time he appointed Bishop Reuss, an indication, perhaps, that the Vatican was trying to keep some balance on the commission. Through his writings, Reuss had made his position known. So had Binz, but not through the force of rational argument. It was Binz who had demonstrated the closed approach, or his loyalty to the church, or to Rome, or to the Holy See, or to the Holy Office, or whatever, by suppressing the NCCM's four-part television series on marriage and the family.

Chapter Four

The Crowleys arrived in Rome on the afternoon of March 24 and took a taxi to the Spanish College on the Via Torre Rossa, chosen because it was a large, new edifice on the outskirts of Rome, where the commission could meet in secret. The Spanish seminarians had not yet taken residence, so there was plenty of room for everyone. But not for Patty Crowley.

Father de Riedmatten, a bluff fellow with a crew cut and dark, horn-rimmed glasses, met the Crowleys in front of the college, greeted them warmly, then told them that the five women on the commission would sleep at a poor convent down the road, on the Monte del Gallo.

Pat and Patty Crowley didn't like that. They believed they were on the commission because they were married, not church officials or employees. In this regard they were unique: the other married couples on the commission, the Potvins and the Rendus, ran church-related programs to teach Catholic couples the rhythm method. Now the Crowleys realized that, throughout this meeting, they were to be like celibates. The two put their heads together. Should they make a fuss? Ah, well, they said, it's not a big deal. The meeting would last only four days. They were sure Father de Riedmatten didn't understand, that the incongruity of the situation didn't occur to him.

So they got back in the taxi, Pat saw Patty to her convent room, then they returned to the college for dinner with other commission members. They ate in the college refectory, simple fare, some chicken, some pasta.

Immediately after dinner, everyone adjourned to their large work room, two classrooms with a portable partition taken down between them, so the conference chamber was rather long and narrow, with everyone sitting around the periphery of the room in a large "U."

The Crowleys hardly knew what to expect, not even what language the commission would use. The Vatican had so far turned down the American offer to fund the hiring of simultaneous translators. But they were pleasantly surprised to find the first meeting conducted in English by a young professor from Notre Dame, John Noonan. Noonan had achieved notoriety in the church for his masterful work on usury, showing how theologians had long condemned the lending of money for a fee, then, under the impact of new folkways and a new understanding of economics, did a complete turnabout.

For more than a year now, Noonan, a 32-year-old bachelor with a strong Boston accent, told the group he had been writing a history of church teaching on contraception. Those in the church who could abide no change had insisted that "the church has always condemned contraception." Noonan confirmed that. Contraception was a fact in the ancient world. Classical authors had written about "potions of sterility" in ancient Greece and Rome, whores in Egypt used various kinds of pessaries, and poor couples who could not handle offspring practiced coitus interruptus, withdrawal. The contraceptive practices "invited the ideas and judgment of Christian moralists from the first century to the present."

But why did the church's moralists condemn contraception? Who made these condemnations? Whom were they condemning? And in response to what problem?

Noonan found that for more than a thousand years, the church was reacting to challenges from three major heretical groups opposing any procreation. Common sense alone compelled the church to put these people in their place.

The church was right to do so, Noonan said, but for possibly the wrong reasons. St. Augustine, for example, had a bias against sexual pleasure that resulted more from a struggle with his own sexuality than from anything Christ taught. And Augustine typified the church's intellectuals in those days, who were convinced that sex was bad, and that sexual pleasure was a no no for everyone, even husbands and wives, unless there was "an excusing good." Procreation was the only excusing good.

Relying solely on written documentation, Noonan made an ironclad case for the church's consistent teaching on the evil of contraception, though it was obvious medieval authors didn't copy patristic teaching. They selected and adapted. Why? Noonan guessed that contemporary problems and tribal traditions had their influence. He noted that these were times when many hostile forces threatened. Life was precarious. There was a population shortage.

Noonan also noted that the church experienced "creative years" in theology and canon law from 1140 to 1260, when the church was fighting heretics called Cathars, who proclaimed the world evil and attacked procreation as a value in marriage. A church lawyer, Gratian, accordingly wrote the canon *Aliquando* in 1142 denouncing contraception. Peter Lombard, writing about 1150 in Paris, adopted this canon in his *Sentences*, a textbook used by every student of theology for the next 400 years.

"Once the basic texts were set," said Noonan, "opposition to contraception was established and perpetuated without need for external stimulus or challenge." They became church law from the twelfth century to the twentieth.

Said Noonan: "There was no suggestion that intercourse might lawfully be for the purpose of expressing love." The only time love was regularly spoken of in connection with intercourse, he added, was to repeat an old warning by St. Jerome (borrowed from the Stoic philosophers) that "the too ardent lover of his wife is an adulterer."

Even so, Noonan pointed out, the church accepted marriage of the sterile. The church taught that a man and a woman might marry, no matter their age. Yet if marriage was for procreation, and the only lawful purpose in initiating intercourse was procreation, how could the sterile have intercourse without sin? Said Noonan: "No theologian dealt with this contradiction between Augustinian theory and the custom of the church."

But in Renaissance Europe, Noonan noted, something new began to happen. In a tract for lay people on married life, Denis the Carthusian, a fifteenth century Flemish monk, struggled with this question: whether love based on sensual delight might be sought in matrimony and marital intercourse. If the marital act itself is good, he reasoned, then it is good to seek pleasure in the act and find love through it. For Noonan, this was "the first Catholic linking of the value of love to marital intercourse."

Through the centuries, theologians would develop this idea. But it had little apparent impact on the size of the average Christian family. "There was no population problem in the sixteenth and seventeenth century Europe," said Noonan, "where colonization of the New World was the solution to population pressures. Plague, infant mortality rates, and bad sanitation made human life precarious, and the preservation of the race a critical matter. A quarter, even a third, of city populations were swept away by plagues in the seventeenth century. Milan is estimated to have lost 40 percent of its population in the plague of 1630. In these circumstances, there were no pressing social reasons for modifying the old rule."

Then came the industrial revolution. A new pattern of living emerged: families no longer needed to be so large; children no longer represented extra hands on the farm, but extra mouths to feed. Urban dwellers, in fact, started limiting the number of their children. The old canon law condemning contraception was still in force, Noonan noted. But no vigorous effort was made to enforce it. Sermons on the subject were rare. St. Alphonsus Liguori recommended that confessors ask a woman only if she has been faithful to her husband and avoid other questions relating to marital life. Neither pope nor bishop bothered instructing the faithful in this regard. Theologians of the era stuck closely to the works of their predecessors. "They produced manuals which were summaries of earlier works. There was little fresh analysis and little attempt to understand the situation sociologically or historically."

Until the end of the nineteenth century, then, the church was not overly excited about birth control. In 1880, Pope Leo XIII wrote an encyclical on marriage; he did not mention contraception. But the modern birth control movement had only begun. A neo-Malthusian league was formed in London in 1876, and, though the medical profession itself was slow to approve birth control, the idea's time had come. The neo-Malthusians sold their program as a humanitarian cause, help to the poor, and a way to avoid excess populations that led to war.

Many bought this idea. Noonan said birth rates in Western Europe proved that: in Belgium, they started falling from a level of 31 per 1,000 in the 1870s to fewer than 20 per 1,000 in the 1930s. At the end of this period, the birth control movement had won the support not only of radical reformers, but also of many doctors, sociologists and Protestant leaders.

Another assault on the value of life? The church thought so. Once again, as in the days of the Catharist heresy, it went into action. Noonan reported that as the birth control movement spread, Catholic opposition became stronger. Rome started urging confessors to interrogate people in the confessional where there was "founded suspicion of onanism." In 1909, the Belgian bishops issued a pastoral letter to the faithful and instructions to confessors on ways to combat "the vice of onanism." In 1913, the bishops of Germany followed suit, the French bishops in 1919. The U.S. bishops wrote a similar pastoral in 1920. Finally, on December 31, 1930, Pope Pius XI issued his encyclical *Casti Connubii*.

Noonan refrained from dubbing that encyclical out of date or even a pointed reaction to a pointed challenge by the Anglican bishops at Lambeth. But he did call this encyclical "a high water mark, a climax rather than the beginning of a campaign." More development lay ahead, moving toward a qualified acceptance of birth control.

To ascertain what happened in the church from 1930 to 1964, Noonan said one first had to ask what had happened in the world at large, at least in Western Europe and the United States.

Items:

• Women had become the social equals of men, leading to freer choices in marriage and an accent on marriage for love, not convenience or security.

• Education had become universal, lengthy, expensive.

• Life expectancies had risen, from 25 in the days of the Roman empire to 69 in Western Europe during the 1960s.

Noonan outlined areas where reputable church representatives had taken positions different from *Casti Connubii*:

• People were rightly giving lovemaking a peculiar new value in marriage.

• In a backhanded way (perhaps without even realizing what he was doing), Pius XII had disapproved of artificial insemination; his objections seemed to be based on the premise that old-fashioned lovemaking was part of God's plan for husbands and wives and that it was good in itself. Pius XII thus contradicted the Augustinian view of sexual intercourse as a mere biological tool.

• Authorities were taking a new, positive attitude toward use of the sterile period. *Casti Connubii* had vaguely mentioned rhythm; bishops and theologians had been guarded about it until 1951, when Pius XII fully approved it if a couple had serious economic, medical or social reasons to avoid offspring.

• Finally, Noonan noted that the gathering of this commission represented another development. He referred to Paul VI's address to the college of cardinals June 23, 1964, indicating that "the matter is open enough to deserve the attentive study of the church in the light of new scientific, social and historical understanding."

Noonan looked up over his large, horn-rimmed spectacles at the assembly. "It is to that reconsideration that I understand you are addressing yourselves, so that you now enter into this historical process—this process of preserving a balance in a complex of values and of selecting options to preserve the central values committed by Christ to the care of his church."

Noonan had stated his view of those values: 1) procreation is good, 2) procreation is never complete without education of the children that follow, 3) human life is sacred. The question: could this commission take a new view of contraception that would not go against these long-standing values?

Noonan's learned talk lasted two hours. Many audiences might have found it too long, too filled with *Wissenschaft*. This audience found it just right. And its general, though soft-spoken, lesson was clear: church teaching on this question had gradually changed, impelled by varying conditions of the times, and always with a view toward preserving basic respect for human life. Were there any reasons new insights could not bring further change? Logically, some members of the audience told themselves, there were none.

Furthermore, an official church body, this very commission, could transcend the limitations of the past. Noonan did not speak about those limitations. But in his book *Contraception*, then on press, he noted that in much of church history, most of the decisions were made for the people by celibate clerics.[19] Now, perhaps for the first time in the modern church, there was a new deal: the pope had seen to it that the majority of members on this deliberative body were lay men and lay women.

* * *

At first the lay men and lay women hung back, unable to say what they felt. The Crowleys knew in their hearts that rhythm didn't work; not only did it not help couples avoid new births, the method also militated against what they saw as a necessary expression of human love between husband and wife. But when Patrick addressed the commission, he was so circumspect that one could hardly guess his position: "Our long identification with Christian families," he said, "gives our report on how family people feel on this subject some evidentiary value. In response to our inquiries, we received a number of interesting letters. . . ." Blah, blah, blah. On he went. He related the history of the Christian Family Movement. He told the group how sympathetic the movement was to large families. Would he ever come to the point? Yes, but not yet.

Patty has since recalled the hesitation she and Pat had at the time. "We hung back," she said. "We didn't know what the church wanted. It wasn't until later that we realized that 'the church' didn't know any more than we did. We were the church."

What did it take for the commission members to arrive at that realization? A good deal of talk. In retrospect, they seemed to be wandering in circles for an unconscionably long time. They were like inexperienced hunters, lost in the woods. Once out of the woods, they might wonder how they could have taken one absurd turn after another. But at this time they were still in the forest, still taking wrong turns, still going around in circles.

Here, for example, was a note from de Riedmatten to commission members as they were about to discuss "immediate action" by the pope:

The main intent in this part of the session is to give the group a chance to formulate its views on the possibility of considering that certain points seem today to be sufficiently settled so that the commissioning authority can intervene, in the manner it considers preferable, this intervention to be of such a nature as to permit as a consequence the solution of several difficulties still pending; furthermore, certain questions which are constantly asked today, either in the form of a doubt or of a crucial question, will be faced up to so that the group will be in a position to formulate, either as a general conclusion accepted by it, or as alternatives, or as opposite conclusions (but reasons given) its opinion on the possibility of immediate action in reply to these questions.

But a majority of commission members were beginning to see they had a lot more thinking to do, listening and learning from one another, before they could advise the pope what "immediate action" to take. They seemed to have a healthy humility. They started each morning with a mass of the Holy Spirit, asking for enlightenment, then worked an extraordinarily long day, starting with major section meetings, then breaking for the day's meal at one and a postprandial walk, then meeting again in general session each afternoon until suppertime. Another meeting after supper lasted until ten p.m.

De Riedmatten had divided the commission members (now numbering 57) into three major sections: one group of sociologists, demographers and economists, another of medical professionals and a third of theolo gians. But after three days, none of the subsections provided any definitive "answer."

Those who attempted to force answers won no admiration from the rest. George A. Kelly, a well-tailored monsignor from New York, swooped into a theological section meeting, read a paper that neatly summarized past papal teaching and zoomed off in a cloud of dust. One American said he was ashamed of Kelly: "He treated the whole thing like a bit of testimony before a Congressional subcommittee." John Marshall said, "Most of us were there in a kind of fact-finding mode. Monsignor Kelly didn't get into the spirit at all." The more prevailing opinion among those who sat through the March meeting: "We don't have any solutions."

Some members considered this progress, of a sort: in the recent past, the church had been handing down easy answers, with vast harm to its credibility. Now, a papal commission was daring to say that in this area of marital morality, there were no panaceas—certainly none this commission wanted to recommend for the pope to proclaim.

The social scientists could report only what "the folk" were doing. The sociologists and demographers had collected a staggering compendium of laws of all the countries of the world relating to sterilization, abortion and birth control; current figures and projections on world population and food production; data on birth control programs, from English rhythm clinics to Korean centers for intrauterine devices.

They reported on various cultural understandings of the concept "love." But, as one expert later told me, "A statement on conjugal love is all right to have, but it's pretty hard to apply it uniformly to a couple living in the slums of Bogota, a rich Italian family and a middle-class American couple. Even we Westerners don't understand one another when we talk about love. The French are wild. They have a full-blown mystique about sex and love. Their expositions were poetry—and prose that was absolutely incomprehensible to an Anglo-Saxon."

Marriage itself? Different understandings of it appeared in different cultures. Marriages in India were still, by and large, arranged by a couple's parents. Africans still prized large families. In Japan, abortions were everyday happenings. Commission members knew that such data about *what was* in this or that part of the world could provide no real guidance to the pope on what *ought to be* on any universal plane.

Most demographers on the commission were alarmed by predictions that world population would double by the year 2,000, an outcome that would have an effect on world hunger and, therefore, on world peace. In the slums of great Latin American cities, for example, the population explosion was acute. Better medical care lowered infant mortality and advanced longevity, and birth rates were rising. Should the commission urge "responsible parenthood" upon the world? Tom Burch advised the comission that that term was "a highly elusive one. . . . Attempts to formulate an ethical ideal of 'responsible parenthood' valid for all Christians should stop short at a fairly general level. An ideal set forth in very specific terms is certain to reflect the situation in a particular time and place, and to that extent will be irrelevant to persons in widely differing social circumstances."

Finally, the experts said they were loath to push populations toward methods contrary to their own folkways, "just for the sake of allowing the most highly developed section of people to live without worrying about their neighbors."

Perhaps the ever-rising birth rate was a problem in the *favelas* of Rio de Janeiro. But birth control was not the only solution, and these experts said the church should beware of giving the Third World the impression it was. Developed peoples and rich nations still had a duty in charity and justice to help underdeveloped nations, economically, politically, financially. This was a bit beyond the competence of the church as church, and in one commission member's words, "so complicated that nothing the church could say would make universal sense."

Rather than have the church deal with birth control in any global sense, the commission's demographers recommended keeping the question of family limitation "on the level of married couples," which put the solution (if indeed there were one) back in the theologians' camp.

Those on the medical section, led by André Hellegers, reported on every known method of birth control, including statistics on each method's effectiveness and its medical advantages and disadvantages. They ruminated about the effects of the pill and of the intrauterine device (often called "the coil" or IUD) on the female reproductive system. Dr. Cavanaugh reported that specialists he consulted agreed the pill was an anovulant; they were not sure it was an abortifacient, important distinctions for the commission, because the delayed passage of an egg was one thing and the killing of a fertilized egg something else. Dr. Hellegers told the commission it was unclear that the IUD was an abortifacient.

Pierre Van Rossum made a strong pitch for the morality of the pill and the IUD. This physician's reasons were not medical but theological—or canonical, for he harkened back to something in canon law: that intercourse always had to be *unitivus et inseminativus,* that is, intercourse had to place the male seed in the female vagina. He claimed that this was why the only birth control methods ever explicitly condemned by the Holy Office were withdrawal and the condom. Said Dr. Van Rossum: "Coitus always unites and always inseminates because of the way that the male functions, but it does not always procreate. From this, it can be inferred that those methods which respect the uniting and inseminating characteristics are permissible and those which separate one from the other, such as coitus interruptus, are not permissible."

Some theologians wanted to know from the doctors whether the pill or the IUD were "against nature." They answered that with other questions: "What do you mean by nature? Isn't much of man's activity interfering with nature, from building dams to performing surgery?"

Father Häring, ever a step or two ahead of his theological colleagues, agreed. According to Patrick Crowley's handwritten notes during one theological section meeting, Father Häring said that, because human nature is also rational, men and women can and should apply reason to every aspect of their lives. Said Häring: "Sex tends to be an expression of love. This is not true of animals."

Claude Thibaut, a research scientist from Paris, also pointed out the difference between animal and human sexuality. Animals go into heat, they copulate, they reproduce their kind. He said men and women make free decisions. And, more often than not, their lovemaking has nothing to do with "procreation" in either an ontological or psychological sense. He talked about the "prodigality of nature in producing spermatazoa and ova, a prodigality which is rendered even more striking by the infinitely small number which finally take part in fecundation; and in addition, 30% of the fertilized ova are lost either before or after nidation."

The point was clear: babies do not necessarily follow on lovemaking "naturally," as morning the dawn. The psychologists and psychiatrist chimed in with their counterparts in physical medicine, noting that couples need to make love, even when they cannot risk having children.

More and more strongly, the numbers began leaning toward the ideas of Bishop Reuss, who contended that in such a complex thing as marriage a couple might reasonably put aside one goal in favor of another, equally important, goal: They might have a duty not to make a baby and still have a duty to make love, as long as the method they used did not interfere with "the substantial integrity of the marital act."

Of all birth control methods, the pill seemed to "interfere" least. Theologically, many members favored the pill. But, for medical reasons, they feared it. So they told de Riedmatten any statement on the pill was "inopportune," even if a state of doubt existed on the morality of the pill.

One who did not believe the pill was permissible under the doubtful law doctrine: Joseph Fuchs, perhaps the most highly regarded moral theologian on the commission. Father Fuchs was a princely German Jesuit, one of an elite minority inside an elite order. For decades a band of German Jesuits had been Vatican insiders, principal advisers to Pope Pius XII, the scholars who drafted many papal allocutions and encyclicals. On matters dealing with sex, Pius XII's principal adviser was Franz Hürth, a German Jesuit. Father Hürth taught at the Gregorian University in Rome; seminaries around the world used his Latin text on the sixth commandment. What thousands of priests knew about sex, they knew from Hürth. And when Hürth grew old, the Jesuits groomed another German Jesuit to take his place, Father Fuchs. Fuchs had his own Latin text, *De Castitate.*

Fuchs was a classical moralist, in the sense that he upheld an objective moral order: good intentions alone are not sufficient; one has to *do* good, too. A newer school of Catholic theologians was more concerned (as Protestants had long been) with basic orientations under the aegis of God's love. But it would be unfair to Fuchs to characterize him as either "conservative" or "progressive." The man was too far learned, too much a scholar, too much a teacher to be tossed into any facile category. His textbook may have contributed to the notion that the church had clear answers to every moral problem dealing with sex. All the questions and answers *were* in his *De Castitate.* But, in an article in the Winter 1964 *Chicago Studies,* Fuchs himself made it clear that the church was not "an answer machine."

When a new moral problem is to be solved by human insight, i.e., through the natural law, one ought not to be surprised when occasionally a solution is not found at once, and perhaps not even for a long time. Perhaps some of the faithful have too mechanical a conception of the church, as though a new question required only the unlocking of an existing treasury of truths? The church . . . is no automaton; nor is the pope, nor the bishops united with him; nor the theologians. The finding of truth presupposes painful search: a search by the human spirit within the facts of the situation. . . .

Fuchs and his commission colleagues were engaged in such a painful search. In his early position papers for the commission, one can see Fuch's dissatisfaction with continuing arguments for or against the pill, because those arguments responded to old questions which may or may not have penetrated the heart of the modern problem: what will help men and women grow together in intimacy?

Fuchs had particular difficulty with one major argument for the pill: it was morally acceptable because it did not interfere with "the substantial integrity of the marital act." Some of his colleagues were trying to apply an old canon law definition—*depositum seminis in vagina.* But the act's integrity required something more than depositing sperm into the right receptacle. If not, said Fuchs, why should a couple limit themselves to the pill? A diaphragm, the coil or spermicidal creams would achieve the same result.

No one yet had the answer to the knotty question. But de Riedmatten was convinced everyone agreed on the necessity for change. In a report to the pope on this meeting, he wrote, "Everybody, conservative or progressive, theologians or lay men, all are convinced of the necessity for the church to make a fresh move in order to face up to the distress of conscience and the needs arising from facts that cannot be denied."

De Riedmatten, however, noted a sticking point: "Any new move could only be within the framework of the teaching of Christ and of the church." He seemed to open the door, then start slamming it shut again by telling the theologians they had to deal with the previous solemn statements of Pius XI in *Casti Connubii* and of Pius XII, who endorsed his predecessor's view in addresses during the 1950s. Were those statements part of the pope's infallible teaching? If so, how could another pope change them?

Father Zalba argued that those statements were infallible and irreformable. "We stand before a practically uninterrupted tradition," he said. When a colleague, recalling Noonan's presentation, noted that some of that tradition was tacit indeed, Zalba conceded that, at least during the past 150 years, all the bishops, reflecting pronouncements from Rome, taught many things "infallibly."

He listed them: 1) the condemnation of onanism, certainly in the form of coitus interruptus, and probably where condoms or diaphragms are used, 2) the proclamation of a primary end in marriage to which other ends must be subordinated, 3) the condemnation of all forms of direct sterilization, and 4) the lawfulness of periodic continence used to take advantage of times of natural infertility.

Zalba believed Pius XII had condemned the pill but, because he voiced this in a mere *allocutio,* Zalba did not consider this an irreformable conclusion. Fathers Perico and Visser tended to agree with Zalba but, wanting to have the doctrine changeless and changeable at the same time, said in different ways that even an "irreformable" doctrine remains open to explanations and new developments.

Father Ford didn't agree. He quoted Pius XI in *Casti Connubii.* He quoted Pius XII quoting *Casti Conubii:* "No indication or necessity can change an intrinsically immoral act into one that is moral and allowable." And: "This prescription is in full force now as it was before, and so it will be tomorrow and forever, because it is not a mere human enactment but the expression of a natural and divine law."

It was difficult to argue that Pius XII's position little more than a decade earlier could be modified. Yet a number of those on the commission tried to prove precisely that. Philippe Delhaye pointed out, citing respected church historians, that popes can teach two ways. They can pass along "Catholic doctrine." Or they can give the church "pastoral guidance." Catholic doctrine is irreformable. Pastoral guidance, by nature a prudential judgment, is reformable. *Casti Connubii*'s teaching on birth control, said Canon Delhaye, was pastoral guidance, and Pius XII made this clear, by implication, when he gave different pastoral guidance by approving the rhythm method—something Pius XI did not do in *Casti Connubii*.

After several meetings on this question, de Riedmatten felt he needed a summary charge. Would the members of the theological section vote on the question? John Noonan, not a commission member but a consultant allowed to attend the sessions, recalled in a recent interview that he was surprised to find de Riedmatten taking a ballot. "It was a pretty solemn moment," said Noonan, "one filled with a good deal of suspense. De Riedmatten went right around the room. I made a tally."

Father Zalba voted for irreformability. Six others agreed with him: Archbishop Binz, Monsignor Kelly (perhaps in absentia), Fathers Visser, Ford, de Lestapis and Perico. But even one of these wanted the door left ajar for a change: Father Visser said even an irreformable pronouncement could remain open to explanations which did not diametrically oppose the original teaching.

Bishop Reuss and six others—Professor Van Melsen, Canons Anciaux and de Locht, Fathers Häring and Auer—disagreed. Moral matters, they said, each in a slightly different way, do not lend themselves to irreformable statements "because the human data develop and change." Tradition is not static, it is life and history. In matters of morals, the magisterium can give directions, but not determine behavior once and for all. Moreover, "The natural law cannot be declared by the church without clearly showing the reasons on which it is based. The day on which the reasons are shown to be false is also the day the conclusion is outdated, except for that part which is covered by revelation."

Father Häring cited a formula recently voted by an overwhelming majority of the council fathers when they passed *Lumen Gentium*, on the nature of the church: *tantum patet infallibilitas quantum patet revelatio*—infallibility reaches as far as revelation does.

Bishop Reuss and several others said that popes who make infallible statements manifest their intentions explicitly; neither Pius XI nor Pius XII did this. Father Ford challenged this. He wondered how *Casti Connubii* could be any more solemn, any more explicit.

At this point, the vote was seven to seven, a standoff. But the five remaining members—Canon Delhaye, Fathers Fuchs and Labourdette, Don Goffi and Monsignor Lambruschini—said the teaching of *Casti Connubii* could be changed. Because of the paper he had already given, Canon Delhaye's vote was no surprise. His reasoning was trenchant: he said that church teachings could change because they have changed. He cited historic examples, the most striking of them the one on usury. Three ecumenical councils and several popes condemned interest on a loan as contrary to natural law. Yet no reputable authority in the church today would make the same condemnation.

Father Labourdette took up the same theme: "With time," he said, "a document concerning very precise moral conduct loses its force because it presupposes situations in which many of the elements have changed. Had not Pius XII already started an evolution? His acceptance of 'regulating births' and his approval of periodic continence already strike a new note."

Don Goffi and Monsignor Lambruschini both noted that when a pope talks about natural law, he is bound by the same factors that bind anyone attempting to figure out a new moral course: the reasons for change which serve fidelity to the truth.

Finally, Father Fuchs said he believed these pronouncements were reformable. Noonan was surprised. He was aware from some things that Fuchs had been saying that he might lean toward change. But to hear him cast his vote. . . . Noonan felt now the matter was settled: a 12-7 vote, a victory for the forces of change.

Not quite. Fuchs tried to stop the commission from leaping too far, too fast. "Declaring these statements 'reformable' does not make them uncertain," he said. "Theologians cannot simply abandon them until they have good reason to do so." He thought such good reasons did not exist. He would not even concede there was enough doubt to qualify the old teachings under the law of probabilism—the principle established centuries ago after much theological debate that "a doubtful law does not oblige."

Lambruschini disagreed with Fuchs. "In my opinion," he said, "the church can make a change here." He looked up and around at the group, at Ford and de Locht and Fuchs, paused for emphasis, then added: "The church, not us."

Fuchs shook his head. He was having problems with this. If he went along with the majority, he would turn his back on a tradition, not only of the church but of his own Society of Jesus. The Jesuit Father Vermeersch wrote *Casti Connubii*. The Jesuit Father Hürth advised Pius XII on his statement to the Italian midwives. And now Fuchs was trying to advise Pope Paul VI. He said, "Simply saying past teachings are reformable does not help the people waiting for an answer. But what is the answer?"

At this point, commission members could agree on only four points— part of the answer, but not "the answer" Fuchs was asking for.

1) *Parenthood should be "responsible."* The Crowleys had difficulty with the phrase, already overused in the U.S., which implied that parents

with many children were not responsible. But commission members intended only this: that a couple could plan to have a specific number of children, depending on a number of common-sense circumstances (financial, social, medical, psychological), and that it wasn't the role of the church or the state to decide for them. No wonder there was unanimity here: there was nothing new about this position. It was Pius XII's position in the 1950s.

2) *Marriage is for love.* In days when parents arranged their children's marriages, this may not have been so true. For whatever reasons—the revolution of rising expectations, a new sense of freedom, the mass media's discovery that people loved love stories—many on the commission talked of a "progressive awakening" to love as "the bond and the spirit of marriage." The Crowleys referred to love as "a mystery," as did Jesus. In this context, they spoke of "the new meaning of sexuality as the language of liberty." They were so convinced that love was "of the essence" of marriage that they wanted a new church statement on the ends of marriage. They would get one from the council in the fall (but not without a battle from Father Ford).

3) *Sex has a positive value.* De Riedmatten reported that one commission theologian expressed "considerable reticence" over this, and that others had "various shades of opinion." But a majority felt that the church had "undervalued sexuality in the teaching on marriage." For some members sex had a value aside from its procreative aspect. "More often than not," declared Professor Thibaut, "a couple's lovemaking has nothing to do with procreation. They are not thinking of making a baby. And they cannot make a baby."

Others on the commission agreed with Professor Thibaut's point. The psychologists and psychiatrists, Doctors Lopez-Ibor, Cavanagh, Bertolus and others, had tried to make clear to the celibates here that this was not part of man's "animal nature," that, for men and women, sex was positive, part of the divine plan. Dr. Cavanagh pointed out that couples need sex, even when they cannot risk having children.

4) *The church must educate young people,* help prepare them for marriage, help them live their marriages. This was self-evident. The church hadn't been doing as good a job as it could have on this. It could do better. De Riedmatten, undoubtedly echoing what he had heard in the meetings, charged: "There has been far too much culpable negligence on the part of Christians up to now, and it is to be hoped that energetic measures will be taken to set this right." No one argued with that.

But they differed on practically everything else. De Riedmatten presented eight other possible courses of action; the members agreed on none, not even that the church should reiterate past condemnations. Perhaps they were unwilling to condemn because of the new spirit alive in the church during the mid-1960s, promoted by Pope John: people didn't need to be told what not to do, but what to do.

Was it opportune to make a statement on the pill? De Riedmatten, one can tell from his report, wanted the pope to make one. The world was waiting for some clear, distinct answer from *his* commission and he thought he saw a way of encouraging those unable to use rhythm. In these borderline cases, he said, the church could recommend that pastors adopt an attitude of leniency, declare the current state of church thinking on the pill, at least, as doubtful.

Few on the commission wanted to go even that far. Aside from the medical uncertainty about possible bad side effects of the pill, Fuchs said, he could find no theological arguments for the pill based on natural law, on previous teachings of the magisterium or on tradition. "Moreover," said Fuchs, "any judgment [he meant approval] on the pill implies a judgment [again approval] on other means of contraception and taking a [new] position on *Casti Connubii*."

In Fuchs' early position papers for the commission, one can see Fuchs' dissatisfaction with continuing arguments for or against the pill. He hadn't liked Dr. Van Rossum's ingenious [and ingenuous] argument for the pill, based on the misappropriated piece of church legalism, that the church could approve coitus that was *unitivus et inseminativus*—but not *procreativus*. He said he still favored periodic continence as the only moral method. What was wrong with rhythm?

The psychologists, psychiatrists and some medical doctors would try to tell Fuchs. John Marshall, who had proved that the temperature method could work among unlettered peoples on the Isle of Mauritius, was among those who tried. "Father Fuchs and I became very good friends," recalled Marshall in a June 1981 interview. "At night, after ten p.m.," he said, "we'd pay the porter to keep the door open for us, and slip out to a local place, something like a working-class pub, crowded and noisy, but it was a place where we could talk over a beer." Marshall confided to Fuchs: despite his espousal of the rhythm method all these years, he was becoming less and less sure that the church should recommend it as the only method. And why not? "Because," he told Fuchs, "it just doesn't work for everyone."

Marshall recalled that Fuchs took a long quaff of his beer and pondered that for long moments; not in silence, for this was a noisy bar, but with an intense look on his face which told Marshall that Fuchs was thinking new thoughts.

* * *

Fuchs would soon have more to think about when he saw the evidence of the Crowley survey, one that attempted to tap the elite of CFM members in the U.S. and Canada. The results, Patrick Crowley told the commission, were surprising. Most couples polled had at least six children. Some had 13. Many felt rhythm wasn't working. Some knew how to use the method, but reported its cost was sometimes overwhelming.

Pat and Patty Crowley told commission members many couples surveyed felt rhythm was "a detraction from the proper development of married love." Commission members could read the vivid, almost choking testimony of many (for the Crowleys had now distributed copies of their questionnaires and letters) and some judged that the Crowleys may have understated the case. One couple with six children, married 13 years, told this story:

He, a scholar, wrote:

Rhythm destroys the meaning of the sex act: it turns it from a spontaneous expression of spiritual and physical love into a mere bodily sexual relief; it makes me obsessed with sex throughout the month; it seriously endangers my chastity; it has a noticeable effect upon my disposition toward my wife and children; it makes necessary my complete avoidance of all affection toward my wife for three weeks at a time. I have watched a magnificent spiritual and physical union dissipate and, due to rhythm, turn into a tense and mutually damaging relationship. Rhythm seems to be immoral and deeply unnatural. It seems to me diabolical.

His wife, writing independently, reported:

My doctor advised me, recommended the basal temperature combined with the calendar method, and was constantly consulted. The psychological problems worsened, however, as we had baby after baby. We eventually had to resort to a three-week abstinence and since then (three years) we have had no pregnancy. I find myself sullen and resentful of my husband when the time for sexual relations finally arrives. I resent his necessarily guarded affection during the month and I find I cannot respond suddenly. I find, also, that my subconscious dreams and unguarded thoughts are inevitably sexual and time consuming. All this in spite of a great intellectual and emotional companionship and a generally beautiful marriage and home life.

Another couple, both 33 years old, married ten years, with three children, wrote:

The "natural law," or whatever pseudo-scientific, theological term is used to describe our physical union, has little meaning to us. We cannot fail to love each other unless we overburden this most intimate relationship with musty phrases like "primary purpose," "your bound duty" and "animal attraction." As Christians we demand more and expect more from our union than "just gifts from God."

We expect the "best" and work toward our mutual sanctification as the means of obtaining this goal. We certainly realize that our mutual love is not the only thing we have in our marriage, yet it is the clearest and least confused event in our lives. As busy parents raising children, we know few moments of complete harmony and personal communion. Our physical and spiritual union, when it does occur, is just such a moment. It should not be subjected to scientific or metaphysical scrutiny. . . . We do not believe that every time a man and wife feel a need to express their love to each other that it is a "call from God" to raise more kids. Neither is it a resurgence of the base and selfish sex drive which has yet to be conquered by pure love. We are frail and lonely people holding to the only mutual concern and affection we really know.

Not everyone responded this way. Some couples said they believed the moral law came straight from "the church" without any contribution from the folks who had to live it. It was not an uncommon misconception in the U.S. church, where Catholics were catechized in rote fashion during their years in parochial schools and were not expected to let their religion work with their reason. One couple, married 17 years, with 14 children, misunderstood the purpose of the Crowley's questionnaire, which was to tell the commission's scholars how the church's teachings were being lived. Wrote the father of this family:

Frankly, we are surprised at the thought of a popular referendum on one of the teachings of the church. Do we next vote on the question of abortion, and then maybe divorce? Our education in engineering, law and nursing, as well as our experience during our life together, has not provided any basis to doubt the teaching of this subject. . . . Of course, should the pope, with the guidance of the Holy Spirit, decide that the teaching is in error, then it should be changed. But our vote should not have any effect on such decision.

Another couple, married 16 years, with ten children:

If the church should for all practical purposes suddenly reverse itself and allow the use of contraceptives, I do not see where the process will stop. If one moral law is changed, then why not change the others? Then why should it not be all right to start lying because it makes things easier in business? Why should it not be acceptable to steal because possession of more material wealth makes us much more comfortable? If one rule of Christianity, a rule that has been held up as a basic moral truth, is reversed, I personally do not see any point in following any of the other laws, rules or customs of the church.

But these responses were untypical. Most couples said they looked for some new approach to emerge. The Crowleys said they hoped this new turn might be like the one taken by their friends, the Mathew Ahmanns, in Chicago:

The end of marriage [wrote the Ahmanns after meetings with their study group] is both personal and social—the fulfillment of the individual partners as Christians and human beings and the perfection of society. The bearing and raising of children are normally the means by which this end is reached; the intent of fruitfulness is normally part of the marriage union. The number of children . . . can be determined, should be determined, by the couple alone; if the decision is made to limit the number of children, this should be done on the basis of Christian charity, i.e., unselfishly, out of a love that sees some larger good to be accomplished by the limitation.

Discussions of the morality of sex in marriage should be based on considerations such as these, not on analysis of the isolated act of intercourse.

Father Häring had been saying this in meetings of the theological section: "Not every conjugal act need seek procreation; the latter is looked for by marriage as an institution."

But if this commission were listening seriously to voices such as these, to Father Häring, to Mathew Ahmann's study group in Chicago, then wasn't the whole question of methods beginning to loom less large?

Yes. Canon de Locht spoke with a fierce clarity. "With the exception of abortion," he said, "no method can be called intrinsically 'bad' or 'good.' They are all unimportant in themselves and their moral significance lies in the life of the husband and wife. Obviously, some methods are theoretically more efficient than others, or more refined (or rudimentary) than others, but these two criteria are not enough to state a general rule." He added: "It is not fertility that decides the moral value of methods; it is the way in which these methods, with greater or lesser merit, preserve the significance and authenticity of conjugal intimacies."

Before de Locht had begun speaking, Dr. Marshall and a few others noted that a young man had come into the room, sat down and begun listening to the proceedings. To be sure, others in the room were not members of the commission, most notably some seminarians who were now helping de Riedmatten with his paperwork, and serving as translators, generally from French to English or from German to English. But this young man seemed different. When he suddenly pulled out a camera and began shooting it became clear that he was no seminarian. He was a Roman *papparazzo*, one of those pesky freelancers who roamed the Via Veneto in search of celebrity shots they could sell to the *Life* bureau chief in Rome or to a wire service.

As soon as de Riedmatten saw what was happening he cried for someone to grab that man with the camera. Marshall made a move toward him and several others did the same. The *papparazzo* dashed to the door ahead of Marshall and ran down the hall with the others in pursuit. For almost five minutes the chase went on, up one hall and down another, into the basement and back up again until Marshall and the others finally cornered the *papparazzo* in a stairwell. Nodding and panting, he surrendered, and said, in Italian, "Okay, you've got me."

They took him out to a courtyard, in the sunlight, and conferred with de Riedmatten. "What to do? What to do?" De Riedmatten decided they should confiscate the young man's film, then phone the police. Marshall took the film, exposed it. Someone else called the cops. Then commission members stood around laughing and wondering how much value the press would put on these pictures. Of this balding, eagle-beaked de Locht? Of the silver-haired Fuchs? Talking about the philosophical final causality of marriage?

The Roman police took their time getting to the scene of the crime, if there was a crime. Marshall and the others relaxed their guard on the young *papparazzo*. Finally, the young man realized that he had his camera. Why should he wait around to answer a *carabiniero*'s questions? He spotted an open gate at the end of the courtyard. He skedaddled.

Marshall and the others looked at one another and laughed. "What of it?" said Marshall. "We've got his film. Let him go." The others couldn't agree more.

When they returned to their seats, however, de Riedmatten told them the press was more than a little interested in these meetings and that the commission had to exercise the greatest discretion. "Tomorrow, we'll see the Holy Father. When *L'Osservatore Romano* has put out the word about this audience the press may be after us to ask us what has been happening here. Now, we can't say what happened, where we are in our deliberations, what tentative decisions we've come to. We are to give no press conferences. No interviews. Even exchanges with our friends should be limited."

Yes. John Noonan and the Crowleys already knew that. Their friend Ted Hesburgh, president of the University of Notre Dame, visiting Rome on another mission, had asked if he could drop by one of the earlier meetings. De Riedmatten had turned him down—Father Theodore Hesburgh, the very man who had helped Noonan get a leave of absence from Notre Dame to attend these meetings in Rome.

Someone asked de Riedmatten if they could share some of the commission documents with outsiders. "No, not possible," he said. "These documents are under the secret of the Holy Office." That, he said, meant automatic excommunication for anyone leaking the documents.

Archbishop Binz agreed. "We have to maintain secrecy," he said.

* * *

The next afternoon they were to have an audience with the pope. But before they set out for the Vatican, de Riedmatten wanted to hear the group's suggestions for further work. He got a whole notepad full of ideas. Obviously, the group would have to meet again. De Riedmatten suggested that he appoint ten members or so, a central committee, to plan for the next session.

But what of all those folk out there waiting for this commission to quiet their anxiety? Somehow, most members were less in a hurry now. Patrick Crowley scribbled on his large yellow legal pad and told the group, "We've learned of the unsettled situation. We suspect others would be reassured to know this, but realize this is not possible. So we think the commission should work hard, meet again and again until a solution emerges in which all can discern the Holy Spirit. In the meantime, couples should be assured that anxiety and dialogue are not the worst things in the world."

This was the same Patrick Crowley who, with the other North Americans, had felt in January that the pope ought to say something definitive right away. Now, many others believed as Patrick Crowley did. One of them suggested the commission ought to publish an exhaustive report of their conclusions, tentative though some of them were.

In September, the Vatican would attempt to do exactly that and distribute the report to more than 2,000 bishops as they arrived in Rome for the last session of the council.

* * *

The Crowleys wondered what the pope would tell the commission. Paul VI, the same Paul who had told the world he hoped to have an answer to its anxieties "soon," would have his only meeting with the commission delegated to give him an answer. But they had no answers.

No matter. This would be no discussion, a mere papal audience, one in which they would do the listening. And so, in a small chamber at the Vatican, the commission members heard the pope address them twice as "Dear Sons," forgetting, or not noticing, that five commission members were women, and tell them that, while there was a pressing need for him "to give guidance without ambiguity" to the church at large, he understood why the commission needed more time.

This was his own doing, he said. It was the pope who wanted the commission's investigations to become broader, it was the pope who wanted different currents of theological thought and men and women from different countries to be better represented, it was the pope who wanted lay men, and especially married couples, to have qualified representatives in such a serious undertaking, and it was the pope who wanted the commission to work "in complete objectivity and liberty of spirit."

"This," he said, "is how you come to be now at a new and decisive stage in your work. We are confident that you will know how to continue it to the end with courage." The pope said he was assured the commission would provide him with the basis for his answer to the anxiety of so many.

In my 1981 interview with Dr. Marshall, he told me this was comforting to de Riedmatten and to himself and others on the commission who had worried about going far deeper into the question than the pope had originally imagined. "At each step forward, as we got deeper and deeper into the mire, each time de Riedmatten went to see the pope he got the same answer: 'Press on.' This ought to be emphasized. Throughout the whole of the agony of the commission the pope insisted on going on, going on, 'in complete objectivity and liberty of spirit,' never insisted on our not touching this or that aspect of the question. Pope Paul has not been given all the credit he deserved."

The pope Marshall described was Pope Paul the intellectual. There was another Pope Paul or, perhaps, many Pope Pauls. And the members of his birth control commission would see these other Pauls in action—or inaction—during the next three years.

Chapter Five

One of those other Pauls was puzzled, according to the solid testimony of some who were close to him, by the news he was getting out of the commission. Soon after the March meetings, de Riedmatten gave him a 58-page report, along with a stack of documentation no less than three feet thick: 26 reports from the theologians and historians, 17 reports from the doctors and psychologists, 16 from the social scientists and demographers.

The pope had wanted guidance; now he was suffering from information overload. He told de Riedmatten, wryly, "The more people I put on the commission, the more complex things become."

De Riedmatten replied, "Yes, and the more one approaches the truth." De Riedmatten, the one who told this story, did not say how the pope reacted to that riposte. But he was right: the reality of the situation was complex, and probably did not lend itself to a simple statement from the pope that would "solve" everything.

As the pope read some of the new thinking that had emerged during the March meetings, he realized the commission was taking him further away from a solution, rather than closer. The pope had originally been concerned about the pill. Now, according to de Riedmatten's report, commission members were producing new thinking that went far beyond this method or that:

On nature. "Nature is not something ready made, it is making itself. Nature is constantly revealing herself. Essence and historicity condition each other."

On the principle of continuity. "It is enough that at any given moment a pronouncement on moral matters should be true 'for the moment.' In any event, reality will never be entirely understood and new aspects are being discovered all the time."

On tradition. "Tradition is open and forward looking. It never ceases to make modifications in its understanding of the fundamental content hidden within its formulations. . . . Interpretations of Holy Scripture which have followed one another provide an excellent example of such modification."

On moral matters. "The role of the magisterium in moral matters does not consist in defining behavior, except by right of prudence. Like the Gospel, its function is to give broad illumination. But it cannot issue edicts of a kind that bind consciences to precise modes of behavior."

This last idea was new to the pope. In effect, de Riedmatten was reporting that some commission members didn't think the pope should attempt to "solve" the birth control question, unless by telling the people of God the problem was theirs to solve. The pope was not sure he could go along with this concept. What of his right and duty to teach the whole church? He was the supreme pastor, a shepherd who was supposed to feed his flock, not send them off to forage by themselves.

But then, he had encouraged the commission's "complete objectivity and liberty of spirit." He couldn't reject it now. Through the spring of 1966, he would continue to give his commission the same kind of encouragement and more.

* * *

On April 20, 1965, de Riedmatten confessed, in a note to Canon de Locht, that he was still having trouble convincing Rome that the pope had to do more than deal with the casuistry of the pill. (The mention of de Riedmatten's dealing with "Rome" was a tipoff, confirmed by subsequent events, that he was now working with the pope's two top curial departments, the Secretariat of State and the Holy Office, rather than directly with the pope.) "I cannot make a definite decision," he told de Locht, "on what should be done next."

The North American members of the commission thought they knew. They met in Washington, D.C., June 4 and 5 and produced a four-page, single-spaced, confidential memorandum for de Riedmatten, outlining the commission's needs. Most notable: they wanted some "systematic, speculative theologians," as opposed to moral theologians, on the commission. Their memo didn't say why the commission needed these men, but their reason is apparent now. In deliberations so far, they could see they were getting into basic questions about the nature of the church and its authority. They couldn't come up with solutions that didn't involve a radical revision of the way Rome had exercised its moral authority for a century. And so they suggested the appointment of three theologians known for their work in ecclesiology, Karl Rahner, Hans Küng and Yves Congar, and of two American Jesuits who specialized in problems of public policy and social ethics, John Courtney Murray and Robert Drinan.

De Riedmatten may have tried to get these men added to the group. In retrospect, these five would have made a big difference during the final fight that was to come. But if de Riedmatten tried, he failed.

Another quarter dictated his next moves. On June 9, Cardinal Ottaviani told him to produce a document which would reflect commission thinking on the four points agreed on in March: responsibility, love, sexuality and education. The cardinal knew commission members were having trouble coming to an accord on birth control methods. Nevertheless, he told de Riedmatten himself to draft a pastoral instruction the Vatican could give to priests, something along the lines de Riedmatten had suggested in his report of the March meeting.

De Riedmatten sent telegrams to Häring, Labourdette, de Lestapis and de Locht, asking them to prepare position papers on the four major points; from these, he himself would prepare "a pastoral instruction." Then, during the week of June 20, they and other commission members would gather in Rome to polish the texts. It seemed that the Vatican wanted to get something ready for the bishops as they arrived in September for the council's final session. This was a strange move; the pope and his curia had wanted to keep the bishops out of this. Now they were bringing them back in? Well, these were obedient men, serving the pope. If he had a new strategy. . . .

When the four theologians met de Riedmatten at the Spanish College Sunday, June 20, a committee of four other theologians were also there with de Riedmatten: Fathers Visser, Perico, Fuchs and Sigmond, his "editorial board." For three days the nine of them worked away at their texts, writing and rewriting. Then another group came in for another three days to chew over the chapters, paragraphs, sentences and words: Archbishop Binz, Monsignor Lambruschini, Canon Delhaye, Father Alfons Auer of the University of Tübingen and four doctors: John Marshall, André Hellegers, J.R. Bertolus and Pierre Van Rossum. (De Riedmatten had wanted Bishop Reuss included in this group, but he was "gravely ill" in Mainz.)

When these men had finished, de Riedmatten himself gave the text a final edit and took it to Cardinal Ottaviani, who then submitted it to a number of Vatican congregations (or departments) so others could check it over before their summer break began on July 15.

What was printed in September was a bore—the inevitable result, perhaps, of a whole phalanx of committees trying to speak for the pope on "a delicate matter." De Riedmatten unwittingly explained what was wrong: "The document represents a total collaboration on the given points, keeping in mind the character of the Authority which might find it helpful to use. Consequently, as soon as a question or a formula statement provoked any controversy, it was systematically omitted."

Pussyfooting around the question, opting for a least common denominator approach to the burning question of the day, these great minds produced, on a scale of one to ten, a tiny two. A few fine sentences graced the final, edited version of the doctrinal document, some borrowed from statements made by Pius XII in 1951. And the pastoral instruction contained a few wise injunctions. This, for example: "The elements of conjugal morality go beyond the problem of what is commonly referred to as 'methods.' " And this: "The moral life of the Christian does not consist in seeking ready-made solutions which dispense with any personal reflection and with any decision requiring personal responsibility."

The instruction made an oblique reference to the pill: "The discoveries of modern science bring one into the presence of new procedures before which moral science remains hesitant. . . . Naturally, recourse to such procedures requires grave motivation or one sufficiently proportionate. Moreover, the couple using them should not forget that . . . the use and especially the abuse of means touching very deeply the physiology of the feminine body may give rise to moral problems of another order."

But after all these meetings, after all the work of all these fine people, it was a letdown to find the commission's first almost published work reduced to a few banalities.

I call the work almost published because both the doctrinal document and the pastoral instruction were included in a curious thing called *The Green Book,* intended for September distribution to the national bishops' conferences in Rome.

When Bishop Reuss saw an early copy of it, he took de Riedmatten and Binz in tow and went to see the pope in protest. He asked Paul VI to withdraw *The Green Book* from circulation. He claimed that the account (in Latin) of the commission deliberations didn't fairly reflect the commission's conclusions. For one thing, *The Green Book* reported that two-thirds of the doctors and psychologists approved of rhythm. Reuss said that, unless he was mistaken, all members of this section now had problems with rhythm. Another example: in the commission, all agreed the conjugal act ought to be *unitivus* and opinion was divided about whether the act ought to be *inseminativus* as well, with a majority opining that it need not be. But *The Green Book* had the commission saying the conjugal act ought to be *unitivus et inseminativus.*

These were minor quibbles. For the most part, *The Green Book* was a fair summary of commission deliberations. Reuss implied to me, some weeks later, that the Holy Office had been up to its old tricks. But no evidence existed that anyone had tampered with the doctrinal statement or the pastoral instruction. And it is hard to see how anyone in the Holy Office could have put *The Green Book* together without the active cooperation of de Riedmatten and several members of his commission. But now Reuss, Binz and de Riedmatten were urging the pope to scuttle *The Green Book.*[20]

Reuss was the main mover here. But what were his reasons? *The Green*

Book was intended to help the pope find a collegial solution to birth control by posing 11 questions to the world's bishops. Reuss believed in collegial solutions. But apparently, he only believed in collegial solutions that were intelligent. In this case he didn't see how the bishops could answer these questions in any but an uninformed manner:

1. Whether and how can we rethink and more aptly rephrase the traditional formula on the primary and secondary ends of marriage?
2. Can we give more importance to the end of marriage (the mutual help and the quieting of concupiscence) by leaning on the notion that husbands and wives relate to each other body and soul together and say that this is justification enough for the conjugal act?
3. Should we give love a higher place in marriage?
4. Should we make more of the personal responsibility of husband and wife in marriage, in regard to both the procreation and the education of their children?
5. Does the natural law rigidly prohibit husbands and wives, for grave personal or social reasons, from using their freedom and their reason to govern the exercise and the outcome of their lovemaking?
6. Since we permit the use of the rhythm method, can we also permit, for rational reasons, the suspension of ovulation, which often happens in the natural course of events?
7. Should such a suspension be deemed equivalent to sterilization?
8. What should we think about the use of a pill that inhibits ovulation?
9. Would it be opportune to raise the age for entering marriage (paying attention to the diversity of regions)?
10. Is it opportune for the supreme pontiff to speak openly about these matters?
11. Is it opportune for the pontifical commission to continue its work?

Ruess told the pope it was unfair to ask the bishops to respond intelligently to questions one through nine, which were unresolved and should only be resolved after further study. As for question ten, Reuss said, there was no denying that millions waited for a quick papal decision. But how much more dangerous than delay would it be for the pope to treat this as a question of church discipline instead of a matter to be worked out by some hard thinking? Reuss said it would not suffice for this pope to recall the teachings of past popes and the Holy Office: a commission majority had already judged those teachings "reformable."

Other reasons may have compelled the pope to act. It is almost certain that elements from the Ottaviani wing of the curia opposed the collegial solution, as Reuss did. Pope Paul probably reasoned this way: if representatives from both wings in the church disliked *The Green Book*, why not drop it? In any event, he stopped distribution of *The Green Book*.

Then he turned from the collegial solution to an old-fashioned, Pius XII-type of decision. The world was waiting for something from him. He would give it. He asked his old friend Cardinal Suenens to help him fashion a simple allocution. "One thing in particular is bothering me," the pope said. "If we make a change, we will go against the constant tradition of the church."

Suenens said Noonan's book would help solve that difficulty. "The church's constant tradition has always been conditioned by cultural circumstances. That's the meaning of our incarnational theology." The pope said he'd like to see Noonan's book.

Cardinal Suenens had a copy of *Contraception* delivered the next day. The next time Suenens saw the pope, he asked him if he had read Noonan. "*Eh beh!*" said Paul, making a helpless gesture at the book. He wanted a nice, neat statement, preferably in Latin. He'd gotten a 561-page tome in English.

And so, Suenens summoned experts from Louvain (in Rome anyway, for the council). Together they wrote a five-page document which, according to Victor Heylen, a Belgian *peritus* who had been editing the marriage chapters for *Schema* 13, "emphasized the continuity of the church's teachings on the value of life but was not closed to practical change."

Suenens gave this to the pope. "A very good text," said the pope. "But I must read it with a peaceful mind." Suenens took the hint and left the papal chambers in an easterly direction for the Belgian College. His paper went south to the Holy Office, to be blue-penciled by someone on Cardinal Ottaviani's staff. The Suenens' statement died. When I later asked Suenens about this, he said, simply, "The pope has the right to use or not use what we prepare for him." But one of Suenens' advisers, Arthur McCormack, a Mill Hill Father and a demographer who was not invited to be on the pope's commission, said sadly, "The pope cannot seem to stay away from the Holy Office."

Perhaps. But neither could he stay away from birth control. During the fourth and last session of the council, three things were on the tables of every *trattoria* in town: bread, a carafe of Frascati and the birth control question.

People were talking, for instance, about Father Häring's recent speech at Notre Dame to a convention of the Crowleys' Christian Family Movement. It was a doozer, a lallapaloozer of a sermon on love and loving parenthood, in which Häring told the couples that, when it comes to expressions of tenderness in marriage, anything goes and that, under the theory of probabilism, given the church's great uncertainty, those who had serious reasons for not wishing another child here and now could use any methods short of sterilization and abortion. Häring's talk was reported on front pages all over the world. Häring was not only one of the pope's favorite theologians, he was also a member of the pope's birth control commission. Maybe this was an important clue, something which would tell the world what the commission might do.

That was precisely what bothered Vatican officials and de Riedmatten, who had warned commission members not to discuss this birth control business outside the commission. Most members were complying. Archbishop Binz wouldn't even acknowledge to priests of his own city that he was a commission member. Father Fuchs wouldn't talk to the press; some reporters were after him, because seminarians at the Gregorian University were buzzing that Fuchs wasn't teaching this fall. They claimed the princely Fuchs had abdicated, because he no longer held what he and the church had taught for years. Even Bishop Reuss, one of the most outspoken members of the commission, was refusing to appear at learned symposiums on this question, though he had somewhat recovered from his illness.

Father Häring, caring less about politics and more about people, danced to the music of his own zither. But neither the pope nor de Riedmatten chastised Häring* for his speech at Notre Dame. He may have been an embarrassment to de Riedmatten and possibly a pain to the pope. But Häring was only one man.

In Rome, however, as the council opened, many "Härings" appeared. Many were taking ever more open positions on birth control, often enough in reaction to those who were pushing to close off debate.

At one private meeting of English and Welsh bishops, for example, the English hierarchy's chief adviser on moral questions, Lawrence L. McReavy, said, "The weight of authority behind the traditional position is so great and so theologically significant that . . . any ambiguity in the reaffirmation of the accepted doctrine which might be construed as a retreat from it would have grave consequences throughout the whole ambit of the magisterium in regard to faith and morals. One has only to think of the millions who must have been refused the sacraments and led thereby to abandon the practice of their religion on this one ground. If the church could have misled the faithful on so grave a matter, with such grave

---

* But John C. Ford would, to the Crowleys, at least. When Father Ford read of Häring's speech, he asked the Crowleys for a copy. They sent a transcript and a tape recording. Ford returned them with thanks, but added, "I can't share your enthusiasm for the contents." (The Crowleys had termed Häring's talk "wonderful.") Ford called it "theologically inaccurate and pastorally very harmful." He deplored a news release on Häring's talk, approved by Häring, because he believed it was "being used to promote the practice of all kinds of contraception among Catholics by showing them how to be 'in good faith about it.' "[21]

consequences and for so long a period, what value or reliability could be attached to her moral teaching generally?"

If everyone in Rome had been speaking in the same accents, the pope's task would have been easy. He would reaffirm the old position. But conciliar Rome was a very different Rome than ever in history. For every Monsignor McReavy, a half-dozen others, more articulate than McReavy, made equal good sense, even better sense, on the other side.

On September 30, as the council took up the marriage chapter in *Schema* 13 once more, Remi de Roo, bishop of Victoria, British Columbia, won applause for his formulation of a principle gaining ground at the council, that the quality of married love depends on a daily renewal of affection:

Married couples tell us that conjugal love is a spiritual experience of the most profound kind. It gives them their deepest insight into their own being, into what they mean to each other, into their mutual communion in unbreakable union.

We . . . recognize also the healing value of marital intimacy. Husband and wife find it is often indispensable when spirits are dejected, when a partner labors under some extreme difficulty, when home life has lost the serenity so necessary for the children's welfare. . . . These are some of the reasons why spouses must never abstain from constant development of conjugal love and its practice.

Speeches like this triggered more talk around the city. At another meeting of the English and Welsh bishops, Charles Davis underlined current confusion over the terms "intercourse" and "marriage." Theologians had been saying the end of intercourse is the procreation and education of children. Exactly wrong, said Father Davis:

The end of intercourse is the establishing and fostering of a marital union. It is the marital union with the pattern of regular intercourse it presupposes which has as its *finis operis* the procreation and education of children to adulthood. Intercourse is linked with procreation not by a one-to-one relation but by a statistical law, whereby a marital union with regular intercourse will result in conception, according to a statistical average.

Hence, the objective morality of intercourse is determined by the "end," marital union. A control of it that does not destroy that end is moral. The morality of the marital union is determined by an openness to parenthood. A use of contraception that fits within those limits, the limits laid down for the use of rhythm, does not violate objective morality.[22]

Some bishops nodded agreement. Some had seen a similar argument from the English Dominican Herbert McCabe, who compared marriage to a rugby match, where one often has to pass the ball backward to move on downfield.

The fact that contraceptive intercourse is less perfect than non-contraceptive intercourse [continued Davis] does not alter this conclusion. Intercourse is a sign of the embodiment of marital love. The sign need not always be perfect. Face-to-face encounter is a more perfect form of communication. This does not mean that it is immoral to use the telephone.

One bishop asked Davis about Monsignor McReavy's argument from tradition. Davis said Pius XII already abandoned that tradition by approving rhythm:

This is brushed aside as a minor point by authors. It is not. It represents a profound change in the theology of marriage, a new understanding of the meaning of intercourse in relation to conjugal love.

The prohibition of contraception is, I suggest, an archaic remnant from an already abandoned theology of marriage and intercourse.

Davis' talk was brilliant, more so than many of the papers presented inside the birth control commission. It is probable that someone gave the pope a copy, that it was added to the stack of papers piling up on his desk, the pile the pope referred to in a remarkable interview with *Corriere della Sera,* the Milan daily, published on October 4.

Popes do not often give interviews. Yet Pope Paul VI opened up to a reporter with touching candor. He was about to leave Rome for a historic visit to the United Nations General Assembly in New York to give "a solemn moral ratification" of the UN. For him, the UN represented "the obligatory path of modern civilization toward peace." It was Paul VI's "no more war" speech, an address as brilliant and moving as that body had ever heard. In the same speech, he would say to the general assembly, the representatives of governments tempted to undertake wholesale and inhuman methods of halting the population explosion, what he should have said (after deploring the useless slaughters and frightful ruin of past wars): "The life of man is sacred. No one may dare offend it. Respect for life, even with regard to the great problem of birth, must find here in your assembly its highest affirmation and its most reasoned defense. You must strive to multiply bread so that it suffices for the tables of mankind, and not rather favor an artificial control of birth, which would be irrational, in order to diminish the number of guests at the banquet of life."

Yet, in a quiet moment with a quiet reporter, toward the end of a long, almost relaxed conversation, Paul VI revealed his feelings about birth control. The pope had greeted Alberto Cavallari with a smile and a joke. "Many are studying us today, trying to understand us. Many books have come out on the Holy See and the council; and some are good, too. But many put thoughts into the church's mind without ever having bothered to ask the church what she really does think on certain matters. And, after all, our opinion should also count in religious matters." The pope smiled again.

Cavallari found Paul VI "in good health, tanned," nothing like the pope he'd seen on Italian television, "tense, cold, palid and anything but spontaneous." But now, sitting at the end of a long table in his private library with Cavallari, he was spontaneous. He simply volunteered to discuss his quandary on birth control: "So many problems! How many problems there are and how many answers we have to give! We want to open up to the world, and every day we have to make decisions that will have consequences for centuries to come. We have to respond to the questions of the man of today, the Christian of today, and there are some questions that are particularly difficult for us, such as those connected with the problem of the Christian family.

"Take birth control, for example. The world asks what we think and we find ourselves trying to give an answer. But what answer? We can't keep silent. And yet to speak is a real problem." He paused. One might expect that, if the pope really thought all birth control "irrational" (as he would claim before the UN), he might now have an easy, rational answer. He did not.

He said to Alberto Cavallari, raising his palms, "But what?"

Popes move largely on precedent. This was one reason why Paul VI was stymied now. He said, "The church has never in her history confronted such a problem." He paused, started to say something, hesitated, then finally blurted out, "This is a strange subject for men of the church to be discussing." He paused, then added: "Even humanly embarrassing." Paul's predecessor had grown up on a farm, he had seen animals mating and he accepted sex as a part of life. But Paul was an intellectual who had spent his youth in sick rooms and libraries. And now he was admitting that this talk of sex and love and marriage troubled him, personally. It was an honest admission and one that not many clerics would make.

Now Cavallari was embarrassed. But the pope moved away from the personal note. "So," he continued, "the commissions meet, the reports pile up, the studies are published. Oh, they study a lot, you know. But then we will have to make the final decisions. And in deciding, we are all alone. Deciding is not as easy as studying. We have to say something. But what? God will simply have to enlighten us."[23]

No evidence suggests that God gave the pope any direct enlightenment on the question. The president of the Church of Jesus Christ of Latter-day Saints claims to receive direct inspiration; Mormons cannot change any doctrine unless the president does get word from on high. Not so in the Roman Catholic Church. Normally, a pope's cues come from Scripture and tradition, tradition embodied in the faith as the people of God live it here and now. Historically, popes have sought special enlightenment in times of crisis from ecumenical (or universal) councils of all the world's bishops on the grounds that the bishops as a whole reflect the faith lived by the people. On this theory, an ecumenical council has been the next best thing to direct revelation. That is why, according to most commentators, a full council, pope and bishops together, enjoys the church's highest teaching authority. Specialists in information theory can give an algebraic formula proving why this must be so; the same specialists could go on to prove that all members of any community, consulting together, have a greater chance of being "right" than a leader acting alone.

This pope's best chance for enlightenment would have to come from the next and final session of the council.

Chapter Six

In the fourth session of the Second Vatican Ecumenical Council, the council fathers wrote a new charter for the church, aimed at turning it from a church of laws, looking inward, to a church of love, looking out. Many commentators believe they did this best in their *Schema* 13, the *Pastoral Constitution on the Church in the Modern World*. It was not a perfect document; the final version sometimes reflected compromise between warring factions. But it put the church on record as favoring a joyful, hopeful posture toward the world God loved. Hence its title, *Gaudium et Spes*, Joy and Hope.

No chapter of that constitution had more meaning, more joyful, hopeful potential for the people of God, than the one on marriage and the family. And no chapter created more controversy between those trying to update the church and those who wanted to keep it "the same as always," which is probably why it received more press attention than all other parts of the *schema* combined.

Before the council, members of the Roman curia had prepared a *schema* on marriage and the family and sent it to the council fathers. It was not full of joy and hope. Instead, according to Bernard Häring, that original document "adopted a hostile attitude to all the questions of our time." And in a censorious, lugubrious tone, besides. One introduction said:

> How false these accusations and malevolent insinuations are toward the church will be clear to anyone who remembers how Christ himself used the ten commandments, the negative precepts, and proposed a renunciation, even to the death of the cross. The apostle, led by the Holy Spirit, warns all the faithful to work out their salvation in fear and trembling. Let those who have given themselves to the equally onerous and glorious task of Christian education listen to these words. . . .

Those who rewrote the document made every effort* to avoid such a

---

*The marriage chapter went through no fewer than eleven revisions before it

110

negative approach, They spoke of sexual intimacy in such positive terms that commentator Norman St. John Stevas could call their document a "death knell for Catholic Manicheism." They did not define marriage as "a remedy for concupiscence" but "a community of life and love." And they tried to avoid the old, legalistic approach to Catholic morality, this despite efforts of older shepherds at the council (perhaps 200 out of 2,200) who had a hard time accepting the council's new vision.

One hundred and ninety council fathers, for example, wanted to insert in the *schema* a canonical definition of marriage's "entitlements": *jus in corpus, perpetuum et exclusivum in ordine ad actos per se aptos ad prolis generationem,* "a right over the body, perpetual and exclusive, for acts in themselves apt for the generation of children."

Members of the subcommission editing the chapter noted laconically that such juridical language was "neither pastoral nor conducive to discussion with the world" and expressed the hope that such humiliating language would also disappear from canon law. "Right over the body" derives from a time a wife was listed with her husband's possessions. It was also a relic of the juridical notion of marriage as a contract, with an exchange of rights and duties. But nowhere in *Gaudium et Spes* did the council fathers refer to marriage as a contract. They preferred the biblical term "covenant."

And, after bitter debate, the council fathers rejected the old dichotomy between "primary and secondary ends of marriage," as defined by Pius XI in 1930, by the Holy Office in 1944 and by Pius XII in 1951.

The council fathers, instead, set conjugal love at the core of marriage: "Such love, merging the human and the divine, leads the spouses to a free and mutual gift of themselves. . . . Such love pervades the whole of their lives. Indeed, by its generous activity, it grows better and grows greater."

---

reached the council floor in 1964, then three more as a result of amendments proposed by the council fathers in 1964 and 1965. In the fall of 1965, the *periti* in charge of these revisions sifted through more than 4,000 amendments (or *modi*), frequently putting in 18-hour days to present a final text to the council by November 16, along with detailed analyses and explanations of how they handled each amendment. The Vatican's Polyglot Press has published these *relationes* and *expensiones modorum*, along with the official texts, in large Latin type. They are a marvel of clear thinking, adroit analysis, and parliamentary civility, which explains, in part, why their editing received such overwhelming approval by the council fathers in their successive votes on the *schema*. But the hard work took its toll. Gerard Philips, the Belgian *peritus* who had a prime reponsibility for *Schema* 13, had a physical breakdown and could not continue to the end of the council.

Therefore it far exceeds mere erotical* inclination, which, selfishly pursued, soon enough fades wretchedly away."

And then the startling statement: "This love is uniquely expressed and perfected through the marital act." The word "uniquely" is a rendering of the Latin *singulariter*, a word which does not mean conjugal love is expressed and completed only through the marital act, but that the act does this beyond all other acts and in a way most typical of the love it expresses and completes. Furthermore, the council fathers warned couples not to break off love and full intimacy when "they find themselves in circumstances where at least temporarily the size of their families should not be increased."

And so, in *Gaudium et Spes*, the council fathers' prescriptions came closer than the church had ever come to dealing with the experience of marriage as loving couples live it. In effect, they put a new blessing on loving intercourse.

This blessing would help the papal birth control commission vault some hurdles. Rather than worry about the theoretical "reformability" of *Casti Connubii* (and, logically, about other statements of Pius XII that were far less solemn than *Casti Connubii*), they could simply cite the council's authority, pope and bishop together asserting the goodness of a couple's lovemaking.

Except for forging this new principle (and, historically, it *was* something new), the council did not attempt to solve specific problems that had perplexed the papal commission for two years. Some fathers wanted the council to scuttle these new ideas about birth control. Time and again, they tried to insert language that would bind marital love to procreation and, despite all the text had said so far, sanction a hierarchy of ends in matrimony. The council rejected these efforts and endorsed responsible parenthood which made the couples "interpreters of God's creative love" and said that "ultimately the married couple themselves" must judge how many children they are to have.

And how were couples to protract the goodness in their lovemaking and still limit the number of their children? The council gave only general guidelines. The final text of November 16, 1965, condemned infanticide and abortion. Beyond that, the council hardly went beyond telling couples to do good and avoid evil, leaving specifics to their conscience. Back in March, at a meeting of the General Mixed Commission working on *Schema* 13, Monsignor Philips had argued successfully against those who

---

*Not that the fathers wanted to put down eros. One late draft had contained a condemnation of the erotic. But, at almost the last moment, one father noted, "Eros in itself has something good about it." The editors agreed and put it to a conciliar vote. The fathers approved the "something good" in the erotic, 2,052 to 91.

wanted to give clear directives on birth control methods. "We have been urging lay people," he said, "to form their own consciences. If we get into specifics here, we'd simply encourage them to be automatic Christians." The bishops of the conciliar commission accepted that as a good reason. Furthermore, the pope had this other commission, this birth control commission.

But members of the Vatican's rear guard could see the bulk of what they called "the faith" crumbling because of this wait-and-see approach, though their notion of "the faith" tended to embrace a whole barrelful of beliefs and notions that did not all deserve the same degree of intelligent assent. In dogmatic theology, scholars talked about descending gradations of certainty: things were "of the faith," or "theologically certain" or "commonly believed." In moral theology, popularizers of the faith, which meant most priests and nuns, who saw themselves as teachers rather than scholars, often ignored the gradations of assent, and just as often ignored the difficulty of applying the so-called natural law to concrete situations. These people were on the business end of the church's answer machine.

But those on the other end of the answer machine, those who had traditionally told the teachers what to teach, were alarmed. Many, like Cardinal Ottaviani of the Holy Office, were lodged in curial dicasteries. Many, like Cardinal Ruffini of Palermo, Archbishop Heenan of Westminster, and Archbisop O'Boyle of Washington, D.C., occupied positions of authority outside Rome.

And some had the authority that authors enjoy. One was John C. Ford. Ford was a tall, stocky, New England Jesuit in his early sixties known for his enormous pride. He once asked Tom Burch, a fellow member of the papal commission, to brief him on a meeting he had been unable to attend. When Burch suggested they discuss it at dinner, Ford replied, "Oh, I never waste my time on social dinners." For years, Ford had been cranking out manuals in moral theology and instructing seminarians to teach what he taught them. Now, if things kept going as they were in Rome, Ford's texts and teachings would become obsolete.[24]

One November 6, he typed a letter to Egidio Vagnozzi, the Vatican's ranking diplomat in Washington, to ask for his help. Ford had to see the pope, to warn him about the mentality of the folk who had seized leadership of the papal commission and were teaching indirectly, but clearly, by implication, innuendo, ambiguity, omission, that contraception is not intrinsically evil. Perhaps the pope did not know some members on his commission "would simply destroy the power of the church to teach matters of morals in such a way as to bind consciences."

I would like to make known [wrote Ford] some of the implications of the strange situation of Canon Pierre de Locht, an influential member of the commission. He has taught contraception to the priests and people of Belgium for some years (I have the documents to prove it); he professes a type of situation morality which is clearly opposed to the decree of the Holy Office of February 2, 1956. And judging by his writings I cannot help but conclude that he is one of those who does not believe that the church has any right to bind the consciences of individuals in moral matters.

Ford said he knew the church's dilemma about birth control, to authorize a change or retain the old teaching. He thought he could help the pope come up with a partial solution, partial because "no matter which way the thing is decided, there are going to be defections from obedience if not from unity."

Ford, then on loan from the Jesuits to the Catholic University of America, was writing from his residence at Carroll House in Washington, D.C. He had no first hand knowledge of current council proceedings, and, possibly for this reason, he made no mention in this note to Archbishop Vagnozzi of the council's *Schema* 13 and its chapter on marriage. It is my guess,* however, based on the urgent tone of Ford's letter to Vagnozzi, that he wanted to talk to the pope about the council, too, its *Schema* 13 and its marriage chapter, which was unacceptable to him.

Vagnozzi did not arrange the audience. But that didn't stop Ford. He jetted to Rome anyway. On November 16, the day the council fathers approved a second reading of the marriage chapter, he was sitting in Cardinal Ottaviani's quarters at the Holy Office, petitioning to see the pope. *Romam veni solummodo ad habendam audientiam personalem cum S. Patre*, wrote Ford in a memo for the cardinal. "I have come to Rome only to have a personal audience with the Holy Father." He whined a bit, wondered in the memo why the pope hadn't wanted to see him. Had Father de Riedmatten told the pope Ford was "a difficult fellow"? That's what Ford suspected. That was why he hadn't been able to see the pope. But no matter. He wanted to tell the pope a leading member of his commission was "a contraceptionist and a situationist." Yes. Canon de Locht. Ford had the documents to prove it, marked appendices I through V, attached to his critique of the commission's pastoral instruction.

It is probable that Cardinal Ottaviani listened gravely to Ford's charges, which sounded like an indictment prepared by the FBI Strike Force on Organized Crime, then decided to use this intense fellow in his own fight with the majority theologians editing *Schema* 13. Carlo Colombo, one of the pope's theologians and a member of both the papal birth control commission and this conciliar commission, had already brought in three

---

*In 1982, I asked Father Ford about these events. He refused to elaborate on anything. His work on this question, he said, was still under the secret of the Holy Office.

other members of the birth control commission, Fathers Fuchs, Visser and Zalba, generally thought to be conservatives. Now that Ford was here, maybe he could help them do something about this troublesome chapter on marriage.

* * *

Which leads up the The Case of the Four Papal *Modi*. Other commentators have written at length about this incident, notably Gregory Baum, Xavier Rynne, Jan Grootaers, Norman St. John Stevas, and Ambrosio Valsecchi.[25] One principal in the drama, Victor Heylen, wrote his own account. All agreed: this tale of political intrigue involved the passions of good men in opposite camps who saw danger ahead for the church and did their best to head it off. Neither side was able to win a complete victory. Neither side was able to head off the danger.

The story probably began November 16, when more than three-quarters of the council fathers approved a second reading of *Schema* 13's chapter on marriage. (The vote was 1596 *placet*, 72 *non placet*, and 484 asking for amendments.) According to council rules, outstanding amendments could be considered only if they were completely in line with the approved text and in keeping with the basic intentions of the council majority.

On November 19, Carlo Colombo made clear he was not content with the marriage text: it said some beautiful things about marriage, but it did not advise priests what they should tell people in the confessional. He proposed an extraconciliar meeting between members of the subcommission on marriage and those of the papal birth control commission who were in Rome (about three dozen people) to talk about the problem.

It is no wonder Bishop Colombo called this meeting "extraconciliar." He wanted to know what the group thought about: 1) the advisability of publishing the council's text on marriage and 2) whether the papal birth control commission had a future.

Bishop Reuss helped settle the answer to the second question by outlining a long list of problems on the agenda. "The papal commission," he said, "still has plenty on its plate." Most at the meeting nodded their agreement with Reuss.[26]

As for the first question, Ford and Visser suggested that publishing the conciliar text in its existing form "would only create confusion among the faithful." Eight others agreed. But the other 28 or so were content to let the text go before the council for a third reading, when it would, no doubt, get near unanimous approval. Colombo and company found no solace in this.

Father Ford had his meeting with the pope November 22. He has declined to report what the pope said. He told the pope the conciliar text, as it then stood, would deny the intrinsic immorality of contraception.

This would shake the faith of many, for it would prove that, on this issue, the church had been wrong. Ford's analysis undoubtedly gave the pope some pause.

Ford's fears found their way to the council, in a form that made them look like the pope's fears, too. Not more than 48 hours after Ford's visit, late in the afternoon of November 24, at a plenary meeting of the Mixed Commission, Cardinal Ottaviani reminded the 70 bishops and almost 100 *periti* and lay observers present that they were under an oath of secrecy. Then he asked Sebastian Tromp, a Jesuit who worked closely with him at the Holy Office, to read a letter from Cardinal Cicognani, the Vatican secretary of state. In Latin, it proposed that the commission introduce four amendments in the text—which could not admit doubt, keep silent or otherwise insinuate that birth control methods condemned by *Casti Connubii* were not still in force. And the text should underline the need for conjugal chastity.

The letter "caused an understandable stir" (Grootaers), "was a cause of great consternation" (Baum), and "a papal bombshell" (St. John Stevas). Xavier Rynne reported "a look of triumph" on John Ford's face, while Cardinal Browne is supposed to have said, *Christus ipse locutus est—* "Christ himself has spoken." Canon Delhaye leaned over and said to Father de Riedmatten, "But is this now the end of your commission?" De Riedmatten said, "Right now, I don't know any more than you do." De Locht (who had also been invited into the meetings of the Mixed Commission two days after Ottaviani had brought in Ford) observed that this would be "a return, pure and simple, to *Casti Connubii.*"

The amendments proposed in this note would have restored the old doctrinal position on primary and secondary ends of marriage that the council had just given the silent treatment. In that aspect, the changes demanded were substantial modifications of the approved text. One amendment, prohibiting contraception in the terms of *Casti Connubii*, would have had council fathers taking a position on a subject they hadn't discussed—and had been advised by the pope not to discuss.

As the meeting adjourned, everyone seemed to be talking at once. Were these amendments a proposal or an order? Did the pope intend that council rules be suspended? Did he want his amendments handled like others? Did these amendments really come from the pope? Or from the birth control commission?

Canon de Locht complained about this last suspicion. "They have a false idea about our commission," he noted in his diary. "It's not fair for us not to be able to tell the Mixed Commission that a majority of our theologians have already decided that past pronouncements of the magisterium are not irreformable."

The next day's meeting ended in another uproar. The chair, Fernando

Cento, a curial cardinal, immediately proposed that the commission accept the amendments without discussion, out of reverence for the pope. John Dearden, archbishop of Detroit, wondered whether and how far these amendments expressed the pope's mind. Canon Heylen went on the attack, asking about the first amendment, one that condemned all *artes anti-conceptionales*. What did the term mean? Wouldn't these "arts" include rhythm? Did the council now want to condemn rhythm? More hullaballoo.

Someone asked Father Tromp to read Cicognani's letter again. He did, then added on his own that the pope wanted the commission to follow the teachings of Pius XI and Pius XII. He said, "There is no question of freedom with regard to doctrine, but only with regard to formulation." Cardinal Paul Léger deplored the proposed amendments, said their adoption would damage the Holy See's prestige and reputation, then got up to leave the meeting. He said he was heading for the papal apartments.

Cardinal Cento suspended debate. He said discussion of the amendments would proceed on the morrow and that the meeting would be closed to *periti* and lay auditors. That decision didn't stick. The pope heard from all sides, not only from Léger, but also from Cardinal Ottaviani, Bishop Colombo, and no fewer than ten lay auditors, who sent him a note saying public opinion would not welcome "a series of last minute corrections added to a text which is already familiar and well known."

Arthur McCormack urged Cardinal Suenens to speak to the pope. Suenens: "I can't. We can't make a fight the last week of the council. We don't want a scandal." McCormack: "We've got one already if these amendments go through." Suenens went.

De Riedmatten also found his way into the papal chambers. If the pope intended to "solve" the birth control question with a papal footnote, did this mean the end of the papal commission? The pope assured de Riedmatten these suggested amendments did not end the commission's work. And more: he told de Riedmatten that the reference to *Casti Connubii* in the marriage chapter "should not stop the commission from continuing to examine this prime aspect of the question."

So the question was still an open one. De Riedmatten got this word out to others and also the news that the *periti* and the auditors would not be excluded from the morning meeting. *L'Avvenire d'Italia* told much of this story in its morning edition November 26. Bishops, *periti* and auditors were sharing copies of the paper when Cardinal Ottaviani called them to order at 9:30. Ottaviani deplored the news leaks about the four papal amendments, then Father Tromp read a second letter from Cardinal Cicognani.

This letter specified that 1) the pope considered the amendments of great importance, 2) the commission didn't have to follow their exact wording, 3) certain things could be added, provided the sense was retained, and 4) the pope would later decide whether the commission's versions were acceptable. Some *periti* believed an exegesis was in order. But the majority didn't bother with that. They devised a practical solution, saying, in effect, "Let's see how much we can neutralize the amendments, then dare the pope to reject what we've done."

No need here to recount the intricacies of the four amendments and describe how the commission's liberal majority modified a few lines of text. Enough to note that Archbishops Dearden and Garrone made a suggestion which allowed the council fathers to: 1) look backward, and thus please Rome, by citing Pius XI and Pius XII and 2) also look forward, and thereby please the rest of the world. The council could point out, they suggested, that the pope had a commission still working on the problem. It was a brilliant idea.

In the text approved on November 16, the council told couples about the importance of conjugal love. It told them to decide on how many children to have. It said transmission of life ought to be determined by objective criteria, standards not drawn up on a basis of biology alone, for human beings reproduce in a way that goes marvelously beyond lower forms of life. The human standard: the dignity of the human person, which preserves mutual self-giving and human procreation in the context of true love. But then the text was deliberately vague: "Imbued with these principles," it read, "sons of the church may not undertake methods of birth control which are condemned by the magisterium."

What methods did the magisterium condemn? The editors didn't intend to say. They could have said the magisterium was in doubt. They decided to say nothing, to leave that impression by implication. But now, in the third papal amendment, the pope's conservative advisers wanted to clear up the doubt. They were proposing a new sentence: *Quibus principiis innixis, filiis Ecclesiae in procreatione regulanda vias inire non licet, quae a Magisterio improbatae sunt vel improbentur*—"Relying on these principles, sons of the church may not undertake methods of birth control which have been condemned or will be condemned by the magisterium." To make things even less doubtful, they proposed adding two papal citations, to Pius XI's *Casti Connubii* and Pius XII's Allocution to the Midwives on October 29, 1951.

In meetings of the marriage subcommission, and in meetings of the full Mixed Commission, they discussed those words *improbatae sunt vel improbentur*. Was this council to endorse all past condemnations, including St. Augustine's implicit condemnation of rhythm? Could this council urge people to give the church a blank check on the future? What was this word, this *improbentur*? Wasn't the future tense of *improbare, improbabuntur*?

At this point, Canon Delhaye noted, one *peritus* blushed a deep crimson. Delhaye believed that the proud *peritus*, a perfectionist no doubt, was embarrassed about his tiny grammatical error, and thereby revealed himself as the author of this papal amendment. The blusher was Father Ford.

This grammatical gaffe gave the other side an opening. They proposed reverting to the more vague present tense of *improbare*, which would return exegetes of the text to asking, "What methods was the magisterium now condemning?" The honest answer was that the magisterium was in doubt. And the best way of proving that was to cite not only the words of Paul VI on June 23, 1964, when he first announced that he had appointed a commission to advise him, but also to add these words to Footnote 14:

Certain questions which need further and more careful investigation have been handed over, at the command of the Supreme Pontiff, to a Commission for the Study of Population, Family, and Birth, in order that, after it fulfills its function, the Supreme Pontiff may pass judgment.

And then the coup de grace:

With the doctrine of the magisterium in this state, this holy synod does not intend to propose immediately concrete solutions.

In this state? What state? Said Canon Heylen, one of those most responsible for the editing of the chapter on marriage, a state of doubt. In the summer 1966 number of *Ephemerides Theologicae Lovanienses*, Heylen wrote a 12-page article on Footnote 14, explaining that the church was in a state of real doubt. "Every translation or interpretation," he wrote, "which implies that the council has reaffirmed the teaching of Pius XI and Pius XII as certain and irreformable does not respond in any way to the real sense of the text."*

Summing up: With the submission of the four papal amendments, the minority had tried to reestablish *Casti Connubii*. The majority used the crisis, however, as an opportunity to knock it down. By including the citation on Paul VI's study commission, they put *Casti Connubii* into a context: there had been a development of doctrine on birth control and it was still going on.

Friday evening, November 26, Cardinal Ottaviani was delegated to take the reconstituted amendments to the pope. He did so and he took along a critical note from Father Ford. He told the pope, "I did all possible to have the commission accept the modifications of Your Holiness, but I was

---

*Some have produced such a translation, in a version of the conciliar documents edited by Austin Flannery and published by the Talbot Press in 1975, a version so tendentious and so counter to the spirit of the council that Joseph Selling, an American lay theologian teaching at Louvain, warned scholars in 1980 to use "supreme caution . . . if Flannery's text is to be employed for teaching about the theology of marriage."

always in the minority. Father Ford could not approve the attitude of the theological commission in this matter." Saturday and Sunday, sccording to Jan Grootaers, majority members were "on pins." They had decided to assert their conciliar independence, but they were not quite sure they could bring it off. But on Monday evening they discovered they'd done it. The council's general secretariat delivered documents to the conciliar sub-commission on marriage indicating that the pope had confirmed the amendments as revised.

Next day, the full text of the *schema* went to the printer. On December 3, council fathers had the *schema* and its *relationes* and *expensiones modorum*. December 4, the fathers voted an overwhelming yes on the marriage chapter, 2,047 *placet*, 155 *non placet*.

This victory kept the doors open. To Canon de Locht, it was a partial victory, because the text was equivocal. He thought the council fathers would have approved overwhelmingly a complete scuttling of *Casti Connubii*. They were not allowed to do so, he said in a December 3 note to the Belgian bishops, because Rome had wanted to assert its authority. The fathers, he wrote, had lost a chance to make a difference in the lives of millions. He had recommended a vote of *non placet*.

But work remained. The pope knew this and said so, strongly, as he began his address closing the council December 7: "And if quite a few questions raised during the course of the council itself still await appropriate answers, this shows that its labors are now coming to a close not out of weariness, but in a state of vitality which this universal synod has awakened. In the postconciliar period, this vitality will apply, God willing, its generous and well-regulated energies to the study of such questions."

As the pope spoke, I stood on a platform not fifty feet away with photographers accredited to the council. I had loved the great hearted Pope John XXIII, and I was not a fan of Paul VI, who seemed to take a pessimistic view of almost everything that came under his scrutiny. But now I was not hearing his wonted tidings of gloom. Now I was hearing his summation of the council just ended, and my heart soared.

The pope was saying, "Never before has the church felt the need to know, to draw near to, to understand, to penetrate, serve and bring the Good News to the society in which she lives; and to come to grips with it, almost to run after it, in its rapid and continuous change." Some may have thought the council "too responsive to this world at the expense of tradition." He didn't think so. This council, he said, was marked by love for mankind. And then this pope gave a paean to modern man that would mark Paul VI, Giovanni Battista Montini, as much more human than his critics believed.

The church of the council has been concerned with man, man as he really is today: living man, man all wrapped up in himself, man who makes himself not only the center of his every interest but dares to claim that he is the principle and explanation of all reality. Every perceptible element in man, every one of the countless guises in which he appears, has, in a sense, been displayed in full view of the council fathers, who, in their turn are mere men, and yet for all of them are pastors and brothers whose position accordingly fills them with solicitude and love.

Among the guises, we may cite man as the tragic actor of his own plays; man as the superman of yesterday and today, ever frail, unreal, selfish, and savage; man unhappy with himself as he laughs and cries; man the versatile actor ready to perform any part; man the narrow devotee of nothing but scientific reality; man as he is, a creature who thinks and loves and toils and is always waiting for something, the "growing son" (Genesis 49:22); man sacred because of the innocence of his childhood, because of the mystery of his poverty, because of the dedication of his suffering; man as an individual and man in society; man who lives in the glories of the past and dreams of those of the future; man the sinner and man the saint. . . .

The pope said secular humanism had in a sense defied the council. But there was no clash, no battle, no condemnation. "The attention of our council has been absorbed by the discovery of human needs (and these needs grow in proportion to the greatness which the son of the earth claims for himself)." The pope asked those who called themselves modern humanists "to give the council credit at least for one quality and to recognize our own new type of humanism: we, too, in fact, we more than any others, honor mankind," a mankind the council had taught him to love more and serve better.

* * *

But many believed the pope hadn't yet learned enough. In December, I interviewed Father Häring, Bishop Reuss, Canon Heylen, Cardinal Suenens, four who could help me understand the council's final texts on marriage, and what to expect from the papal commission and the pope. All struck the same chord: they were pleased with what the council had achieved. But they were not optimistic that the pope would make the right decision about birth control.

I saw Father Häring at the Redemptorist headquarters on the Via Merulana, the same place Francis Xavier Rynne Murphy called home during the four council sessions. Häring had always been forthright with me. Now he seemed somewhat chastened by events of the past week. Though some liberals were eager to blame "the Ottaviani crowd" for the

Papal Modi Affair, I gathered from Häring's account that it was Paul VI himself who had tried to brake the council. "We won a minimal victory," said Häring, "by keeping the birth control question open."

"What about the papal commission?" I asked.

"The commission majority is on the side of change," he said. That was a happy report to me, for it was news I needed: commission members had been close lipped about the direction they were headed. But reporting this news gave Häring no joy. His pale blue eyes looked watery and sad. Maybe he was tired. The last week of the council had been a terrific strain.

"And the pope?" I asked.

"It would be difficult for the pope to give an opinion opposite to the commission majority," said Häring. "But I do not think we are going to convert him to any view outside the juridical view."

* * *

Without prompting, Bishop Reuss expressed the same reservations about Pope Paul. I was meeting with Reuss at the Villa Stuart. "I think the Holy Father is worried about confusing the people," he said. He paused. Then he blurted, almost angrily, "And so we must search for," he paused for emphasis, "the truth!" He said he was sad about this, because he knew the problem was far too complex. No one could come up with "the truth," a simple formulation to "solve" the problem for "a juridical minded pope."

"And in the meantime?" I asked.

"I do not think we can or should conceal the fact from the people that there is some doubt in the church on this question. Anyway, they already know there is if they have been reading the press. And so, this is what I have told my priests." He handed me a copy of an article he had written for pastors of his diocese. It was in German, so I asked him to summarize. "In essence," he said, "I say to pastors that in this stage of real doubt, they can hardly tell a couple using contraception that they are sinning, especially if they do not believe they are sinning. I am not even sure they are. *In dubiis, libertas.* 'In doubtful matters, liberty.' Therefore, it would be wrong to question them about this in the confessional. Couples in this stage should go to communion without going to confession."

This was a breakthrough, said Reuss, from the rigorist position of recent decades, a position which frequently kept conscientious couples away from the sacraments. In a sense, he explained, this represented a return to the Holy Office's first known reply to this question, in 1822. The Holy Office then counseled leniency in the confessional. Rigorism set in later, under the crusading banner of the embattled Pius XI and his chief adviser in moral matters, the Belgian Jesuit Arthur Vermeersch. Vermeersch, he said, probably drafted *Casti Connubii.*

"And," I said, "the church has been fighting to keep it on the books ever since." Reuss nodded. "And why does the church fight so hard?"

Reuss paused, then said slowly, "They believe that the church cannot change. If it does, the authority of the church will suffer."

I said, "Won't the authority of the church suffer if it doesn't change?"

"Naturally," he said, nodding again rather sadly.* I waited. At length, he added, "We have two problems facing us: 1) whether our principles are correct, and 2) whether any couple has the right to decide on a solution for themselves."

"Is contraception wrong," I asked, "because *Casti Connubii* says so, or because it is wrong in itself?"

"Because *Casti Connubii* says so," he replied.

I was startled. That put the church's strictures against contraception in the same category as other disciplinary rules. Did the church have any right to do that? Could the church make something a serious sin that wasn't sinful in itself? The council just ended had already touched on that. October 27, when the fathers were discussing the church and the modern world, Louis Morrow, bishop of Krishnagar, India, asked, "How can men and women of today understand that God is good if we continue to teach them those who eat meat on Friday will go to hell? An infinitely regrettable contempt for the authority of the church is the result. Let us not speak falsely or irrelevantly about mortal sin. Let us continue our *aggiornamento*, our updating, by simplifying our legislation."

The fathers applauded, and more. They endorsed the idea that they should go home and do something about the rules of the church, rules that bound people under pain of mortal sin if, for example, they ate meat on Friday.

* * *

I visited Belgium the second week of December and had lunch at the

---

*Some church intellectuals were beginning to see "the authority of the magisterium" as the issue most important to the pope. Hans Küng had a conversation about it with Pope Paul VI in December 1965 and told me about it some months later. "If someone could show the pope how the insights of the birth control commission were only a development of *Casti Connubii*, then he would be able to say something tomorrow. But of course, they are not a development. To say so would be dishonest." Küng said he urged the pope to say that *Casti Connubii* was a mistake, an understandable mistake for Pope Pius XI to make. "The world," Küng said, "will not make a big furor over this. Everybody makes mistakes. It's no sin to err."

The trouble was, Küng told me, that in a triumphalistic church, traces of which remained in the Roman curia, "error still seems to be the greatest sin of all."

Cafe Royal in Louvain with Victor Heylen and a mutual friend, Charles Moeller, an intimate of Cardinal Suenens, who had just been assigned to the Holy Office in Rome. Canon Moeller's appointment was one of the nice outcomes of the council. He was a warm, open man of vast culture, and the pope wanted him to bring some of that openness to the Holy Office, a place staffed by a group who normally looked on the world with the eyes of, say, detectives from the Los Angeles Police Department who had spent too many years on the vice squad.

Moeller came along to enjoy the lunch and serve as an interpreter when Heylen's English failed him. Heylen was an ebullient fellow, a council peritus who, when Häring's health faltered during the council, became chief editor of the chapter on marriage. Heylen ordered a beer, then identified the villains of the council's last days: Zalba, Visser, John C. Ford. All three, he said, seemed to be crusading.

"For a cause?" I asked.

"No," said Heylen, "for their own vindication, for a vindication of the ideas they have been teaching all these years. They obey the pope when the pope obeys them." Heylen said Ford had double dealt with the mixed commission. "Ford kept telling me and others that we had 'a good text, a good text.' At the same time, he was working away on the third floor [in the pope's quarters] quietly, secretly."*

I told Heylen I was not sure the pope didn't agree with Ford on birth control.

Heylen nodded. "Yes, the pope is a juridic theologian, and that is the difficulty. He does not have a theology, but, rather a closed juridic system." To illustrate, he cited the pope's statement of June 23, 1964, admitting theoretical doubt existed about the church's position on birth control but insisting that, in the meantime, Pius XI's and Pius XII's norms should apply.

Heylen explained that birth control was in the area of natural law, contraception was either right or wrong in itself, but not because of a ruling by the magisterium. But the pope felt he was stuck with his predecessor's rulings. Why? Because, he explained, the pope's theological training came from strong canon lawyers. "That's why he insists on applying this canonical notion, the lawyers call it *possessio juris*, to a field where it simply does not belong.

"This," said Heylen, "is the very first question the papal commission on

---

*A few days later, Ford told me over the phone—I had found him "hiding out from reporters like you" at St. Mary's Hospital in Walla Walla, Washington—that he could "easily see where some might think there was some double dealing involved, but actually I had to go along with an entire text if I saw no real possibility of changing it."

birth control should answer, whether the notion *possessio juris* ought to come into a question of natural law. You cannot take a notion from positive law," he said, "and apply it to the field of natural law."

But that, I suggested, is exactly what the pope seemed to be doing. The most disputed sentence in the final version of the marriage chapter seemed to prescind from the rightness or wrongness of contraception entirely. *Filiis ecclesiae, his principiis innixis, vias inire non licet. . . .* "This prescription," I said, "is intended for 'sons (or children) of the church,' not for everyone."

"Exactly," said Heylen with a broad smile. "This is not a doctrinal statement, but a pastoral directive, made to avoid plunging the church into laxism. But interpretation of pastoral directives is possible. For example, the church decrees pastorally that I should go to Mass on Sunday and abstain from meat on Friday. But, if I am ill, I can certainly use my own judgment and stay in bed on Sunday, or eat meat on Friday."

"Do you mean, Canon," I said levelly, "that contraception may be like eating meat on Friday? OK, if it's done for a good reason?"

"Exactly," he said. "But it's not an arbitrary decision. You just use common sense. You use the commonly accepted human principles for solving any dilemma situation where you have conflicting values at work."

I wondered whether the notion of *epikeia* came into play here.

Heylen brightened when I used the word. "Yes," he said. "Juridicism is an abstraction and, therefore, a deformation of the real. The canonists all realize this, and that is why they all accept the notion of *epikeia* so readily."

For good historic reasons, no doubt, the word *epikeia* doesn't have an English equivalent, though the concept has classic origins. Aristotle recognized that general laws have particular exceptions, especially if one has to act immediately. And so he named a "virtue," *epikeia*, that helped govern the peculiar quality of discernment needed when a person must decide whether the law applies or does not apply. Thomas Aquinas, leaning on Aristotle, defined *epikeia* as "a kind of higher rule for human actions." His example: the law says that loans must be repaid. But if a madman lends you his sword, then demands it back while in the grip of madness, you'd be practicing *epikeia* by not giving it to him.

But in Anglo-Saxon tradition, the law is the law. People follow it until lawmakers change it. No one ever tells them about *epikeia*.

And so, in 1964 and 1965, when an onerous church law proscribing contraception came up for review, Catholics living in the Anglo-Saxon tradition, those unfamiliar with *epikeia*, had more than a passing interest in "repeal" of that law.

The big question was, could humans repeal God's laws? Well, sometimes, as, for example, God's law: "Thou shalt not kill." According to the just war tradition, peoples could "repeal" that one in self-defense. Trouble was that for decades, churchmen had been reiterating Pius XI's doctrine that contraception was intrinsicially evil, which meant that it admitted of no "repeal" or exception. In Pian terms, contraception was more evil than killing. This put Pope Paul VI in a difficult bind.

But the pope's liberal advisers at the council were trying to free him from that idea. Canon Heylen and those who understood what they were voting on when they ratified the words *Filiis ecclesiae . . . vias inire non licet* believed they could help the pope establish contraception as positive rather than divine law. Then it would be easier for Catholics everywhere to practice *epikeia*, to say that, in this instance, the law does not apply.

* * *

The day after our lunch at the Cafe Royal, Canon Moeller took me to Cardinal Suenens, a man we both considered the church's number one cardinal. Suenens was a man of vision and courage, a man who could, and did, exercise leadership, above all, in this birth control question. During the 1958 Brussels World's Fair, Suenens called the world's doctors to help find a means of birth control the church could accept and throw its moral weight behind. He held a colloquium that year, a modern counterpart of the famous Malines Conversations sponsored by another great churchman who had also been the cardinal-archbishop of Malines-Brussels. Desiré Joseph Mercier had gathered leading intellectuals of post-World War I Europe to talk about cooperation among the Christian churches. This first major ecumenical dialogue of modern times had launched the ecumenical movement that was now capturing all Christendom.

Based on his first colloquium, Suenens wrote a book, *Love and Control.*[27] It was not radical. In it, Suenens talked about "a spirit of neo-Malthusianism that was sweeping the world" and about "the evil of sexual emancipation." But he also made a strong case for the new, personalist values moderns were finding in marriage-for-love (which contrasted with traditional arranged marriages still in vogue in many parts of the world). Suenens said the church was wrong to tell couples, "The more children, the better." What if a couple had good, conscientious reasons for not wanting more children? For a churchman in 1960, Suenens had surprisingly liberal views. He scored the severe "all or nothing" approach many were preaching to Catholic couples, and wrote, "Married couples must be able to translate their love into physical activity and gestures, even though they are obliged to abstain from the final act of love."

Since *Love and Control,* Suenens had been gradually changing, as he made clear in his widely read comments during the third session of the council, the one in which he pleaded with the fathers not to allow "another Galileo case."

In our conversation, Suenens admitted his evolution on birth control. I didn't ask how he had changed his mind, partly out of awe—he was very tall, with penetrating eyes sunk deep in his craggy skull—and partly because I already knew that, in long conversations with "his men" on the birth control commission, he asked them radical questions. He felt many in the church would need time to accept the radical answers he had received. "Still," he said, "I see progress and evolution." He mentioned Noonan's book, praised Noonan, and added, "I checked to see if he quoted me correctly, and he did, in all seven references. Even when he said I was wrong, he was right."

"But what about this period of indecision?" I asked.

He said, "We have to let time take care of this. I remember when Ogino first announced his discoveries. There were some moral theologians who immediately denounced the rhythm method. Then, after a few years had passed, the moralists got used to the idea and began offering tentative approval. I think the same thing may be happening now. How long have we been reconsidering the question on the basis of the discovery of the pill? Two or three years? Let's give it a little more time."

I guessed a majority of people would be likely to accept the pill before the pope would. "The pope is on the conservative side as a theologian," replied Suenens. "On the birth control question," he added, with candor unusual for a cardinal, "the pope hasn't grown. But I must say in his defense that he is concerned about the people. He thinks we are living in a dangerous time, because the people are not prepared for change. I think the pope would announce the tentative judgments of the commission, except for one thing: there is such a great possibility of abuses." But he said he was sure the council's marriage chapter "helps us arrive at a partial solution. It's a personalistic approach. . . ."

Did he think the church's old norms should be considered "doubtful law"?

He raised his eyebrows. "Why . . . no," he stammered.

The previous day, Heylen had given me four good reasons why the church was in a state of practical doubt. Now I was trying to see if Suenens would also admit the doubt. "And why not?" I asked.

Suenens replied, "Because the pope said they were not."

"Do you really believe that?" I said.

Suenens' eyes glazed over. "Sometimes," he said, "grace illumines reason. It is like, well, sometimes I go up on the tower of my cathedral here in Malines, and I look out over the countryside, and I cannot say exactly what that object is in the distance. Then I take out a map and look at it, and I see that the tower of"—he mentioned a place name I was unfamiliar with— "ought to be in that spot, and then I can see for sure that indeed that is the tower of "—he mentioned the place again. Suenens' eyes searched mine.

"Faith is a map," he said. "We use it to help us see better. This is an old idea. St. Thomas Aquinas said it. *Credo ut intelligam.* I believe so that I can understand."

"But do you think this really applies here?" I persisted. "We're not talking about belief, but about a question of the natural moral law."

Suenens repeated an old answer, one I had heard in ninth-grade catechism: "The church is the defender of the natural moral law."

I said the outstanding philosopher at Louvain, his own man, Albert Dondeyne, considered this "a bizarre and dangerous idea."

Suenens raised his eyebrows again, quizzed me a bit about my background, nodded, then said, "You know a lot about the church. But please do not push too hard. Everything will happen in due course."

Chapter Seven

After Footnote 14, the world was watching.* Now Pope Paul VI had to encourage his birth control commission by calling an extended session. Previously, he had authorized three- or four-day meetings. Now he gave the commission two months, plus a budget. That meant more secretarial help for de Riedmatten, more copying machines for the pages upon pages of reports that he had to make for everyone on the commission and, above all, skilled interpreters and simultaneous translation equipment. In previous sessions, the commission had limped along with Roman seminarians whispering halting translations in the ears of those who couldn't understand the speaker. Now, de Riedmatten could hire specialists otherwise employed at the UN's Food and Agricultural Organization headquartered in Rome, being careful they sign agreements to reveal nothing heard inside the commission meetings.

The fifth session of the pope's commission resumed on April 13, 1966. The theologians came first. The others would arrive in May and stay until late June, and now "the others" would include 14 new members, cardinals and bishops appointed by the pope, "to give the new pastoral emphasis to the deliberations." Some suspected the 14 would help tone down the radical element that worried Father Ford. Canon de Locht took this personally, as he probably had a right to, though he was unaware Ford had complained so directly and so specifically about him to the pope himself. He grumbled in his diary, "We already *had* a pastoral emphasis."

Cardinal Ottaviani was named commission president and there were two new cardinal-vice presidents, one liberal, one conservative: Julius Doepfner, archibishop of Munich, and John Carmel Heenan, who had been made a cardinal February 22, 1965. There were four other cardinals: Suenens, Valerian Gracias of Bombay, Joseph Lefebvre of Bourges, and

* Footnote 14 may be one of the most celebrated citations in history. It made church history, at least: the reference to the existence of a papal commission working on an open question marked the first time any council had allowed a footnote that did not refer to 1) sacred scripture, 2) one of the church fathers, or 3) a previous papal encyclical.

129

Lawrence Shehan of Baltimore. The bishops were Carlo Colombo, the pope's theologian, John Dearden of Detroit, Claude Dupuy of Albi, France, Thomas Morris of Cashel, Ireland, Jose Rafael Pulido-Mendez of Merida, Venezuela, Jean Baptiste Zoa of Yaounde, Cameroon, and Karol Wojtyla, of Krakow, Poland. Wojtyla attended no meetings. Archbishop Binz and Bishop Reuss were already on the commission.

These episcopal appointments may have triggered foreboding among the emerging majority, but their euphoria at the conclusion of the council overcame their paranoia. They plunged ahead, convinced that the council had given them the impetus they needed to free Catholics from the protectionism of the church's rulebook mentality.

In general, the council had set the church on a new path: the people of God were in the world; they would start saying "yes" to the world instead of "no." The council had also written a positive blueprint for marital morality by proposing responsible parenthood as an embodiment of personalistic rather than naturalistic values. The fathers blessed a couple's lovemaking as good in itself, procreation aside. They also refused to declare that procreation was the "primary end of marriage." This was a subtle commutation of the sentence St. Augustine imposed on couples centuries earlier, a subtlety not lost on commission members. And so, this commission got down to business.

The theologians met every day until the end of April, tried to focus more tightly on unresolved issues. They began discussing one of the most basic questions: what makes an action moral or immoral? They could have discussed this for weeks. They spent two days in a fascinating dialogue, principally Father Fuchs, Häring, Zalba and Alfons Auer, the leading moral theologian at Tübingen, going round and round, settling nothing, opening new questions instead.

Zalba proposed several knotty issues revolving around the principle of totality and its application to the morality of birth control, and several more about pre-moral evil: can a good man or woman ever choose the lesser of two evils as a modified "good"?

Häring enjoyed the arguments as much as anyone, but he also pointed out that the group was talking about an abstraction—"the objective order of things." He hoped they would not forget the objective order included human beings, charged with the grandeur of God who is love.

Zalba wondered whether this group could reduce every criterion to the concept of love.

The theologians were caught up again in the council dialectic, in the tension between love and laws. For centuries, of course, the church had "made law." Now, certain elements were asking what it meant for the church to make law. Did church law "bind consciences," as Father Ford and the traditionalists contended, and could such law bind under pain of mortal sin? Did a Catholic who disobeyed such a law go to hell? Or was church law designed to lay down an ideal Catholics could use in forming their consciences but ignore in a concrete instance when the norm did not seem to apply?

De Riedmatten knew the commission had to resolve this question, for Paul VI had been talking about the church's "laws" as if they bound Catholic couples in conscience. Weeks before, de Riedmatten had assigned theologians to consider both sides of the question and present position papers to the commission. April 21, theologians heard a paper written by Philippe Delhaye, but delivered by Jan Visser, because Canon Delhaye had been detained at Louvain.

According to Delhaye, the pope would have "a perfect right to make a positive ruling on something which has been doubtful under the natural law." He could prescribe rules, could lay down a Christian ideal and try to prevent laxism. In fact, wrote Delhaye, "doesn't the church do this when it obliges people to go to mass on Sunday?" To Delhaye, such a move on birth control would have certain advantages. "It would put to rest the doubt which is becoming more and more intolerable and doing the greatest harm to the authority of the church. It would put things off until such time as the positive law could be modified and/or abolished. It would assure a merciful solution in extreme cases (for a law does not oblige insofar as it is impossible)."

But, said de Locht in rebuttal, how could a papal statement put aside real doubt? The law *is* doubtful, he said. Couples knew this. Theologians knew it. Some bishops and cardinals had expressed their doubts on the council floor. Even Pope Paul had publicly expressed hesitation. Insisting now on the old law would throw the church into legalism. It would tell people the church's moral code was some extrinsic overlay. Said de Locht: "If the church were to say the pill were acceptable, the pill wouldn't become acceptable the day the church said so. The pill would be acceptable in itself. It isn't pronouncements from the magisterium that make things good or bad."

He added, "You can't legislate morality just by laying down some rules. Above all, it is necessary to inculcate a moral sense by emphasizing the fundamental virtues: charity, justice, prudence, responsibility, the essential values of love and of marriage."

Visser came right back with contrary arguments. He said the presumption of truth lay with a law that had been in effect for some time. Those who wanted to change it had to provide proof, not a mere doubt, that the old law was bad. "It is imprudent," he argued, "to toss aside the observance of a norm because of doubt alone. The burden of proof here falls on the one who doubts. . . . If we rejected the traditional doctrine on the basis of this doubt, there would be heavy consequences. There would be few moral truths which could not be called in question on this basis."

Some minority members didn't believe the pope could change the teaching, even if he wanted to. John Ford contended that the commission was constituted in order to help the pope. He did not believe it could help him unless it restricted itself to the limits required of any pope. Popes were also bound by the magisterium's teaching.

But not even Ferdinando Lambruschini, who worked in the Roman curia, could accept this notion. During these discussions, Monsignor Lambruschini told his colleagues why it was not enough, given the current doubt, to hold to the law. "It will be good," he said, "if we can come up with reasonable corrections of past formulas, without saying that contraception is bad because it is against nature, and against nature because it is bad. Obligations which are said to rest on the natural law ought to be understood by everyone on whom they are imposed."

Most of the others scored the notion that formulations of the past, even the recent past, had to handcuff pope and church. Fuchs: "Continuity of a teaching doesn't consist in repeating what has been said before in other circumstances but in continuing to see if these earlier pronouncements actually took permanent values into account. We are not talking about fidelity or infidelity to prior teachings; we are trying to see if there are some truly new perspectives which would require new responses." Again, Fuchs inveighed against the church's rulebook mentality. How much better, he said, to take a larger view, to teach the larger laws of fundamental morality: charity, justice, prudence, responsibility.

And so it went: for another week, the theologians disputed the meaning of the natural moral law and the criteria of morality, and the limits of church authority in such an area. They tried to look deeper at the nature and meaning of sexuality and the underpinnings of norms the church had evolved. They asked whether and how far men and women could intervene in their biological processes and what motives justified such interventions. Recalling that time, Auer told me at Tübingen in June 1981, "We had a biologistic approach which was metaphysicized. This resulted in a *natura metaphysica* of sexuality. From there it was possible to arrive at logical deductions of great detail by way of a superficially impressive goosestep."

At first, Fuchs was unable to fault these old logical deductions—naturally enough, for it was he who had been making many of the deductions. Auer told me, "Father Fuchs hesitated for a long time. He had a hard time. He kept telling me, 'Give me better arguments,' and, obviously, with the time going, the arguments were formulated more clearly. Finally he said, 'Yes, we can put it this way.' "

The theologians were moving from an ancient classicism which viewed all ideas and most definitions as eternal and unchanging, to an awareness

that men and women are part of history, that ethics change as the world
and people's awareness of it change. Pope John XXIII helped start the
theologians on that tack by his original use of the scriptural phrase "signs
of the times." For Pope John, this meant the Holy Spirit speaks to the
church not merely through Scripture and tradition but also through contemporary events and trends. In this way, as commentator Peter Hebblethwaite has suggested, "history, what was going on, edged its way into
theology."

John Courtney Murray, an American Jesuit, was a principal conciliar
proponent of that notion. This historical consciousness, he said, helped
the church take a stand on religious liberty in 1966, one close to a position
Pius IX condemned in his 1854 Syllabus of Errors. "Truth," said Murray,
"is an affair of history and is affected by all the relativities of history." Over
a Roman lunch in the fall of 1965, Father Murray suggested to me that
resolution of the religious liberty issue had "transferential implications"
for those trying to work out the birth control question.

Now the classical scholars on the commission were moving to the view
that "ethics is nothing more than human culture," a concept obviously tied
to human history and the gradual evolution of human understanding. At
one time, the church approved of slavery, in fact as well as in theory. (Jesuits at Georgetown, which was founded in 1789, once had slaves.) But
moralists, deepening their understanding of what it meant to be a human
person, later found reasons to disapprove. If culture and ethics were not
identical, some were saying at least this: that human culture had invaded
human ethics. Some theologians here preferred this ethics to the old de-
ductive approach, Auer's "superficially impressive goosestep."

John Noonan's views also helped. De Riedmatten asked him to sum up
his views on birth control and the natural law from a historical perspective. He said that applications of the natural law have changed as the world
has changed. He enumerated some of these changes: 1) People were living
longer: life expectancy in the Roman Empire was 27 years; in the 20th
century, it had risen to about 70 in most Western countries. 2) Social mores
were changing: courtship patterns and free choice in marriage had made
love a common ideal in marriage; more and more youngsters were attending high school and college, a change which affected the meaning of education in the classic formulations of the ends of marriage. 3) Almost everyone was learning more about sex—medically, biologically, philosophically,
theologically. Doctors once thought intercourse during pregnancy was
harmful; now they knew it did not endanger the fetus. Philosophers once
thought every act of intercourse was *per se generativus;* now they knew
that only a relative few of any couple's lovemaking sessions would result in
new life. The council fathers had recognized that sex in marriage no longer
had one purpose, but many.

On Friday, May 6, after four weeks of meetings, de Riedmatten proposed that the theologians each spend a half day preparing brief provisional answers to two questions:

1) Is the teaching of *Casti Connubii* on contraception irreformable?
2) Is contraception intrinsically evil, according to the natural law, so that it can never be permitted in any case?

The theologians had voted last March on the first of these questions and the vote had been 12-7 against *Casti Connubii*. Now de Riedmatten gave the theologians six minutes each to present their best arguments. They did, in an intense meeting, and then they took a "provisional" vote. This vote was 15 to 4, negative, on both questions.[*]

The vote was significant, because 1) it signaled a swing to the side of change by three theologians who had voted the other way a year before, and 2) it represented a further move by Josef Fuchs, who had said a year before that *Casti Connubii* was reformable, but that that didn't mean the church should reform it; this year, he added his voice to those saying the teaching was changeable, and the church ought to change it.

John Noonan took notes on the vote and helped specify, in a written memo to the members, what meaning lay in the ballot against *Casti Connubii*. He said *Casti Connubii* had asserted certain permanent values, but that subsequent generations could distinguish "from the rule against contraception, a rule which serves, defends, embodies and fosters those values, but is not identified with them. In the course of development, a contradictory rule may come to serve the same values." He quoted Cardinal Newman: "Religious ideas develop by a combination of opposites. To grow is to change and to be perfect is to have changed often."

* * *

In de Riedmatten's summary report of this phase, he said the group had reached all the substantial conclusions it was likely to reach. In remaining meetings, members should work on implications of their conclusions, and ways to express them. De Riedmatten summarized the high points of the theologians' conclusions so far.

He pointed out that the commission was not divided into two equal camps, that members basically agreed: the church ought to change. Only a

---

[*]Alfons Auer, who had pressing duties in Tübingen, flew to Rome to vote on a Saturday morning, returned to Tübingen, then to Rome again Monday. Auer recalled that there was not only an air of emergency about his vote, but of utmost secrecy, too. He was stunned, however, when he returned to the Spanish College Monday to have Fuchs greet him with this: "The result of that secret vote? It's in the newspaper today."

small number disagreed. He recalled that the pope had picked the members. "The conclusions that the members came to . . . were the result of a long and mature elaboration. . . ."

De Riedmatten said those who affirmed the intrinsic malice of contraception admitted they could not prove their position. But the minority members claimed that only strengthened their case: in such difficult situations, they said, the simple faithful need help from the magisterium.

Answers to these views abounded; majority theologians would have a chance to reiterate them in June, when the entire commission, including cardinals and bishops, would gather.

Before that plenary session, however, would come more section meetings. There would be a meeting of the medical section, May 2 to May 6, of the demographic section, May 4 to May 7, and a pastoral week, May 9-13, under the presidency of Archbishop Dupuy.

In meetings of the medical section, several of the physicians teamed up to report on the IUD, the intra-uterine device known widely as the coil. The big question, for this commission, was whether the coil acted as an abortifacient. If it did, the commission could not approve it. Research indicated that the IUD did not act on the fertilized ovum. In that sense, the IUD was not abortifacient. Perhaps that meant partial approval was possible. But some doubt remained about the way coils prevented conception. Finally, the group said it could not speak of *the* IUD "as though there were only one with a uniform mode of action." These coils came in no fewer than a half dozen shapes; apparently, some coils acted in one manner, others differently.

Later, on both philosophical and medical grounds, the commission would come close to giving a non-abortive coil qualified approval. But this commission's principal, pastoral thrust was pointed a different direction. This commission wanted to take the church out of the answer machine business. It wanted the people of God to grow up. Giving them even a qualified approval to use this method or another would have made things too easy. More than one member had expressed horror over headlines about "the Catholic pill." Would there also be a Catholic coil, shaped perhaps like a cross?

One way the commission came to conclude it would endorse no particular method: by scrutinizing a method that had long been identified as "the Catholic way," rhythm. The Crowleys had helped members do that in 1965, by letting them see their early survey. Now, they presented the results of another survey, based upon replies from more than 3,000 couples from 18 countries. It was not a random sample: for the purposes of the commission, it was better than a random sample, because these couples were among the world's most earnest Catholics: most were members of the Christian Family Movement; 290 were subscribers to *St. Anthony's*

Messenger who responded to a 1965 article entitled "The Church Calls for Facts."

But these professedly fervent Catholics did not give rhythm a good report card. Only 42 percent of the CFM couples said rhythm helped them regulate their family size. And 63 percent said practicing rhythm harmed their marriages in varying degrees because of tension, frustration, sexual strain, loss of spontaneity, arguments, irritability, discouragement, insecurity, fear of pregnancy. The couples from the *St. Anthony's Messenger* sample were even more negative about rhythm. Less then 10 percent of them said, "Rhythm works, and we have a positive reaction to it." About 25 percent said, "Rhythm works and we have a negative reaction to it." About 65 percent said, "Rhythm does not work, and we have a negative reaction to it." A majority of this group found rhythm unnatural—"unnatural to have barriers built up and to have couples avoid one another during periods of abstinence, unnatural to have the wife become policeman and be forced to assume the dominant role, unnatural to have a husband who travels or who needs comfort and security by reason of daily stress be denied when he needs love the most. . . ."

Donald Barrett produced an elaborate analysis of this data (he acknowledged significant help from people on the Notre Dame campus) and he distributed a 23-page report to the commission. He said he had found many couples now relying on the pill, about half of them after consultation with a priest. Barrett wrote, "There is confusion about what the church and priests have developed to rationalize the pills, and most cannot appreciate why their use must be limited in a moral context. But once a couple takes the pills, then a more secure and positive view of self, conjugal relations and family life tends to arise. Very few couples report feeling that use of the pills is immoral."

André Hellegers added that his surveys showed women going through menopause had the hardest time making rhythm work, thus making it "least applicable at precisely the time when it is most necessary."

Dr. Cavanagh, who had given little previous indication that he thought the church should change, came forward this week with results of a survey he had done. When during any month, he wanted to know, does a woman experience "a peak of desire"? Other researchers—he cited Ellis, Kopp, Davis, Terman, Beach and Tinklepaugh—had come up with varying answers. Some had reported that many women surveyed didn't know when they hit their peak. But Cavanagh was convinced his results were better and more reliable because he had polled 2,300 women—all users of rhythm. "These women were answering the question with introspection. All of them were quite self-conscious of ovulation . . . over a period of years," Cavanagh said. Seventy-one percent of the women sampled registered their greatest sexual desire at the time of ovulation.

Cavanagh's conclusion surprised even himself: "Rhythm is more psychologically harmful than other methods because it deprives a woman of the conjugal act during the time of her greatest desire." In a note to Cardinal Heenan some days later, he would say it even more forcefully:

Abstinence as the only means of controlling conception has left Catholics immature emotionally and impoverished financially. It has left them insecure, rebellious and frustrated. Serious psychiatric disorders have arisen as a result.

The Crowleys tried to make sure Vatican officials saw their figures. They sent copies of their survey and identical letters to the pope, to Cardinal Ottaviani, to Cardinals Doepfner and Heenan, to Bishop Reuss and Archbishop Binz. "Rhythm does not promote unity in marriage," they stated. They also reported that "almost all of the couples hope the church's position will change. . . . Married people who have written to us and who have discussed the subject with us are thoughtful, mature, responsible Christians. They love the church and are devoted to its teachings. . . ."

That week, de Riedmatten asked a question he hadn't intended to be humorous, but Patty Crowley and many others couldn't help but giggle. On May 11, de Riedmatten set aside a day for a conference on "the psychology of love" and proposed a topic that sounded like a title from James Thurber: *L'act conjugale, est-il necessaire pour le couple?*

J.R. Bertolus, the Parisian psychiatrist, stammered over that one. "Is sex necessary?" he said. "But, how could it not be necessary? It is the privileged part of conjugal life. . . ." Patty Crowley found Father Ford's frowns about this proof enough that the commission needed less help from celibates and more from other married couples. She applauded de Riedmatten for commissioning reports by Don Goffi and Philippe Delhaye on the "consensus of the faith" as a source of marriage doctrine.

Canon Delhaye's presentation surprised many, even Patty Crowley, because Delhaye had found an official report that confirmed the Crowleys' findings. Delhaye told the commission that in February 1964 the Vatican's state department, at the pope's request, had asked the world's bishops what their people believed about birth control.

Bishops' conferences in each country reported back: birth control was the major pastoral problem in "developed countries." In the so-called "undeveloped lands," where many were ignorant of basic birth control methods, a majority of couples practiced withdrawal, and abortions were common. Delhaye told the commission that "a fervent minority accepted 'the heroic solution.' The majority reacted with doubt or indifference." In all the reports that came in, Delhaye kept coming across "the same two curious expressions":

It used to be that people talked to their confessors, knowing that they were wrong. Now they do so knowing they are right.

The faithful accept other laws and see themselves as sinners when they transgress them. Here, they invoke the impossibility of the law, their conscience and God's mercy.

Canon Delhaye believed the council's chapter on marriage had partly reflected the consensus of the faithful. He implied that the commission might reflect more of that consensus in its final report to the pope.

One way the commission could do this: by continuing to listen to its lay members. It listened with frank fascination to Albert Görres, a physician and a professor of psychology at the University of Mainz, West Germany, who spoke bluntly about the feelings of his own colleagues. These people believed there was "something bascially wrong, absurd even, or at least questionable" about the church's position on birth control.

> They have in fact been very hurt and have taken great offense at the fact that questions of the greatest importance for life have up until now been decided apparently without theological discussion and according to the opinions of one or two of the Holy Father's private theologians or of a curial authority.

Dr. Görres talked about the sense of liberation felt by Catholic intellectuals: to think the pope would set up a commission!* It was an admission, he said, "that neither the pope nor a curial authority can have a ready answer at hand on every occasion for every moral question. Areas of uncertainty and indecision exist also in the church of God." Görres shared what he had been hearing, at professional gatherings, at conferences, in conversations with priests and laypeople:

- The unanimity that existed up until now among moral theologians was deceptive, conditioned by censorship. What went counter to certain definite textbook opinions either received no *imprimatur,* or was censored, or was not even published.
- The study of moral theology has for generations repelled thinkers who were aware of problems, and has attracted an assortment of timid, often scrupulous ultraconservatives.
- Many moral theologians see their task as collecting arguments post factum for a conclusion which is apparently already firmly established *ex doctrina ecclesiae.* Thus arises the paradoxical situation that many moralists, in a teaching based on natural law, no longer hold its natural law basis as certain, but must fall back on the argument *ex doctrina ecclesiae.*

*One of my more outspoken friends at the council, Gerard Van Velsen, bishop of Kroonstadt, South Africa, said that Holland's tremendous housing shortage had helped push the discussion along faster there than in other places. "In Holland," he said, "you may have an entire family of four or five persons living in two or three rooms. In this sense, I am amazed that the pope, who has several hundred rooms, has thought about the problem at all."

• People know sexual morality of the thousand-year period after Augustine was subject to serious errors, so an unchanged tradition in the strict sence can be assumed only for the most basic principles. The historical distortions of sexual morality are not only the result of an underlying, still more or less active, Manicheism, Platonism and Stoicism, or of deficient and even fantastic medieval biological ideas, or of a logically unsatisfying physicalism, but also a result of a celibate psychosis.

Görres credited Maximos IV, the Melkite patriarch, for that coinage. He defined celibate psychosis as "a state of mind arising out of the psychic situation of the cleric, one that keeps him from viewing marriage and sexuality with an unprejudiced and comprehensive eye." He said he suspected some moral theologians of being "emotionally handicapped . . . even by unconscious stirrings of resentment, envy and aggression."

Görres questioned the standard appeal to "the consensus of the bishops of the world in questions of marriage morality." Was this consensus "as real as alleged"? He cited the case of Galileo Galilei. Bishops of Galileo's day apparently agreed that Galileo's teachings were contrary to their common theological convictions. Many in the church today regretted that. They also rejected many "moral convictions" of the past:

Moral theologians [said Görres] have justified with great confidence things which their successors today reject as outright immoral and un-Christian: witch trials, tortures, burning of heretics, slavery, forceful violation of the consciences of unbelievers and heretics, suppression of colonial peoples and, in the present connection, the castration of choirboys, this last over a period of centuries and with the approval of popes.

Finally, speaking as a psychologist, Görres warned the group about a current pseudo-solution proposed by some important theologians, that the traditional teaching remain objectively binding, but that couples may apply subjectively mitigating circumstances to decrease their responsibility. Görres asked, "What is to be gained from such an approach?" Good married people didn't want quick, easy absolution. "They want to know what kind of an attitude God demands of them. They are unable and unwilling to claim for themselves the mitigating circumstances that apply to neurotics and psychopaths."

John Ford fumed through much of this. He lashed back in a memo summing up the week's conclusions. Some doctors, he said, "spoke beyond their competence by offering moral opinions based on a misunderstanding of what the moral teaching of the church means or by criticizing the moral teaching of theologians without really understanding very much about it." Father Ford suggested the doctors wouldn't have been so free-wheeling if they hadn't learned of the "provisional show of hands on Friday, May 6, by which the great majority of theologians favored the reformability of *Casti Connubii,* and were ready to deny the intrinsic malice of contraception." Ford said that news had given the doctors apparent relief. To Ford, there was something shady about that: "And even more important is it to realize that they felt relieved because, in their opinion, the traditional doctrine many times prevents them from doing what, according to medical ethical standards, would be the best thing for their patients." To Ford, something as real as "the best thing for a doctor's patients" should cede to something as abstract as "the irreformability of *Casti Connubii.*"

But Ford offered little criticism when women took the floor during de Riedmatten's "pastoral week." (What can a man do when a woman says, "This is how I feel"? Listen.)

De Riedmatten had told the women to focus on the psychology of the conjugal act, periodic continence, total abstinence and the role of possible conception in the meaning of the conjugal act, and to express themselves "clearly, absolutely, fearlessly."

Madame Kulanday began. She reported on a survey she took in India. Indian women gave an emphatic and unanimous "yes" to the question, "Is intercourse an important part of marriage?" She told the group, "Women desire intercourse in marriage. It binds the husband and wife together. Women have equally strong urges. After two or three babies it becomes possible for the woman to live her sex life in a minor key, but she still has to rise to her husband's needs. They all recognize that intercourse has a binding force and keeps their love aflame."

Madame Rendu, who had taught rhythm for years, talked about the psychology of abstinence. Periodic abstinence didn't hurt a couple's sex life, she contended. In fact, it probably helped. Dr. Hellegers nodded his agreement and noted that rhythm, unlike other methods of contraception, probably helped a couple avoid reducing sex to the banal.

To Patty Crowley, that point was interesting, but it had nothing to do with the church's imposition of periodic continence—in some cases, even total continence—upon couples as a matter of faith or discipline. She said the church ought to promote love:

I think a couple has a natural rhythm. A couple knows that at certain times more than at other times, everything "seems right" between them. These times—a rhythm of their own, they are not regular, they cannot be turned off—they are signs of love. . . . No amount of theory by men will convince women that periodic continence is natural. We have heard some men, married and celibate, argue that rhythm is a way to develop love. But we have heard few women who agree. Over and over, we hear women say that the physical and psychological implications of rhythm are not adequately understood by the male church.

Mrs. Crowley reminded her largely male audience that women go through menopause, when menstruation is no longer regular. She quoted from one of the thousands of letters she received:

How can we tell when or if another period will be? I am 46, my husband 54; we both have to work. I well know at this age there have been many "change-of-life babies." We want to live within the laws of the church, yet we don't know how. My husband and I are growing further apart all the time because of fear.

She added, on her own:

The wife who is unsure, who is afraid of another pregnancy, is not a true love-mate and can come to resent her husband, intercourse, in fact, her whole life.

Then Patty shifted gears, to say what "free and responsible Christians" felt about children: "Couples want children and will have them generously and love them. They do not need the impetus of legislation to procreate. It is the very instinct of life, love and sexuality."

Colette Potvin nodded vigorous approval, then seized her chance to further the education of these clerics. She described herself as "simply a wife, married 17 years, with five children." She had had three miscarriages and a hysterectomy; perhaps from that point of view she had a clearer view of marriage than the scientists and theologians. She looked up at the group, hesitated a moment, then dared a needed preamble: "To understand woman, you need to stop looking at her as a deficient male, an occasion of sin or an incarnation of the demon of sex, but rather as Genesis presents her: a companion to man."

Where I come from, we marry primarily to live with a man of our choice. Children are a normal consequence of our love and not the goal. The physiological integrity of the conjugal act is less important than the repercussions of that love on the couple and on their family. And that conjugal act is the principal way we have of showing our love for each other.

Colette Potvin said she wanted the commission to get away from methods. "We don't live our married lives around a method," she said. Rather she wanted the commission to ask what sex means in the lives of Christian couples, ask how sex is a part of God's commandment to "love one another."

Because no one had dared speak so plainly, she would. Directly and with no false modesty, she explained what lovemaking meant to her and Laurent. "Marvelous moments," she said, "when each of us accepts the other, forgives the other and can give the best of ourselves to the other." The morning after such a communion with her husband, she said, she felt more serene, more patient with her children, more loving to everyone. Nothing contributed more to her family equilibrium. She described the spiritual sense of well being that accompanied what she called "the conjugal orgasm": a sense of joy, a feeling of accord on every level—and all of it accompanied by "a rainbow of wonderful tingling sensations."

Some theologians were overwhelmed. She obviously touched some hearts as well as some minds. De Riedmatten filled the awed silence that followed with the quiet observation, "This is why we wanted to have couples on our commission."

But de Lestapis was worried. He was the French intellectual here, full of grand abstractions. Next day, he said he feared the commission was starting to "idolize" the couple. "The couple," he said, "has become a state of grace and contraception their sacrament . . . and the result is a sort of intoxication, a practical obliteration of the sense of God, a mystification in the psychological order, a devaluation of procreation." He puzzled many of the lay people present. Patrick Crowley noted on his yellow legal pad that de Lestapis seemed to be engaged in a filibuster. But de Lestapis, a figure of awe to many when they joined the commission in March 1965, had lost much of his influence with this group.

Toward the end of this pastoral week, Archbishop Dupuy, who came to the meetings earlier than his expected arrival on June 20 with the other new episcopal members, distributed some questions: 1) What do you think has been agreed upon? 2) What still seems to be a matter of disagreement? 3) What are the points and conclusions you wish to see in our report?

All but five of the group asserted the need for change. All but five believed rhythm "suitable only for the relatively few, an elite, who have a very strong Christian formation and a low sex drive." Barrett summed up responses to the Dupuy questionnaire, the same Barrett who had written in January 1965 that the pope had to speak immediately, even before the full commission began its work. Like most of the others, Barrett had changed.

So, too, had Father Perico, the Jesuit from Milan. He told the commission, "The more I hear the confessions of good Catholics on this matter," he said, "the more I feel it necessary for the church to change. I would dare say my own penitents have made a contribution here."

If the change does not come, said Professor Van Melsen, pastoral teaching would be "sterilized, paralyzed, leading to loss of any positive way for confessors to be effective, to loss of contact with the better Christians, and even to 'a ghetto church.' "

But what change did these members want? De Locht had the most interesting suggestion. Picking up, perhaps, on Madame Potvin's cue, he said he wanted the church to discard its negative orientation and help couples develop a more adult understanding of the other values and responsibilities of marriage. Said de Locht: "We preach a morality which doesn't have much to do with reality on the one hand and, on the other, a pastoral indulgence which keeps couples on an infantile level. We talk about a pastoral theology of growth toward an ideal and tell couples, 'You're not making it, but keep trying anyway.' At the same time, we can also turn around and ask for a kind of heroism. But the most facile calls to heroism are made in the most dubious wars."

Patrick Crowley was as straightforward as de Locht:

I think we agreed that the sense of the faithful is for change. No arguments were presented on the side of the status quo other than the one that Rome has spoken once and to change would undermine the magisterium. I must say I heard no other argument and I don't think this is a good argument to support an otherwise objectionable position in what we like to call the pilgrim church. . . .

Crowley said the commission ought to create a pastoral statement, based on one already written by Bishop Reuss, that would underline the importance of conjugal love and all the positive values of marriage. He added:

The preponderance of testimony from the lay members showed that change is anticipated and great problems will arise if no change is made. If the church fails in this, much of the progress made by the council will be lost. If the church, that is, the members learn that change was refused when reason seemed to dictate change, I think the authority will be undermined more than by any change.

Our report should tell how many members of this commission have changed their views during the course of these dialogues.

The changes of view were clear to Crowley. In the beginning, neither he nor his wife nor many others thought change possible. Now most members were not ony saying it was possible, they were saying it was mandatory.

Why had so many changed their views? And what had brought about that change? Others would soon ask the same questions.

* * *

The group took a week's vacation, while de Riedmatten and his steering committee stood back from their discussions to figure out what more they needed to do before the cardinals and bishops arrived on June 20. De Riedmatten suggested that his colleagues develop formulations that would be of value to the cardinals and bishops and, ultimately, the pope, "who alone will decide the position of the church."

De Locht wondered why it was so self evident that the pope "alone" should decide. He believed de Riedmatten was reinforcing a long-standing tendency in Rome to isolate the pope in sovereign decisions. But de Locht was a good soldier. He started working on a summary.

So, too, did Ford, with the help of Germain Grisez, an American philosopher Ford brought to Rome and lodged in a *pensione* on the Via del Seminario. Assisted by this bright, vigorous layman, Ford turned out a prodigious amount of work. For at least a week, he and Grisez labored over a Latin text, *Status Questionis: Doctrina Ecclesiae ejusque auctoritas,* The State of the Question: The Doctrine of the Church and Its Authority. De Lestapis, Visser and Zalba signed it, then Ford turned it in to de Riedmatten May 23. De Riedmatten skimmed it and sighed. It set a tone completely opposed to the majority. He asked Fuchs, Sigmond and Delhaye to prepare a rebuttal.

Most of Ford's documents simply reiterated past teachings. Of ancient theologians, to whom contraception was "a damnable vice, an anticipated homicide, a serious and unnatural sin." Of modern popes, even Pope John XXIII (though Pope John spoke on birth control only once, in a discussion of the population problem in his encyclical, *Mater et Magistra*). Of the Roman curia which, Ford contended, answered questions on this matter 19 times between 1916 and 1928 "and almost as many times" since.[28]

As for the question itself, "why is contraception always seriously evil?" Ford first admitted that he could not present clear and cogent arguments based on reason alone. The admission drew little comment from the others. This was a sophisticated group; they knew many conclusions of the natural law did not win absolute consensus even from the best thinkers in or out of the church. Reasonable disputes were raging on capital punishment, nuclear war, racial justice, abortion, euthanasia, business ethics. But that didn't mean the church could not attempt to intervene on many of them, as 20th century popes had in their social encyclicals, and as this pope was attempting to do on birth control, no less difficult a question.

"The question," said Ford, "is not merely or principally philosophical. It depends on the nature of human life and human sexuality, as understood theologically by the church."

This was precisely the question. Historically, the church (and especially churchmen) had been afflicted with the notion that sex was suspect. In the 17th century Francis de Sales reminded his people that "marriage is a great sacrament, but it is the holiness of the fruit it produces which permits a just compensation for recovering from the fault one incurs by reason of the delight taken." Several centuries later, Ford was telling the commission there was no necessary relationship between sex and love. "Conjugal love," he wrote, "is above all spiritual (if the love is genuine) and it requires no specific carnal gesture, much less its repetition in some determined frequency." A father and a daughter can love each other, he said, "without the necessity of carnal gestures." His conclusion, though unexpressed, was clear: "So why can't husband and wife?"

To many commission members it was the final proof that Ford did not understand what the council fathers were driving at when they said mar-

ried love is "uniquely expressed and perfected through the marital act."
Nor did he understand the council's new ecumenical thrust. According
to the council, all Christians were part of the pilgrim church, included in
the category "people of God," and guided, as Catholics were, by the Spirit.
Even on birth control? Ford didn't see how that was possible.

If contraception were declared not intrinsically evil, in honesty it
would have to be acknowledged that the Holy Spirit in 1930, in 1951
and 1958 assisted Protestant churches and that for half a century
Pius XI, Pius XII and a great part of the Catholic hierarchy did not
protest against a very serious error, one most pernicious to souls; for
it would thus be suggested that they condemned most imprudently,
under the pain of eternal punishment, thousands upon thousands of
human acts which are now approved. . . . These acts would be approved for the same fundamental reasons which Protestantism alleged and which Catholics condemned.

Ford wondered whether this proposed change would not trigger "very
grave doubts about the very history of Christianity." For him, Catholics
didn't base their faith in the Holy Ghost, the Holy Catholic church, the
communion of saints, the forgiveness of sins or life everlasting, Amen,
but in the rules on "substantially intact intercourse" fashioned for Pius XI
by the Belgian Jesuit Arthur Vermeersch in 1930.

* * *

On May 23, de Riedmatten brought in two of Rome's best Biblical scholars, Ernest Vogt, rector of the Jesuits' Biblical Institute, and Stanislaus
Lyonnet, also from the Biblicum. Father Vogt was an Old Testament
scholar, Father Lyonnet an expert in the New Testament. Each was asked
what Scripture had to say about birth control. Apparently, the Bible contained no relevant teaching, nothing more than God's suggestion to Adam
and Eve that they "shall be two in one flesh" and his command to "increase
and multiply."

The Old Testament had only one possible reference to contraception:
the story of Onan, slain by God because he spilled his seed on the ground.
Vogt told the commission most exegetes believed the story had nothing to
do with marital morality, but with Onan's failure to comply with Judaic
law: he married his late brother's wife and "God slew him" because he
shirked his duty to carry on the family name. In the New Testament,
neither Christ nor the sacred authors said anything about birth control.
Lyonnet listed all the sexual sins mentioned in the New Testament. It was
impossible, he said, to prove that any reference had anything to do with
contraception.

* * *

The commission members felt they were getting close, but to what? They weren't sure, but an air of urgency pervaded the hallways of the Spanish College. De Riedmatten was scurrying about and distributing papers and calling emergency meetings. He checked in with Fuchs, Sigmond and Delhaye to monitor their progress on the rebuttal to Ford's paper. He found them working proudly. Though Ford's report had indirectly impugned their loyalty to the church, they had nothing to feel guilty about. They had taken their mandates from the pope seriously, had done some honest rethinking of the church's positions on sex and marriage and had made their decisions based on what they thought would help people, not hurt them.

On May 28 Fuchs, Sigmond and Delhaye turned in their report. It asserted church teaching was "in evolution." It underlined the insufficiency of former explanations of the natural law. People do not have to take material nature as a given; they can make it better. "Churchmen," they said, "have been slower than the rest of the world in clearly seeing this as man's vocation." There was no sound basis to fear that change would cause a loss of trust in the church's teaching authority or make it possible to raise doubts on every other doctrine. Such change would rather be "a step toward a more mature comprehension of the whole doctrine of the church."[29]

They reviewed the criteria for human intervention in biological processes of nature and set down some norms of right reason:

"The responsible procreative community" is always ordered toward procreation; this is the objective and authentic meaning of sexuality and of those things which refer to sexuality (affectivity, unity, the ability to educate). So we can speak of the "procreative end" as the essential end of sexuality and of conjugal life.

But this procreative end does not have to be realized by a fertile act when, for instance, parents already have children to educate or they are not prepared to have a child.

Sexuality is not ordered only to procreation. Sacred Scripture says not only "increase and multiply" but "they shall be two in one flesh," and it shows the partner as another helpful self. In some cases, intercourse can be required as a manifestation of self-giving love, directed to the good of the other person or of the community, while at the same time a new life cannot be received. This is neither egocentricity nor hedonism but a legitimate communication of persons through gestures proper to beings composed of body and soul with sexual powers.

They even said a couple making a conscientious decision to avoid conception had a duty to use the most efficacious means. "In this matter," they said, "the rhythm method is very deficient. Besides, only 60 percent of women have a regular cycle." As for the alleged relation of contraception to abortion and other sexual aberrations, this report treated them as red herrings. They noted that "abortions are more numerous in areas where contraception is neglected."

De Locht wrote in his diary, "The talk of the past few days has confirmed for me the general feeling on behalf of a change. What seemed clear enough for some years now has become enriched by an impressive, justified convergence of views." The key word was "justified." Indeed, de Riedmatten had gone to see the pope and returned with a message: "Tell all the members that they are not employees of the church. This commission is the church in dialogue with itself."

Others in the church were interested in that dialogue. Cardinal Ottaviani, for one. Father Ford had been telling him the commission threatened to destroy the magisterium. And Ottaviani, who tended to think the magisterium and the Holy Office were identical, took this as a personal threat. He had an official in the Holy Office, Josef Tomko, sit in on every session of the theologians, never offering an opinion but taking copious notes, something de Locht believed could have intimidated some of the theologians.

The Vatican secretary of state was also concerned. Amleto Cicognani asked one of the commission theologians for a confidential, inside report. The theologian gave the cardinal an accurate account, and Cicognani said, "Well, the procedures all sound correct to me."

They were. De Riedmatten was a good secretary. He imposed nothing on the members. Rather, he created a climate for the freest possible interchange and then recorded members' views, often with a vote on key propositions that helped advance the inquiry. On June 3, for example, he presented the group with two new questions:

Does it seem opportune for the church to speak on the birth control question without delay?

The answer: unanimously yes. Many added: "On the condition that the church talk about an evolution here. Silence would be preferable to a repetition of the old teachings."

Is the church in a state of doubt concerning the received teaching on the intrinsic malice of contraception?

Thirty said yes, five no. Hellegers said, "The debates have convinced me more of the intrinsic danger in irreformable statements than in the intrinsic evil in contraception." Bishop Reuss said any further harping on *Casti Connubii* without giving new reasons for its strictures against contraception, which was probably an impossible task, would do the church more harm than good.

One alarmed defender of the status quo suggested a compromise: the church could "preserve the ancient teaching by reaffirming tradition and then making a special exception for the pill." No need, then, to repeal *Casti Connubii*, he said; the pill didn't exist in 1930. The majority frowned on that ingenuous suggestion. They had decided much earlier not to recommend any method, not the pill, not even rhythm.

* * *

John Carmel Heenan was also concerned. Dr. Marshall had been giving him private reports about the commission's progress, and Cardinal Heenan could see some change in the wind. But how? Why? Heenan was puzzled. He wasn't due in Rome until June 20, but maybe he'd better go immediately, attend some commission meetings, see for himself. First, though, he had to prepare for whatever changes might come. He drafted a pastoral letter for the people of England and, on June 5, published it in *The Catholic Herald*.

In the pastoral letter, Heenan spoke as a father to his children, tried to explain how "truth can remain the same, while our knowledge of it is always increasing."

Some of our notions of right and wrong have also undergone change. At the beginning of the last century, according to English law, children were put to death for stealing and men hanged for forgery. Today, it is thought wrong to hang a man even for murder. . . .

What did this mean to the faithful? Heenan reminded them how the birth control commission began, how husbands and wives, scientists and doctors, theologians and pastors of souls were invited to offer the pope their insights. "Nobody," wrote Heenan, "will be able to say that he did not listen to his priests and people. When he speaks, the pope will have availed himself of all sources of human wisdom and knowledge . . . [and] loyal Catholics will all accept his verdict."

Heenan asked for prayers "that God will guide the Holy Father and members of his commission to wise and compassionate conclusions."

The British press took the letter as a clue that a decision on birth control might come soon. Some reporters caught Heenan at Heathrow Airport about to board a plane for Rome. He wouldn't talk to them, but an aide was permitted to say Heenan was going to attend the last meetings of the birth control commission, which was about to give the pope its final report.

The Guardian's Geoffrey Moorhouse commented on the pastoral letter, on Heenan's departure for Rome and the likelihood of the pope's listening to his commission. That same week, he noted, 500 Catholic laymen from 18 countries had petitioned the pope for a change in the church's teachings. He quoted a piece of the petition:

The church cannot take the responsibility before history of minimizing one of the main problems which humanity must face, let alone of constituting an obstacle to general research into real solutions: humanity expects a positive moral contribution from one of the great spiritual forces of the world.

And so, the morning of June 6, Heenan was in Rome. He not only attended this semi-final meeting of the experts at the Spanish College, he presided as well. De Riedmatten had asked him to, out of deference and respect for his rank. This wasn't a bad idea. This meeting would be a dress rehearsal for their June 20 meeting with the cardinals and bishops. But Heenan was in for a shock.

De Riedmatten had asked Father Ford to present the theological arguments for no change; he tapped Father Fuchs to give the opposing view. De Riedmatten could hardly have picked anyone but Ford: he was the most vocal, most articulate member of the minority. But Ford's manner would not win any uncommitted votes—or even the sympathy of Cardinal Heenan, who was on Ford's side before he arrived in Rome. Ford was scathing, bombastic, rhetorical, almost savage in his attack on those who wanted change. The princely Fuchs was cool, brief, scholarly, quiet in his defense of an intelligent, reasoned approach.

Heenan must have been puzzled. He hadn't had time, as the others had, to rethink things, and he couldn't ken what had happened to the certain teachings he remembered from his seminary days. Worse, he was hearing his own stock arguments couched in the worst possible way.

Ford's position was mainly an argument from authority, for he admitted he couldn't defend the old natural law approach any longer, and an assertion that the church couldn't change because it would never do for the church to admit it was wrong:

The Catholic church was established by Our Lord to show men the true way to eternal life. It could not be in substantial error for so many centuries, or even for one century, imposing under pain of mortal sin the heaviest burdens in the name of Jesus Christ, unless Jesus Christ was in fact imposing these burdens. . . .

When Ford finished the arguments from authority, he went *ad hominem*:

Among the theologians who are defending contraception are some who conceive human nature as subject to an evolution so complete that there "does not exist any fixed concept of nature." There are some who do not seem to admit that intrinsic evil is necessarily connected with the choice of any external actions. There are some who permit in certain circumstances suicide, abortion, fornication, masturbation and adultery. There are some who defend the principle that the end specifies the means, explaining this in a way that is practically equivalent to "the end justifies the means." There are some who seem to be defenders of situational morality.

There are some who seem to deny that the church can teach infallibly in matters of natural law. There are some who seem to deny that the magisterium of the church is competent in any event to bind the consciences of the faithful to any particular behavior in any concrete case.

Ford repeated his memorized litany of abuses that would logically follow changes advocated by his colleagues: premarital sex, oral intercourse, mutual masturbation, sterilization, homosexuality, abortion.

Fuchs dealt with little of this. Ford had presented a caricature of his views and those of his colleagues, and Fuchs ignored the parody. Instead, he simply tried to summarize the factors that had led him and the others to rethink the traditional doctrine:

. . . a realization of the one-sided and incomplete character of previous views on sex, the insufficient biological understanding of the past, the fall in infant mortality rates, changes in society (marriage, the family, the status of women) and, above all, perhaps, a more profound vision of man's mission: man need not simply accept in a passive way the gifts of nature as something sacred. As one created in the image of God, he should look at his responsibilities and cultivate and humanize his gifts according to their total human meaning. And so, many facts have led to this deeper reflection, this more profound understanding of human nature, of sex, of marriage.

Ford was silent, miffed perhaps, about being ignored rather than refuted directly. But the meeting rolled on. Donald Barrett and Raymond Sigmond gave the conclusions of the demographers. That group was now composed of four priests and 12 laymen, sometimes augmented by physicians and theologians, and they, too, favored change. They said falling death rates and medical advances contributed to wild population growth in many parts of the world. Some families might have as many as eight to 12 children, and almost all would live to maturity. They called this situation impossible "for any nation which desires order rather than chaos, human dignity and peaceful community." They favored fertility control "as a way of bringing population growth within the scope of human values."

According to their report:

. . . without such a reduction in fertility, economic and social planning for a dignified, Christian existence becomes hazardous. . . . Mexico is now growing at 3.5 percent a year. At this rate, in 200 years it would have 35 billion people. In certain countries where fertility regulation is not available, the number of abortions appears to be rising swiftly, e.g., an estimated 1,000,000 a year in Brazil alone, and most of these are induced abortions; Catholics in such countries of middle- or upper-class status use contraception, according to the research, regardless of the frequency of mass attendance or reception of communion.

The demographic section recommended that the church take a reasoned approach to birth control so it might speak against policies in certain countries (such as massive sterilization and abortion programs) that militated against human dignity. "What is needed," their report said, "is the presence of the church, dialogue with the world, which present doctrinal thinking tends to restrict, weaken."

Such a view was a byproduct of the council, which had recommended that Catholics get involved in the world and help make it better, rather than stand apart and condemn it for being bad. Documents like *Casti Connubii* had expressed the old view, and those writing the report for the demographic section made that connection. They added, "In contrast to the thinking at the time of *Casti Connubii,* contraception which is widely practiced in the West has not [led] and is not likely to lead to race suicide.* With present death rates, 2.4 children per family is about all that is needed to stabilize a population."

Getting involved, in this context, meant Catholics should cooperate with non-Catholics and support their own governments' birth control programs, "provided some licit methods are offered, provided they are effective and promote responsible parenthood. . . . Catholics simply must participate for their own good and to bring the influence of Christian values upon their communities."

The only thing holding up such involvement: a final resolution of the church's classic view that contraception was intrinsically evil. The commission was in the process of reforming that view. It only remained for members to persuade first the incoming cardinals, then the pope, that such a reform was wise. Some wondered how they could: it had taken many commission members months to come around to their new view. And they were looking forward to a mere week with the cardinals.

One thing stood in the way of reaching the pope and the others, according to J.R. Bertolus and Paul Anciaux, reporting on behalf of the psychological section: the church's classic fear of sex. Dr. Bertolus said he believed that the core of the birth control problem was the inability of most Catholic moralists to accept sex as good. Fearing sex themselves, they tried to put a lid on it for married couples. "We must take the guilt out of sex before we can humanize it," said Dr. Bertolus.

* Certain members of the commission believed Arthur Vermeersch, the Belgian Jesuit who had drafted *Casti Connubii,* had convinced Pius XI that the whole world was in danger of birth controlling itself out of existence in 1930, this because Belgium was reeling from the aftershocks of World War I. Many young men who would have been fathers of young families in 1930 had lost their lives in the war. The birthrate in Belgium had dropped alarmingly.

Paul Anciaux agreed. He said much of the church's understanding of sex was based on pre-Christian pessimism toward sex and the body. He applauded the commission's efforts to go beyond the latent dualism that looked upon human sexuality as "an animal act to be controlled by the spirit." Canon Anciaux tried to set down a more positive definition of chastity. When couples have to abstain from sex, he said, they will—because of their love for each other.

But the obligation of prolonged abstinence by reason of some lame moral prohibition seems harmful in a great many cases. And we are not dealing here with human weakness. We are dealing with the reaction of those who see these moral imperatives as somehow contrary to the fundamental values of marriage.

Anciaux admitted that some members of the psychological section believed couples who had difficulty were overly influenced by "the hedonism of the day" and not possessed of enough "Christian fervor." He added: "But most others, theologians and other couples, reject this position categorically."

Cardinal Heenan, growing impatient with all this on-the-one-hand, on-the-other-hand business, called for an immediate vote, one that would have no ambiguity. Should the church change its position or not? What methods are licit? "We should make a unanimous recommendation," said Heenan. "That ought to impress the pope." The others tried to explain that voting couldn't settle "open questions." At present, there were no answers. Heenan, who had been cranking away at the church's answer machine for decades, almost went into a panic.

He tried to concentrate on those who now had the floor. De Lestapis and de Locht had each been asked to take the other's side. What, de Lestapis was asked, would be the pastoral consequences of change in the church's teaching? De Lestapis could hardly conceive of such a thing. His talk focused on the need for more education. Of young people. Of couples. Of priests and confessors. Of a married elite who could train others. De Locht was told to consider the consequences of no change. He, too, had a hard time visualizing this possibility—which would be profoundly regrettable:

These old norms will be less and less accepted in a blind way. People will discuss them and they will find them doubtful. More and more, they will challenge the power of the church to make pronouncements with an irreformable certainty on moral questions. . . .

Though he was having a hard time "visualizing possibilities," de Locht would become prophetic:

I must mention a pastoral consequence whose seriousness we cannot minimize. What will happen if the magisterium makes a decision contrary to the conclusions reached by the great majority of this commission? Our group (which was constituted by the magisterium) and others outside of the commission have done their research. What if the word gets out (and it will!) about the split between that research and the verdict of the magisterium? This poses a particularly grave problem.

Heenan had a sense of *deja vu*. During the third session of the council he had railed against theologians who seemed to be usurping the authority of the magisterium. Now here they were again, personified by de Locht, telling the magisterium how to scatter its incense:

In a world [de Locht continued] that tends to deal with the great human problems, including the demographic problem, by establishing plans of study and international collaboration, Christians are going to find themselves more and more in isolation. The church has already helped couples come to the notion of responsible parenthood. It has already helped discover the human and spiritual demands of the conjugal community. Now the forces opting for the status quo would be telling couples that they cannot adopt a solution that is not, in itself, seriously sinful. The church would then leave these couples in a state of permanent culpability and force many of the most mature and thoughtful of them to lose confidence in the magisterium.

That was too much for Heenan. When de Locht finished, he burst into a 10-minute diatribe, scolding de Locht for not following his assignment, for not even trying to be a temporary advocate of the status quo. "Fifteen to four," he cried, referring to the theologians' vote on the intrinsic evil of contraception. "This means nothing. We have to ask about the value of the 15 and the value of the four. How many examples do we have in history where heresies held almost unanimous sway, while only a few held fast to the truth, which finally triumphed in the end? I have read the papers you have written. They should have taken a more intelligent tack. I wonder what you were doing with your time?"

With this, Heenan adjourned the meeting. Most of the others filed out of the room murmuring and shaking their heads. What kind of "seeking for the truth" was this? De Locht took de Riedmatten aside. He couldn't proceed in this climate. He would not speak as scheduled on the morrow. An hour later, there was a rapping on the door of de Locht's room, Room 26 on the second floor. It was Cardinal Heenan. He begged de Locht's pardon. He hadn't wanted to hurt anyone's feelings. He and de Riedmatten had had a long talk, and he wanted to say now that his words didn't translate well into French. Now, Heenan said, he was tending to agree with the majority.

De Locht accepted Heenan's apology and the next day, June 7, Heenan expressed his regrets to the whole group.

The debate continued. De Locht and de Lestapis continued their discus-

sion. De Locht kept insisting the church had to bring people to new insights that could help them and their marriages. "The whole church, the
faithful as well as the magisterium, have to live through a period of growth
—with a feeling of joy and of a new responsibility."

De Lestapis foresaw a three-way split in the church between:

1. *The conservatives,* who would follow the old way for different reasons, more security, more need for an objective rendering of the divine
law.

2. *The self actualizers,* those who would "seize responsibility" for their
lives. The church would have to caution these "adults" (de Lestapis himself
put the word in quotes) against "the hardenings always possible to the
individual conscience."

3. *The free spirits,* who would speak of "a new morality without inter-
diction or obligation."

For de Lestapis the question would be: "Which of the three groups
would come closest to the meaning of authority and Christian liberty?" He
said he didn't know.

But the meeting ended on a high note. The discussion was free and full,
with almost everyone suggesting how the church might tell how it had
changed.

Fuchs had almost the last word. "Many confuse objective morality with
the prescriptions of the church," he said. "We have to realize that reality is
what is. And we grow to understand it with our reason, aided by law. We
have to educate people to assume responsibility and not just to follow the
law."

Heenan didn't understand. He would rather see something closer to
blind obedience. "The real scandal," he said in conclusion, "is that we don't
have any certain doctrine any more, the clear voice of authority. It is urgent
for the pope to speak."

Some members shook their heads. Heenan couldn't let go of the controls.

Chapter Eight

Most of the commission's episcopal members trooped into the Spanish College Sunday night, June 19. The theologians had been preparing reams of documentation: reports of the previous meetings, dating back to 1963, many of the position papers written by the experts, a detailed 66-page analytical index of the 1966 meetings. De Riedmatten had written a summary report, but some of the theologians found it hard to understand, thin in places; it hardly reflected the majority's best arguments. Some theologians told him this and kept their fingers crossed in hope.

Canon de Locht wrote in his diary, "When I think of the next six days, I think of the film 'Twelve Angry Men.' " There would be a few more than twelve in this group, but, to de Locht, they were like a jury: the bishops had come "with their own histories, their own problems, their own psychological bent, come to face a crucial question, one that occupied us for years. How will they react? How will they change?"

No one knew. But John Noonan, whose Boston Irish upbringing had taught him about political prognostication, made some guesses. He figured Archbishop Binz was probably on the side of no change, Archbishop Dearden for measured change. Cardinal Shehan had never gone on the record. Neither had Cardinal Gracias. Cardinal Heenan was right, Cardinal Doepfner left. The votes of Cardinal Ottaviani and Cardinal Suenens would nullify each other. Among the cardinals, the swing man would probably be Cardinal Lefebvre. But Noonan knew him to be a conservative and one of the cardinalatial members of the Holy Office. Bishops Reuss and Colombo would be "paired." Archbishop Wojtyla of Krakow had missed every meeting. Morris of Cashel probably leaned right, Dupuy of Albi left. That put only two other bishops in the doubtful column: Pulido-Mendez representing Latin America and Zoa representing Africa.

They met Monday morning with de Riedmatten and 26 other members of the commission: ten theologians—three members of the minority and seven members of the majority—ten scientists and three couples. Cardinal Ottaviani presided. He said they had two things to consider: the magisterium and the intrinsic malice of contraception. He said he knew there were doubts, but he hoped this commission could resolve them without harm to the magisterium. As for intrinsic malice, the cardinal, a genuinely pious man, prayed for light from the Holy Spirit.

De Riedmatten surprised the theologians who had seen his report the day before. Evidently, he had stayed up all night to produce a new version, a masterful short history of the commission and its findings. De Riedmatten said:

Birth control was the church's biggest pastoral problem, a worldwide phenomenon, probably here to stay. To deal with it, the commission had been meeting, and growing, since October 1963, and members had often wondered if they would ever sort out all the complexities.

For a time, they had been bogged down in the old dispute regarding the ends of marriage. After the council's last session, however, they transcended that question and kept sight of two basics in marriage: *bonum prolis et amor conjugium*, the good of the offspring and the love of the couple. The commission had taken some time to come to the most basic question. In June 1964, members had looked at the pill. In June 1965, they'd considered temporary pastoral solutions. Finally, they reached to the root: the idea that contraception was intrinsically evil, which prevented Catholics from applying the principle of totality.

This classic notion had undergone some development and expansion in the twentieth century church. At one time, the church had forbidden amputations, kidney transplants, even small pox vaccine. In the 1950s, Pius XII approved these medical practices and justified them with the principle of totality. In brief, this principle affirms that the part always serves the whole and can even be sacrificed in service of the whole. If malfunction of one part of a person's body threatens the whole, a physician can employ surgery or pharmacotherapy to the benefit of the whole. The totality of the organism justifies manipulation or excision of the diseased or malfunctioning part. But Pius XII limited this argument to pathological cases; one could not apply it to a well functioning part of the body, such as sexual organs (as in direct sterilization) or to pregnancy (even if related complications threatened the mother's health).

Now the commission was attempting to extend that principle to the totality of a marriage. Having children was a part, but not the whole, of marriage. But that wasn't all there was. Members would agree that one cannot do evil to achieve good. But contraception was not evil, at least not an intrinsic moral evil. The act, like the amputation of a person's leg, might belong in the category of a physical, or pre-moral, or ontic evil. But if it could help an entire marriage. . . .

And so, said de Riedmatten, little by little they grew, matured on this question. In March 1965, the commission was divided. But the process had produced such convergence of thought, such development, that one could speak of a commission consensus, not unanimous, but substantial. For the first time, the commission had essentially clarified the debate.

In the first place, said de Riedmatten, members were talking morals, not faith. The church had said contraception was bad because it was against the natural law. Pius XI had taken no other position. But commission theologians had voted, 15-4, that contraception was not intrinsically evil. Such a judgment, said de Riedmatten, meant the morality of contraception depended on the totality of the human act of which it was a part.

De Riedmatten gave a fair summary of arguments against this view:

1) The church's ordinary teaching authority had condemned contraception for a good reason: to protect the sources of future life.

2) This notion depended not on biology, but on metaphysics: the natural order established by God, and life itself, of which God was the sole master. Men and women could not falsify the act meant to transmit life.

3) And finally, once this norm is set aside, then gates are open to sexual aberrations. De Riedmatten quoted two laymen on the commission: "Contraception today, sterilization and abortion tomorrow."

On the other side, de Riedmatten reported these arguments:

1) Revelation had nothing to say about contraception, and the church had never made an infallible declaration about it—indeed, it has never made an infallible declaration about any moral question, not even on any point already contained in Revelation.

2) There are other duties in marriage: a) the good of offspring already born and b) the need for couples to express their love by an act essential to its expression, the sexual act which, like all God's works, is good. De Riedmatten passed on a refutation of the view that contraception attacked "future life" by asking two questions: What life? What future? Science had proved that most acts of intercourse were not "ordained to procreation." Rhythm was a contradiction: couples had a duty to love one another carnally. But the church was telling them they couldn't use some of the means necessary to exercise that duty, under the pretext that using contraceptives was an attack on a life that didn't yet exist. And finally:

3) The traditional teaching against contraception was exaggerated; the tradition hadn't been constant. Furthermore, in this case, the church had made a mistake. No one should be shocked or scandalized. Perhaps the church shouldn't have given the faithful an impression it could never be wrong. The church had been wrong in the past. History was rich with examples.

De Riedmatten reported virtual unanimity on several other points: The church shouldn't try to make decisions on every method of contraception. And no one on the commission was saying the church should leave everything to the individual conscience. There *were* norms and the council had set them down: "Means should be determined by objective criteria, taken from the nature of the person and his acts, which preserve the complete sense of a mutual giving and of human procreation in the context of true love."

Some theologians on the commission had even added three more objective criteria for selecting a proper birth control method: 1) it should be as close as possible to "the natural," 2) it should express love and respect for the partner's dignity, and 3) it should work.

De Riedmatten asked the bishops to have special regard for an idea promoted by the council: the witness of the faithful. Some oldline commentators had customarily divided the church into two parts: the church teaching and the church taught. No more. The council had redefined "church," as the people of God. And, when the people of God turned to marriage questions, married people ought to be among the teachers. As one theologian expressed it (the thought would have been banal if it hadn't been so revolutionary in the church of 1966): *matrimonium pertinet ad conjuges,* "marriage belongs to husbands and wives."

Finally, de Riedmatten discussed the doubting church. A majority of the experts believed the church was in doubt, otherwise why a commission, appointed by the pope, who was also in doubt? De Riedmatten passed on a nagging question, proposed by Father Zalba, one of the conservatives who was trying to save the pope's authority: "If the guardians of the faith find themselves in such a state of doubt, I believe they ought to say so publicly. In a matter so grave, practical, heavy with consequence, the faithful have a right to not be constrained any longer under pain of mortal sin by the magisterium, if a certain objective obligation does not still exist."

De Riedmatten's wish: that this commission, now augmented by bishops from around the world, could help the pope say what he had to say —publicly.

Had de Riedmatten served too rich a meal? At first, there was a great silence, while the bishops tried to absorb what the secretary had said. None of the cardinals, none of the bishops wanted to take up knife and fork. Finally, Bishop Colombo did. Though a bishop, he was not new to the commission, and, therefore, a little less shy than the others. He asked whether anyone knew much about the history of *Casti Connubii.*

Cardinal Heenan said he was sure Pope Pius XI had been worried about race suicide. Cardinal Suenens confirmed that; he said Father Vermeersch, the Belgian Jesuit who drafted *Casti Connubii,* was his teacher, and he had been terribly concerned about the drop in Belgium's birth rate. Father Zalba seemed alarmed at the way the discussion was going. Wouldn't anyone note how far the commission had strayed from *Casti Connubii*? He would. He read a passage from it, for emphasis.

But Cardinal Ottaviani seemed intrigued with the others' line. "I think it would be a good idea," he said, "to find the background papers drawn together for the writing of *Casti Connubii*." Perhaps, he said, the history of that document would help this commission reinterpret the encyclical.

De Riedmatten said he had tried in vain to find the papers. He had asked for a search in the Vatican archives and received only the dossiers that followed *Casti Connubii*, but nothing that had gone before. Cardinal Ottaviani said de Riedmatten ought to try again. (De Riedmatten would, but no one at the Holy Office seemed to know what had happened to the Vermeersch papers.)

Cardinal Gracias said Cardinal Heenan was right: he remembered that in 1942, Winston Churchill also worried about the falling birth rate.

This was getting them nowhere. De Riedmatten turned to André Hellegers and asked him to give the report from the medical section. Dr. Hellegers did, and he was followed by J.R. Bertolus, who said that the psychologists and psychiatrists had been most concerned about helping couples come to grips with the demands of love, as well as with sex. Even if couples had perfect freedom to choose any means of birth control, he said, they would then have to start engaging in much deeper dialogue with one another.

The cardinals and bishops listened respectfully. De Riedmatten curbed his impatience. The bishops, too, needed time. But the next day, de Riedmatten told them he hoped to hear their thoughts.

Monsignor Lambruschini spoke. He thought the group should present the pope a unanimous opinion. "We don't want to embarrass the Holy Father with two views," he said. "Then, he would probably feel obligated to settle on the old doctrine." Lambruschini was close to the pope. He knew what he was talking about. Giving this indecisive pope two views was like giving him nothing, or too much.

How could the commission come to a unanimous opinion? Lambruschini put the onus of change on the minority. He said the minority should not find it hard to say that contraception was not intrinsically evil. "After all," he said, "not even homicide is intrinsically evil, but only in certain determined circumstances." He felt the minority theologians were too simplistic. They had only to realize that even contraception could be justified, according to the three classic criteria of morality: *oggetto, circonstanze e fine*, "object, circumstances and outcome."

Cardinal Doepfner said he understood the importance of Lambruschini's view. Nevertheless, he said, it was necesary for all to express themselves. And then he spoke his mind: "Contraception is not intrinsically evil," he said. He gave closely reasoned, succinct arguments. Contraception is a *malum physicum*, which can sometime be allowed to occur if it contributes to a person's greater good.[30] To Doepfner, there were often circumstances when contraception would work for the greater good. Often, there was greater danger to a woman's health if she risked the uncertainties of rhythm than if she used some mechanical or chemical means. And often, abstaining from sex could help split a couple; better for their conjugal unity to use the pill or the coil.

Doepfner spoke so simply, so matter-of-factly that he made others wonder why there had been so much fuss. If only everyone could see and express himself or herself so clearly as this:

As for *Casti Connubii*:

1. Formally, it is not a definition *ex cathedra*.

2. We are not talking about rejecting an encyclical, but completing it and helping it evolve. In Paragraph 23 of *Casti Connubii*, there is a general principle on love as the supreme value in marriage. We could expand on that and apply it to new facts. We did it (in the conciliar debate on religious liberty) in the case of an analogous doctrine, "No salvation outside the church."

3. It is clear from the acts of the council that the object of the infallible magisterium is not natural truths as such. It pertains to the church to give the faithful directives and precepts even in this field. But these directives can and must be changed according to scientific progress and the changing circumstances of life.

Cardinal Gracias sighed. For years, he had upheld the church's traditional doctrine, in face of desperate birth control programs sponsored by the Indian government. Would he have to backpedal? "If the church changes here," he said, "then there will be a crisis in Christendom, and the church's enemies will rejoice. But . . . there is a resurrection after every death. The church will survive. And we must find a way to help couples." To him, the pill—but no other means of birth control—seemed acceptable. Gracias said he was impressed that most of the theologians generally agreed on change. He was sure that Father Fuchs, for instance, the leader of the majority, hadn't held this view a few years before. What had happened?

Before Fuchs could respond, Bishop Colombo jumped in. Two cardinals back to back, both siding with the majority. This would not do. He played his strongest card. He couldn't agree that church authority didn't extend "to the matter of the natural law, unless it were revealed." On these questions, he said, the church has always taken moral positions. Were the bishops to say the church had been wrong? The church could not err on such an important matter as birth control. Admitting error, the commission "would endanger the very indefectability of the church, the teacher of truth in those things which pertain to salvation. Wouldn't this mean the 'gates of hell' had in some way prevailed against the church?"

According to Patrick Crowley's handwritten notes of this meeting, Bishop Colombo said "the *sensus fidelium* is less important than the authority of the Holy Father."

Patty Crowley spoke up. "On behalf of women in general," she said, "I plead that the male church carefully consider the plight of at least one half of its members, who are the real bearers of these burdens." She said she was uncomfortable with the nay-saying. "Couples are generous. Christian couples want to have children. It is the very fruit of their love for each other. What is needed is to rid ourselves of this negative outlook on marriage and move on to the joyful, positive sides of it, with all its psychological and spiritual values. Couples can be trusted. They will accept the progress of a change, and they will have increased confidence in the church as she helps them grow in love and demonstrates her trust and confidence in them."

There was momentary silence. These men were not used to women who intervened in theological discussion. But Mrs. Crowley had given them something new to think about. De Riedmatten saw no hands in the air. He called upon Fuchs to respond to Cardinal Gracias: how and why the sudden change?

Fuchs rose and spoke. "All the *periti* of 'the majority' have made this change, some sooner, some later. And I am not the leader of the majority, as Cardinal Gracias assumes from reading some of the commission's documentation." For the past few years, he said, he had tried to explain the doctrine propounded by the magisterium. He implied he had had his doubts about it in 1963. In the 1965-66 school year, he had stopped teaching at the Gregorian University, because he feared taking responsibility for teaching a doctrine he couldn't accept. For the same reason, at the end of 1965, he had told staff people at the Gregorian University not to reprint his textbook, *De Castitate*.

He said some of the commission's documentation contained reasons for his change of view. However, he would summarize here. His understanding of the natural law had deepened. "We are not only supposed to conserve the givens of nature but turn them to the good of the whole man. I have always insisted on the connection between every marital act and procreation, but these acts must be interpreted in different ways (and often are). Tradition tries to protect the fundamental good of human procreation in marriage. But history shows that the way in which this protection occurs can change. There has been an evolution in doctrine since *Casti Connubii*, under Pius XII, and at Vatican II. And this evolution has been moving in one direction, away from the notion that each contraceptive act is intrinsically evil."

Fuchs said there were no other reasons for his change, or the church's. Everyone on the commission, "both from the right and the left, agreed that the pill presented no special moral case."

"Well, then," Gracias asked, "how do we decide what means *are* acceptable?"

Fuchs said the council had elaborated some objective criteria on "responsible parenthood" and on the methods couples could use. In practice, once a couple decided they had a duty not to have a child, they also had a duty to choose the most efficacious means. But every means, said Fuchs, had a negative aspect, even periodic continence. Morally speaking, a couple should choose the means with the least negative element, be that element biological, hygienic, psychological or whatever. Not everyone would decide in the same way at the same stage in their lives; couples obviously needed education and instruction to help them figure it out.

Joseph Lefebvre, cardinal-archbishop of Bourges, rose to speak. In the minds of many, he was a member of the Ottaviani camp. Not now. Patrick Crowley said his intervention was "a turning point." The cardinal surprised everyone when he said: "It appears, after looking at the documents given to us, that it wouldn't be too rash to go along with the majority." Lefebvre said that in taking this new position the church would not throw away old teachings but deepen its understanding of them.

Things seemed to be going the way Cardinal Suenens had hoped. He stepped in to suggest: "We bishops are not super-experts, but pastors. We cannot remake in two or three days all the study and reflection done by the experts in two or three years." He wondered if the theologians could give the bishops a basic statement. "Do a precise text," he said, "Then we can make a nuanced judgment about it, see how that might be received by the church." (De Riedmatten nodded. He suggested that the theologians could have a report for the bishops in a few days; then the bishops could edit that, provide nuances they felt necessary.)

Another bishop in Noonan's question-mark column spoke up: Jose Pulido-Mendez, bishop of Merida, Venezuela, concurred in Suenens' strategy. He also agreed with Cardinal Doepfner's views and those of Father Fuchs. But he said he didn't think the commission ought to praise contraception. Perhaps a phrase like "opportune conception?"

Another from the Third World had the same semantic difficulty: Jean Baptiste Zoa, archbishop of Yaounde, Cameroon, asked what they would do about the negative connotation of the word "contraception."

Canon Anciaux agreed. It would be good to avoid the term in anything meant for publication.

Canon de Locht had another, somewhat similar suggestion: better not to talk about putting aside traditional criteria, but about adding others. That had been a part of the problem, he said. Churchmen talk about one criterion and throw everything else into a subordinate category. The traditional, he said, should harmonize with other new approaches.

Now there seemed to be general agreement with the Suenens proposal. Some wanted the theologians to produce one text. Some minority theologians seemed willing. Father Ford was silent. Someone else suggested the theologians produce a majority text and a minority text.

Cardinal Heenan thought that was a terrible idea. There ought to be one text, he said, with some input by minority members. Heenan was an astute politician, who felt that Lambruschini's assessment of Paul VI at the very beginning of this session was correct. Giving the pope two reports would paralyze him. No one argued. That evening, the majority theologians started working on the final commission report.

But if anyone thought that all minority members would play along with Heenan or even Suenens, they were made aware Wednesday morning that for Father Ford, the game would be hardball.

He'd perked his ears the day before when he heard some bishops say they didn't like the word "contraception." So Ford used it now—17 times—in a slashing speech on behalf of life.

He said that contraception violated the natural law, but not because humans are forbidden to manipulate most of creation: they can and do. Rather, he said, "right reason recognizes the moral evil in a physical intervention in this particular natural process for the purpose of preventing life . . . a human intrusion into a domain which belongs to God." Ford asked, "Why did the church always teach this doctrine?" He answered his own question with a piece of stirring oratory:

> Not as a simple reaction against various heresies. Not because the fathers and theologians accepted the Stoic philosophy. Not because, abandoning the principles of the Gospels, they followed some philosophy of nature which is now obsolete. Not because they were ignorant that some conjugal acts are sterile while others are fertile. Not because they thought contraception violated an obligation to produce children, to increase and multiply. Not because they believed every conjugal act must have a procreative intent. Not because they feared the depopulation of the world.
>
> But because, reflecting on the scriptures and what they found there about the nature of human life and the nature of Christian chastity, they saw that contraception was a violation of human life and Christian chastity. From the very moment that contraception is first mentioned in Christian literature, no father, no theologian can be quoted who did not acknowledge, as it were spontaneously, that contraception violated Christian chastity and violated the inception of human life. Many used the analogy with murder.

Ford recalled perhaps the most famous painting in Rome (and a favorite of the pope), Michaelangelo's Creation of Man on the ceiling of the Sistine Chapel: ". . . God stretching out his finger to touch the finger of Adam and transmit new life to him. This is the moment we are talking about—the *fieri* of a new life. This is the moment of conception," said Ford, his voice softening with reverence. He went on:

Contraception (that is, contra-ception) involves a will which is turned against new life at this moment. It is against this life, in advance, that is, against its coming-to-be, its *fieri.* Your conception is your very origin, your link to the community of living persons before you, the first of all gifts received from your parents, your first relationship with God as he stretched out his finger to touch you.

In my opinion, there are different ways of expressing the underlying substantial truth: like life itself, the inception of life belongs to God. To attack it is to attack a fundamental human good, to intrude on God's domain. That is why the will to contracept, though essentially different morally from the will to abort, is nevertheless similar to it. And it is noteworthy that among the Catholic theologians who defend contraception today, there are already some who defend therapeutic abortion in certain difficult cases.

Your Eminences, Your Excellencies: we live in a world where human life is cheap and is becoming cheaper. Fifteen million abortions a year? At least. It is only one step from contraception to abortion. Some Catholic theologians have taken it already. In the present controversy, the stakes are very high. They are not only the fundamental good of new human life and the chastity of Christian marriage, but the teaching authority of the church of Christ.

Who would disagree with Ford? Surprisingly enough, quite a few. Among them: Cardinal Shehan of Baltimore, who seemed to ignore Ford's emotional appeal. His own cool plea asked the others to recognize that the church has always followed two laws, one of continuity, one of progress. "The church grows," said Shehan. "The church develops. And the *sensus fidelium* plays a big role in that development. The church must recognize how marriage is lived today." He reported on a straw poll he had taken recently among the pastors of Baltimore. "The most intelligent answers," said Shehan, "were on the side of change. Many spoke about the anxiety of their good couples." Ten percent expressed no opinion. Seventy percent wanted the church to change on birth control. Twenty percent said the church couldn't change because of the magisterium's consistent position in recent times.

For Cardinal Doepfner, too, the magisterium seemed a major problem, but it was one he could deal with. This Wednesday morning, he spoke again and said that most commission documents dealt less with the need for a change, more about modification of the old teaching. Doepfner hailed this "true progress," noting that the theoretical change being proposed was small, though the practical change was important.

When I first saw Doepfner up close in Rome, he reminded me of Bishop Bekkers of 's-Hertogenbosch—a robust man with a ruddy complexion and thinning, straight black hair, a man who knew how to give orders. He was a leader at the council; now he was a leader in the commission. He said no one need fear what might happen to the church if it made major modifications. The council had recently produced a statement on religious liberty that reversed the nineteenth century teaching that there is no salvation outside the Catholic church. "No scandal came of that," said Doepfner. "Quite the contrary."

He addressed Ford's oft-repeated appeal to the Holy Spirit's guidance of the church and his even-more-often-repeated question, "Was the Holy Spirit at Lambeth, and not therefore with the Roman Catholic church?" Doepfner said it was bumptious for anyone to try to say what the Holy Spirit can or ought to do. "In recent times," he continued, "we have in practice tended to make the church's 'ordinary non-infalliable teaching' into an infallible teaching. Doesn't it follow that a non-infallible magisterium can make a mistake? Or, that the church could not learn something in this matter from the separated brethren, as it has done in a number of other questions during the council?"

More Doepfner: It wouldn't make any difference if Ford were right, that the church had taught something mistaken on this question "so long, so solemnly, in such a fundamental manner, in the name of Jesus Christ." Once the church asked, then learned from couples, especially women who had made the sacrifices, the church is obliged to change, Doepfner said, "so that we do not impose on others any further sacrifices that we know in our hearts are not necessary."

Doepfner concluded: "We are right to fear the reactions of the faithful and of the world. But there will be a reaction in any case, whether the church changes or not." Therefore, it was nothing to worry about. What was needed: "to find the truth and then to present it in a truly pastoral way."

Claude Dupuy, archbishop of Albi, agreed with Shehan and Doepfner. He said he had evolved on this question. He had been disturbed. Now he felt he could help troubled couples who wanted to live a full Christian life. "They should be delivered, not from the obligation of living the Gospel, but from this guilty anguish in which they are engulfed, which makes them despair and feel that holiness is only for those who live outside the married state."

John Dearden, archbishop of Detroit, had helped produce the council's chapter on marriage. No one had to convince him that the church had been making long overdue progress on this question. He did not think the others here needed any oratory. He made one major point: "It is meaningless now to talk of religious liberty on the basis of what Pius IX said a century ago. It is just as meaningless to speak of marriage based on the words of Pius XI."

Bishop Colombo frowned at Dearden's intervention. If Dearden didn't want anyone to belabor the words of Pius XI, then he, Colombo, would present a detailed exegesis of *Gaudium et Spes*, the document that Dearden, and many of the others here, had spent so much time on during the council. The words Colombo cited called for conjugal chastity, which, to Colombo, meant abstinence. He would be "ready to accept any innovation as long as it would fully safeguard conjugal chastity, because a certain number of human beings does not make as much difference to God as the holiness of his church." However, he did not believe the commission had yet found a formulation the church could use that would ensure conjugal chastity.

Casti Connubii, he said, had condemned contraception to safeguard that chastity. Did anyone know "another discipline"* that would give the same assurance? Colombo said he did not have much confidence in humanity. "People cannot fully actualize the moral law in marriage," he said, "because they lack the supernatural infrastructure. Better not to leave things up to the subjective responsibility of individuals unless we can change the moral law. And up to now the magisterium has held that this natural law is also the divine law."

Archbishop Zoa asked for the floor. He had been in John Noonan's doubtful column. Here, he had no problem accepting changes worked out by the commission. He didn't think his people in Cameroon would either. "The fear of scandalizing people by a change is a problem of old Christians. In our country, there is no risk of scandal. We are first generation Christians." One man could not speak for all Africa. But Zoa's opinion encouraged those who wondered how the winds of change would blow in the Third World.

So did the intervention of Michel Dembélé, director of the ministry of planning in Senegal, a layman and a close associate of President Leopold Senghor, a devotee of Pierre Teilhard de Chardin. He said he felt those advocating the status quo were "underestimating the dynamism and the maturity of Christians." Change, he said, would help involve Catholics in Africa (and elsewhere) in the world's work.

When Cardinal Heenan took the floor toward the end of Wednesday, he said he thought the church had moved on to a path which was altogether too fashionable. There were too many theological journalists about, and theologians who wanted to be TV stars. This aside had little to do with the

---

*Colombo used the phrase *un'altra disciplina*, which may also be translated, "another teaching." But the thinking it takes to translate the phrase makes one ask, "Can any 'teaching,' can any 'discipline' ensure chastity?" The question leads to other questions about the efficacy of what is sometimes called "moral education" and about the difference between teaching and mere pronouncements.

discussion. But Heenan, the hardliner up to now, admitted he was starting to feel some ambivalence:

Although my heart tells me that at almost any cost, we must bring relief to the magnificent Christian couples who are finding the discipline of the church intolerable, my head warns me against accepting too readily the arguments of converted theologians who now argue against the accepted doctrine. I stress that my caution and reserve is only toward the theologians . . . professional theologians who until a few months ago, not twenty or thirty years ago, dogmatically taught the old doctrine. I do not doubt their sincerity or their integrity. But I find it hard to be impressed with the intellectual force of their arguments.

I think they have changed their opinions not so much because they regard their former reasoning as false but because, like the rest of us, they are moved to compassion when they see the plight of so many married couples. They are moved by the problem of ordinary parents who love each other and love each new child but conscientiously hold that in this stage of civilization, they should not be forced to control the size of their families only at the cost of continence.

On this I take my stand. I am quite sure that relief must be brought to Catholic couples and I cannot bring myself to accept that the thermometer and the calendar are a good way of keeping men and women from mortal sin. I cannot believe that extraordinary means of this kind are demanded by our blessed Lord.

But Heenan did not see how the church could "downgrade contraception from mortal to venial sin." Contraception, if an offense, was "an offense against God, not against the pope and the church." The solution? Heenan said he believed "science which has brought us the problem . . . must bring us the solution."

It was an extraordinary bit of buck passing. Tom Burch knew what the problem was. Heenan had already mentioned the pope's fear: that a change in the church's teaching might damage the church's credibility. How, Heenan had asked, could the church change its stand and avoid losing its moral influence? Or, if the church did not change, how could it preserve its authority over couples?

Now, Burch stood up and called Heenan's stand "hypocrisy." He was angry and he didn't care who knew it.* Some of the translators from the

---

*Almost 20 years later, Burch told Arthur Jones, a correspondent for the *National Catholic Reporter*, about his feelings at the time. "I think my very strong reaction was, 'What the heck's going on here? You guys are saying that you might have been wrong for nigh on thirty to forty years on some details about methods; you've caused millions of people untold agony and unwanted children; brought on

UN's Food and Agricultural Organization nodded encouragement to Burch. After the meeting was over, one of them would come over to Burch and thank him, "On behalf of millions of others around the world."

When Heenan said that the solutions must come from science, he was referring to the hard sciences, such as chemistry. But this—an easy preference—would have made no growth demands on the people of God. It also slighted the hard thinking theologians, demographers, psychologists, psychiatrists and others on the commission had done for the past few years, or as Heenan would have it, months. But more than thinking was involved. Politics would occupy the commission for the rest of that day.

Wednesday afternoon, the episcopal members of the commission told the experts they wanted to meet privately. They wanted to discuss a proposal by Thomas Morris, bishop of Cashel, who had realized, after listening to the comments of the others, that possibly nine of the 15 favored change. Bishop Morris said he was troubled with the notion that the church was going to recant. "We should not limit our view to the question of recantation," he said. "We should have the choice between two alternatives, the traditional and the doctrine proposed in replacement."

No one was proposing "a recantation." And the theologians were even now working on the statement Morris was asking for. That, apparently, was not enough for this Irishman. He said this matter was too grave for the pope to decide alone, even aided by this commission. He wanted a collegial decision, a secret vote of the world's bishops.

According to the minutes of that meeting, probably done by de Riedmatten and/or a colleague, Cardinal Ottaviani, who was presiding, thought this an excellent idea. This question concerned the whole world. Therefore, let all the bishops decide. "We could speak of a simple evolution," he said, "no change in doctrine really."

"Years ago," said Cardinal Heenan, "this would have been a very good idea. Now, it's too late. We couldn't keep it secret." Cardinal Gracias agreed. Heenan went on: "We would have to give all the bishops all the texts of the commission and then give them time to study. The process would take at least five years."

Cardinal Doepfner said, "If we ask the entire episcopate, then the state of doubt would be evident." (This was a curious lapse in logic by Doepfner.

stresses and strains and tremendous feelings of guilt. You've told people they were going to hell because they wouldn't stop using condoms, and now you're saying maybe you're wrong. But you want to say it in such a way that you can continue to tell people what to do in bed?'

"I think at that point the absurdity became very clear. My feeling was that what the church was most concerned with was exerting its own authority. It was not terribly concerned with human beings at some levels."

Consulting the world's bishops about the doctrine of the Assumption in 1950 didn't imply Pius XII had any doubt. But it is significant that Doepfner believed the church was in state of doubt and, perhaps more important, that he did not think some churchmen here would admit it.)

But Cardinal Lefebvre had the best argument against this worldwide ballot. The bishops could have dealt with this at the council, but didn't, he said, because the pope wanted to put birth control in the hands of this commission. "Would it be reasonable to suggest to the pope that he give the question back to the bishops now?"

Cardinal Shehan said such a consultation with the bishops might give an eventual decision the force of an infallible statement. "Do we want that?"

Cardinal Ottaviani called for a secret ballot and found that only three others agreed with Bishop Morris. Eleven voted against Morris' motion to poll the bishops.

In effect, this was an 11-4 vote to send the recommendations of the commission right on up to the pope. But this group was afraid to do that. Cardinal Lefebvre tried to sum up the majority's feelings. "I know you are disturbed (as I am) over the annoying consequences of a change." He knew some felt that a change might shake the authority of the magisterium and encourage laxism among the faithful. "But this is not the real problem. What it important, above all, is to discover the truth so that we can enlighten those who are waiting for some guidance."

It was time to put church politics aside, Lefebvre said, and talk again about the issues. Lefebvre said, "Science has demonstrated that most conjugal acts are infertile, that they must, then, have another meaning and another goal than procreation, and that these acts can contribute to a deepening of love and self giving. This does not contradict the traditional doctrine. Rather, it deepens it."

Cardinal Suenens had been hanging back, possibly because his role in starting this business had been so important. He said he was struck by the inability of those defending the traditional view to present any but the feeblest arguments based on natural law. "This law is supposed to be available to everyone, but only Catholics see this application." He pointed out that the 1930 Lambeth Conference didn't actually approve contraception. In effect, the Anglican bishops let couples decide. Given that responsibility, they worked things out "for a half century." Suenens said the church should do likewise: listen to good Catholic couples, let them work things out. "We are considering this problem now precisely on behalf of those couples who want to live a good Christian life and not for those who are seeking a way out."

Suenens recalled how the church and the commission had come to their revisionist view. Three moments:

1) *The discovery of the female cycle.* He said the church had labored

under a masculine illusion, trying to define the conjugal act's meaning from this side alone. On the feminine side, the conjugal act is not *aptus ad generationem.* "The conjugal act is not the act of one, but of two. And so, we cannot say that every conjugal act is 'open to generation.' Once we learned that, the breach was made."

2) *The council's blessing on responsible parenthood.* "If parents were to regard this as a duty, then they also had a duty to find a means of birth control that would work. That opened the door. Now we have to figure out how we are going to get through it."

3) *The future.* He said he did not think it possible to translate *Casti Connubii* into modern terms. The church ought to talk about "an evolution, open and at the same time moderate," not look for Cardinal Heenan's "scientific solution." This was a classic case: a conflict of duties. He praised a "pastoral text" Archbishop Dupuy was working on, one that spoke of this problem in precisely those terms.

Suenens tried to help the others understand what they saw as a sudden turnabout by the moral theologians: their change hadn't just happened in the last few months (as Cardinal Heenan seemed to think).

For years, they have had to come up with arguments on behalf of a doctrine they were not allowed to contradict. They had an obligation to defend the received doctrine, but my guess is they already had many hesitations about it inside. As soon as the question was opened up a little, a whole group of moralists arrived at the position defended by the majority here.

We have heard arguments based on "what the bishops all taught for decades." Well, the bishops did defend the classical position. But it was one imposed on them by authority. The bishops didn't study the pros and the cons. They received directives, they bowed to them, and they tried to explain them to their congregations.

Someone moved to adjourn. Someone else suggested the bishops tell the theologians to keep working on their summary document. Archbishop Dupuy reminded the others that he was drafting a text, something people at large could understand. Cardinal Doepfner said he hoped one text or another would refer to "the suffering undergone by couples who have passed through heavy ordeals by reason of their fidelity to the church."

Bishop Morris of Cashel took this personally. He muttered to de Riedmatten as they filed out of the room that he had condemned so many to hell. He wanted off the commission.

* * *

Thursday morning, June 23, de Riedmatten handed out French and Latin copies of the commission report, which its editors, Auer, Sigmond,

Anciaux, Labourdette, Fuchs and de Locht, called *Schema documenti de responsabili paternitate*, a draft document on responsible parenthood (see appendix B). It was only thirteen pages long and it met the wishes of Cardinal Suenens and the others. As those who heard it read aloud that morning could judge, it was "open but moderate." The document used new, postconciliar concepts to explain to Tridentine Catholics how and why the unchanging church could change:

As God became man, so his church is really incarnate in the world. But because the world, to which the church ought to represent the mystery of Christ, always undergoes change, the church itself necessarily and continually is in pilgrimage. Its essence and fundamental structures remain immutable always; and yet no one can say of the church that at any time it is sufficiently understood or bounded by definition.

The church draws understanding of its own mystery not only from the past, but . . . assumes within itself the whole progress of the human race. The church is always being made more sure of this. What Pope John XXIII wished to express by the word *aggiornamento*, Paul VI took up, using the phrase "dialogue with the world," and in his encyclical *Ecclesiam Suam* has the following: "The world cannot be saved from the outside. As the Word of God became man, so must a man to a certain degree identify with the forms of life of those to whom he wishes to bring the message of Christ. He must share the common way of life—provided that it be human and honorable—especially of the most humble, if he wishes to be listened to and understood."

The document gave reasons for change. The people of God had "a better, deeper and more correct understanding of conjugal life and of the conjugal act. . . . The magisterium itself is in evolution. . . . It is natural for man to put under human control what is given by physical nature." There were legitimate methods "of reconciling the needs of marital life with a right ordering of this life to fruitfulness in the procreation and education of offspring." And there were objective criteria for determining those methods, though "every method of preventing conception, not excluding either periodic or absolute continence, carries with it some negative element of physical evil."

The document recognized that reasons for change may vary in different parts of the world. "Universal principles and the essential values of matrimony and married life," it said, "become actual in ways which partially differ according to different cultures and different mentalities." The authors may have been thinking of reports by Tom Burch and the other demographers and social scientists on the varying mores of the Orient, Africa and Latin America. The differences indicated that local churches should try to work things out locally, setting up research centers and discussions "between families, representatives of the different sciences and pastors of souls."

Palpable tension followed the reading. Some there believed this would be the moment of truth. Bishop Colombo asked for the floor. He had questions for the theologians. His first was a presentiment of problems to come. Ford had charged that the commission was trying to "take away" the magisterium's power to bind consciences. Colombo looked over to Fuchs. He wanted to know: "Does the magisterium have the authority to proclaim in the name of Christ moral positions not only on the level of principles but also applications of those principles, as, for example, the question of abortion?" ·

Fuchs responded. "Yes. The church did so in council and continues to do so."

That wasn't enough for Colombo. The council's condemnations had been entirely too restrained. He asked: "Is there any absolutely certain criterion that we can use to prove that moral teachings proposed by the ordinary magisterium are infallibly true and irrevocable?"

Fuchs could have inveighed against past papal pretensions. But he was characteristically terse: "No. Theology does not propose an absolutely certain criterion as clear and simple as the question implies. I have not yet been able to find a theologian who can exactly describe in so many words, *a priori*, what the Holy Spirit, in assisting the church, is able to permit or not permit in the church." He added that the church can give criteria, but it is often difficult to apply those criteria in concrete cases.

Cardinal Heenan, too, had questions. One demonstrated he hadn't quite understood the meaning of the term he, and many others, had been using for decades: "Can it be said that contraception is intrinsically evil, but permitted for sufficient reasons?"

Fuchs replied: "If contraception were intrinsically evil, it could never be licit. All methods of contraception contain some evil, biological, psychological, et cetera, even periodic or continued abstinence. But this evil [Fuchs called it *malum physicum*; others call it ontic evil, some pre-moral evil] is permitted if some proportionate good demands it." He added: "In a case where a couple may use rhythm, they may also use other contraceptive means, if these means seem to be indicated, for example, if rhythm is hard to apply."

Heenan asked, "What means?"

Fuchs said, "That would be determined by the couple, depending on their circumstances."

Bishop Colombo had another question: "Is contraception to be admitted only in certain extreme circumstances, or is it to be admitted as a norm both for couples and for the actions taken by governments to solve the demographic problem?"

Fuchs said, "The commission is not proposing a solution only for limited application. We have tried to work out a way of reconciling in a truly human and Christian way the duties of procreation with the needs of the couple, for the good of the couple, the children and the family as a whole. The methods should be worked out by the experts in such matters, biologists, psychologists, spiritual directors. I point out that rhythm is not the better method in every case, its educative value notwithstanding. As for governments: nothing should stop them from making birth control available. But the demographers and the theologians on the commission insist that governments not impose this on their people. This would take away the peoples' freedom to make their own decision."

Dr. Rendu said he had difficulties with Fuchs' downgrading of periodic continence. Critics claimed the method hadn't worked. Rendu said it hadn't been tried. Rendu talked about his experiences with the temperature method. (He preferred not calling it "rhythm.") He had seen this method help couples grow in love. He had seen how it helped wives know themselves better, psychologically, and how it helped them have, not prevent babies. "It would not be wise or useful for the church," he said, "to change its teaching before it sees that our experience (limited, certainly, but perfectly valid) proves how couples can regulate their families and grow in love and in divine charity."

Dr. Potvin confirmed Dr. Rendu's experience with the temperature method. But he also knew that it didn't work for many, not just individuals, but "a whole, important part of the population, laborers, foresters, others."

Patrick Crowley, a good lawyer who could cut to the heart of things, helped change the course of the debate. He said everyone had had a chance to make his or her position clear on various forms of periodic continence. Now he added, "In the nineteenth century, the church was reported to have lost many working men because it was slow in speaking on the social problem. We cannot risk the loss of married couples now, by delaying a change. We seem to be held back by a teaching that is in grave doubt. All seem to admit that the reasons which support the teaching have lost their validity and force." Crowley admitted he was getting impatient. "This problem seems to have been escalated into a position far beyond its importance. War, peace, poverty, social justice seem more urgent. So let us help the Holy Father scuttle this question so we can get on to the work of bringing Christ to the world with his law of love."

The group seemed to respond to this. Cardinal Lefebvre said that no one needed to repeat his or her reasonings again. "I am satisfied with the text," he said. "It needs a few pastoral precisions. Contraception is a modality, not a principle, of marriage. The church has not been wrong. It took a position in the past based on the knowledge it had."

De Riedmatten, noting the general nods at this, took Lefevbre's words as the sense of the house and judged the commission would be ready in the morning for the cardinals and bishops to vote on three questions: 1) Whether all contraception was intrinsically evil. 2) Whether they could affirm that contraception, in the way the majority theologians described it, could be affirmed in continuity with tradition and the declarations of the magisterium. 3) Whether the magisterium ought to speak as soon as possible.

Next morning, before the vote, Cardinal Ottaviani wanted discussion on the questions. He was voted down. Cardinal Heenan protested that the questions were not clear. Cardinal Doepfner, who had fashioned them, argued that they were perfectly clear. Heenan, reddening, said they were not. For 45 minutes, everyone had something to say about the questions. In doing so, they each revealed, wittingly or not, how they would cast their secret ballots. Finally, they voted. Nine bishops said contraception was not intrinsically evil. Two said it was. One said it was, but with a reservation. Three abstained. So the score on the first question was nine to three, with three abstentions. A clear win for the forces of change.*

On the second question, it was nine to five with one abstention. This was a clear majority, but not a good sign. If five episcopal members saw the recommended change, no matter how reasonable it was, as a sharp break with past teaching, could the pope accept it? Maybe he could not cross this bridge.

On the third question, the vote was fourteen to one. After all this, the pope had to say something. Perhaps he could adopt some version of the commission report along with Archbishop Dupuy's pastoral letter intended to supplement that report.

The commission adjourned. It was the feast of St. John the Baptist, the pope's name day, and this commission's cardinals were scheduled for an eleven o'clock audience at St. Peter's. But the bishops who stayed behind talked with the theologians. Would a separate pastoral letter create serious misunderstanding—that laypeople needed a statement more vague than the document produced by Auer, Sigmond, Anciaux, Labourdette, Fuchs and de Locht? What would the pope think of two documents which may or may not say the same thing? The group agreed to wait and see what Dupuy produced. Another session was scheduled for five o'clock.

---

*The nine were: Doepfner, Suenens, Shehan, Lefevbre, Dearden, Dupuy, Mendez, Reuss and Zoa. Heenan, Gracias and Binz abstained. Ottaviani, Colombo and Morris affirmed the old view.

At five, a team of newspeople descended on the Spanish College. The press had been making demands at the Vatican's Sala Stampa. Everyone knew the papal birth control commission was in session. Television people wanted footage, and de Riedmatten was directed to give it to them. In front of the cameras, de Riedmatten said yes, the commission was meeting and had almost concluded its work. He was almost ready to give their report to the pope, who would decide—what? De Riedmatten shrugged. He wasn't authorized to tell the press anything substantial.

De Locht looked on this scene with some reservations. He complained in his diary that this would only heighten the world's expectations, while it was entirely possible that the commission "will give birth, perhaps to a mouse. Who knows how long it will take? And those who authorized this are strutting about. Poor church!"

In the meeting that followed, the bishops said they had no great difficulties with the text of the majority theologians. Father Ford and the minority theologians were strangely silent. Cardinal Shehan requested non-bishops to leave, presumably to give the others more freedom to speak. But the discussion was brief. The bishops liked the document. Only one rose to say vehemently that the pope would never agree to it.

It was Bishop Colombo. "His Holiness will never accept the proposition that contraception is not intrinsically evil. He would only agree to this: a letter to the world's bishops telling them their people 'are not to be disturbed. It is not necessary to disturb couples who practice contraception. Close your eyes.' "

Several bishops groaned. After all this. Bishop Reuss, who had participated in recent editing sessions, tried for a compromise. He proposed another formulation: what if they said contraception was illicit, but that, in certain serious cases. . . ? The bishops said they ought to sleep on it, take up the question in another private session in the morning.

The theologians learned of all this at dinner. They grumbled about the turn of events. Again, said de Locht, the commission was more concerned with the prestige of the magisterium than the real needs of the people. Bishop Reuss heard the rumblings (and the next day, he would withdraw his offered compromise). De Locht wondered: what kind of commission was this, whose report would change based on everyone's varying guesses about the pope's readiness to accept it or not?

Saturday, June 25, the last day's work. Archbishop Dupuy began by reading his pastoral letter. It won almost complete acceptance and congratulations from all. It was a good job (see Appendix C), not too filled with sermonizing, but, according to some of the commission's more honest members, too full of praise for past popes' teaching on marriage.

In fact, the pastoral letter was, in part, a diplomatic attempt to convince one man, Pope Paul VI, that the papacy itself was the great instigator of progress, the promoter of research:

All this teaching, it must be stressed with joy, has, in many countries, produced lay and Christian family movements which have contributed very powerfully to a deeper understanding of marriage and the demands of the marriage union. It has also stimulated pastors and laymen, theologians, doctors and psychologists to undertake a more rigorous investigation of the conditions and difficulties involved in a more exact and generous observance of the laws that must govern the family, and of the meaning and value of human sexuality.

As gently as he could, de Locht wondered, "Which came first? The teachings of the magisterium or the new self awareness of couples around the world?"

Dupuy met that objection with whimsy. "Perhaps," he said, "the magisterium encouraged the research by opposing it." But he didn't want to change what he had written.

He had reason to be proud. The church, he wrote, did not want to condemn interventions regulating conception done in a spirit of true, reasonable and generous charity. If it did, "other goods of marriage might be endangered."

. . . So what is always to be condemned is not the regulation of conception, but a selfish married life, refusing a creative opening out of the family circle, and so refusing a truly human—and therefore truly Christian—married love. . . .

As for the means that husband and wife can legitimately employ, it is their task to decide this together, without drifting into arbitrary decisions, but always taking account of the objective criteria of morality. These criteria are in the first place those that relate to the totality of married life and sexuality. . . .

It will always remain true that for Christians, procreation confers the dignity of cooperating with God the creator, and that children will always be a great good and a joyful responsibility. Husbands and wives will only be convinced that they should deprive themselves of them with the greatest sorrow.

Several, including Cardinal Lefevbre, wanted to delete what looked like a eulogy to rhythm. Dupuy wanted to retain it, "perhaps," said de Locht, "to keep some falterers in line." That night, Dupuy took the eulogy out, because it went against the advice of almost all commission experts, advice based on reasons studied at length and ratified by a vote.

But Dupuy made sure the text thanked those whose past "sacrifices and faithfulness" made progress possible. The church took time expressing its new insights, the text said, because the church did not want to act hastily. As Dupuy and the others would learn, there would not be much danger of that.

* * *

They realized their work was almost over, and with that realization came a sense of relief. There was even a small reconciliation among the theologians. For two days, Father Zalba had been giving valuable textual suggestions to the theologians of the majority, and Father Visser was translating Dupuy's pastoral letter into Latin. The commission celebrated that night with a festive dinner at the Spanish College. After the dinner, the Potvins stayed up most of the night with Archbishop Dupuy and a few others working on a last revision of the pastoral document. On Saturday, many of them packed their bags, said goodbyes and were off.

Sunday morning, de Locht wrote in his diary that the battle was won: "It will not be possible any longer to reaffirm the general condemnations of contraception," he wrote. But he also wondered what the pope would do. "I do not understand what excuse he can use to impose on the church his own personal option. The research he set in motion does not make sense if he does not take it into account. Why, then, would he have asked for it? Will he accept our conclusions only if they lean toward a reaffirmation?"

* * *

After they returned to Chicago, the Crowleys would receive a short note from de Riedmatten, telling them he had an audience with the pope on July 4, and thanking them for their work. Then, nothing more from Rome. They wondered what was happening.

Chapter Nine

June 28, Cardinal Deopfner and Father de Riedmatten took the commission's final report to the pope. Cardinal Ottaviani trailed with another report, something that would mistakenly come to be called "the commission's minority report." It was not, it was Father Ford's May 23 demurrer. The commission's episcopal members had agreed not to submit majority and minority reports, just one report of the commission. But Ford and Ottaviani felt they had a right and a duty to warn the pope away from it.

By early July, it was clear to Cardinal Doepfner, even before he knew of Ottaviani's end run around the commission, that the pope had been listening to others. He wrote Bishop Reuss July 8, "I want to take this opportunity to thank you again for the tireless efforts you have made toward the clarification of the burning problem of marriage, this without regard for your own health. May God grant that everything will go for the best and that the church will not miss a great opportunity. Unfortunately, during my last audience, I gained the impression that the holy father is very uncertain and hesitant in the whole question."

Neither the pope nor de Riedmatten revealed what transpired during de Riedmatten's official audience July 4. De Riedmatten gave few clues when he spoke on Italian television that evening to talk about the commission's historic charge. He talked about birth control as *regolazione di nascita* and defined that phrase as meaning "simply that husbands and wives ought to consider the duties of conception in a spirit of responsibility." He did report that the commission had finished its work, and that the pope would make the final decision, which would not be "sensational."

That Delphic statement could have meant anything, but, as with most such statements, what de Riedmatten then had in mind was later clear: the pope was turning away from his commission's recommendations. Still, maybe the pope hadn't made up his mind. *Comincia adesso la fase di giudizio*, de Riedmatten told the reporters of RAI. "Now begins the period of decision."

It was not a decision the pope would be allowed to make on his own. He was lobbied, right, left and center. In late July, Bishop Colombo wrote

Bishop Reuss, telling him "a minority has made proposals through Cardinal Ottaviani to the holy father." Colombo enclosed the proposals. Reuss was alarmed. They were piecemeal solutions, remedial quackery. Colombo tried to justify this move on grounds that "the pope would otherwise see himself forced to reaffirm the traditional solution." Reuss immediately wrote the pope, saying the suggested formulations that had come to him from the minority "are not even acceptable for pastoral instruction."

Reuss sent a copy to Cardinal Doepfner, and Doepfner wrote back, "The uncertainty, indeed, the anxiety of the holy father is very considerable and I have serious concerns that a hesitant half solution will be the result. We must pray fervently."

* * *

Catholics the world over, however, were not waiting for word from Rome. Life did not stop during the pope's "period of decision." A growing number of priests, even some bishops, were advising couples who had good reasons for practicing rhythm that they could use other methods approved by their physicians. Cardinal Doepfner published a pastoral guide for priests of his diocese which said couples who could not forego contraceptive intercourse were not necessarily in a state of sin and should not stay away from the eucharist.

Many priests and bishops were saying the same thing. James P. Shannon, former president of the College of St. Thomas in St. Paul, Minnesota, and then an auxiliary bishop residing in Minneapolis, was piloting a chartered Cessna 180 around the state of Minnesota, telling people that the council had already helped resolve the birth control question, in favor of full, loving intercourse; if couples had good reason to avoid children, they should use their own judgment on the means. Charles Curran, a moral theologian at the Catholic University of America, was teaching seminarians that the church was in a state of doubt, the sort of doubt that results in freedom of conscience for the individual couple.

Using one's conscience was a novelty, in American Catholicism, at least. But that notion began to get more attention. John Cavanagh, the American psychiatrist on the pope's commission, and James McHugh, a priest then directing the U.S. Catholic Conference's Family Life Bureau, put together a symposium on "Marriage in the Light of Vatican II." It included a long paper on conscience by Warren Reich, a moral theologian at Catholic University, who pointed out that people should not conform blindly to the doctrine of the church.[31]

External actions are not commanded for their own sake. To be moral acts, they must be the concrete expression of internal consent to a moral value which is internally perceived and pursued in the untouchable depth of the human person. Not uniformity of action but inner acceptance of truth is the important element in the formation of conscience. The church may not force the truth on any man, for in man's relationship to truth coercion has no place whatsoever. . . .

The church teaches, guides, and leads, with the realization that each individual, who finds himself conditioned by a greater or lesser degree of religious and psychological freedom, is liable to respond in a different way.

Dr. Reich, now director of a bioethics program at the Georgetown School of Medicine and Kennedy Institute of Ethics, noted that "the church's educative activity is a formative one prior to the judgment of conscience. When the individual finds himself at the moment of moral judgment, when he must decide what his response to God will be in this situation, he confronts God in an intimacy which admits of the presence of no third party."

This was precisely the line Father Curran took in August in lectures at St. Gregory's Abbey in Shawnee, Oklahoma. The *National Catholic Reporter* published his remarks and, on the basis of that story, William J. McDonald, rector of the Catholic University, called Curran to account. The faculty at CU's School of Theology backed Curran and resolved that they had no reason to suspect his orthodoxy. But Monsignor McDonald and the U.S. bishops who legally governed CU kept their eye on Curran.

Curran was not alone. Privately, if not publicly, priests in every part of the Western world, at least, were telling their people: the church is in a state of doubt; follow your conscience.

Ingenuously, the pope decided to resolve that situation by announcing there was no doubt. October 29, he appeared before members of the Italian Society of Obstetrics and Gynecology during a papal audience at St. Peter's. The pope averted to birth control—"a very delicate question." He knew people awaited his decisive pronouncement, but he could not make one at this time. His commission had given him its conclusions, he said, but he did not consider them "definitive."

Why not? "Because," he said, "they carry grave implications together with several other weighty questions both in the sphere of doctrine and in the pastoral and social spheres which cannot be isolated or set aside, but which demand a logical consideration in the context of what precisely is under study." The pope was speaking bureaucratese, but commission members who read those words in *L'Osservatore Romano* understood all too clearly. The pope didn't intend to follow their advice, not, at least, without much more thought. And, in the meantime, what were Catholics to do? The pope had an answer:

. . . the norm until now taught by the church, integrated by the wise instructions of the council, demands faithful and generous observance. It cannot be considered not binding as if the magisterium of the church were in a state of doubt at the present time, whereas it is rather in a moment of study and reflection concerning matters which have been put before it as worthy of the most attentive consideration.

America, the Jesuit weekly edited in New York, found that statement puzzling. "In a nutshell," said *America*, "it is hard to see how a doubt about doctrine, if it is a genuine doubt, can be dissipated without the explicitly doctrinal type of statement the pope said he was not making on October 29." But perhaps this was good. In the past, the Vatican had been too prone to release "instant certainties." To *America's* editors, "the magisterium is undergoing important changes in its self image, and it may be unavoidable that these changes will manifest themselves in temporary ambiguity and some resulting turmoil of consciences."

The editors of *Commonweal* solicited John Noonan's interpretation of the pope's remarks. Noonan's judgment: the pope had given a disciplinary ruling. It was something like the meatless Friday rule. Good Catholics ought to follow this legal directive. But Richard McCormick, one of the most respected moral theologians in the U.S., took some exception.

Once it is shown that there are intrinsic reasons (good and probable) why the church may change her teaching on contraception, it would seem that the foundation for a certain obligation has ceased to exist—precisely because the obligation never derived in the first place from a legal directive, but from a teaching or doctrinal statement. If the teaching statement becomes doubtful, does not the obligation also?

Father McCormick claimed the pope had repudiated the existence of doubt, but only "verbally."

. . . a careful reading of the address (wherein the pope said explicitly that he was not making his decisive statement on contraception) will lead one to the conclusion that it could not have been a doctrinal or teaching statement. . . . Only an authentic teaching statement is capable of dissipating a genuine doctrinal doubt. And that is why I would agree with the many theologians who contend that the matter of contraception is as of now, at least for situations of genuine conflict, just where it was before the papal address, in a state of practical doubt.

This may have been easy for McCormick to handle. He was one of those subtle Jesuits. But the average layman was simply confused. A Mr. Bruce Stewart wrote to *The Tablet* in London:

Surely after three years of not finding out, of discussion, disagreement, dismay and a certain acrimony, no finality, a special commission and a remaining inability on the pope's part yet to give an answer, we have a least arrived at a "state of doubt?"

I can see now that we are going to have arguments on what constitutes a state of doubt as head-splitting as the arguments themselves on what constitutes a right use of natural law. Well, roll on the fog: but as any city chap would agree, if the amount of doctrinal certainty involved in the traditional teaching were our bank balance, we wouldn't get much joy out of the manager.

It reduces the mere layman to a state of, well, my Roget seems to offer a couple of dozen alternatives, but none of them, I regret to say, is either "study" or "reflection."[32]

Charles Davis, England's brilliant theologian, didn't have such a whimsical reaction. The pope's statement had such a violent effect on him that he resigned from the priesthood. For him, that statement "illustrated the subordination of truth to the prestige of authority and the sacrifice of persons to the preservation of an out-of-date institution." To Father Davis, the pope was being dishonest. "One who claims to be the moral leader of mankind should not tell lies."

Davis thought things over for a month, then decided to leave not only the priesthood but the church as well. He had a discussion with Cardinal Heenan, then, December 21, made his decision public, lying a little himself in the process. He told the press he wasn't leaving because of the pope's most recent statement on birth control, or because he wanted to marry (which he did in very short order). But that papal statement did help him realize how radically the official church was opting for "authority at the expense of truth."

The British press treated the news as a sensation. And, though many Catholics in England and the U.S. were sad to see Davis go, they were also proud of him for calling a spade a shovel.

* * *

Meanwhile, back at the Vatican, advocates of both sides were urging the pope to act immediately. Giacomo Perico, the Jesuit moral theologian from Milan who had been a member of the commission's majority, wrote a piece for *Aggiornamenti Sociali*, and then arranged to have it republished in *La Civiltà Cattolica*,[33] a Jesuit monthly whose articles invariably had the semi-official blessing of the Vatican. He hoped the piece might nudge the pope into a move.

Those on the other side did not have to deal with the pope in such an indirect manner. Cardinal Ottaviani, as secretary of the Holy Office, saw the pope at least once a week. And so, few in Rome were surprised when they heard that the pope had appointed another, secret, commission to advise him on birth control. This one, headed by Ottaviani, was purportedly composed of 12 members, all conservatives. Their task: to help the pope write an encyclical that would "settle the question."

Across Europe, the bishops who had had high hopes that the pope's original commission would help him confront the question in a realistic way were buzzing. Would the pope repudiate the commission that labored more than three years on this? February 4, Josef Elchinger, bishop of Strasbourg, wrote to Bishop Reuss: "In Rome, it must be understood that the recommendations of the commission cannot be ignored. Otherwise, we will have followed a false procedure. We should not be afraid to say this, because we must be servants of the truth in order to avoid even greater evil." To such as Bishop Elchinger, things were that desperate.

* * *

Others also believed the situation called for extreme remedies. One was Leo Alting von Geusau, priest of the Diocese of Groningen, and director of the Dutch Documentation Center off the Piazza Navona in Rome. Father von Geusau had given me sources for my first story in *Time* on the church's re-evaluation of its strictures against birth control, and he had helped me on several stories after that, often by providing reports and speeches at the council that would have been otherwise unavailable. Now, somehow, he had gotten copies of the commission's concluding reports, Dupuy's pastoral statement, the so-called majority report, the so-called minority report, and the rebuttal written by Fathers Fuchs, Delhaye and Sigmond. Should he make these available to the world press?[34]

Naturally. He had been doing the same since the council began, on the grounds that the people of God had a right to be informed about the doings in their own church. Giving the reports of the birth control commission to the press was hardly a new departure for him, but just as benignly subversive. He knew knowledge was power, and that publishing these documents would give millions of Catholics power in an area once reserved for higher authority to decide.

Von Geusau approached Henri Fesquet, one of the best journalists at the council and correspondent for the French daily *Le Monde*. Strangely enough to von Geusau, Fesquet was horrified at the thought of dealing with the reports, but he turned von Geusau over to another editor at *Le Monde*, who was poring over the documents when Gary MacEoin, an Irish-born American journalist and the author of more than a dozen books, showed up in Rome December 13.

Von Geusau told MacEoin what was up. MacEoin read the reports, surprised that such a great majority of the commission had opted for change. He had no difficulty with the idea of leaking the reports. But he didn't think turning them over to *Le Monde* would help. "*Le Monde* won't print the reports in full," he said. "It will do a news story. And then the world will pick up a truncated version of that story and get things all garbled. That could do more harm than good. Why don't we arrange to have the *National Catholic Reporter* print all the reports in full? *Le Monde* can have its scoop in Europe on the same day." MacEoin believed that *NCR* might agree to provide summaries to the U.S. national press and to the news agencies, "so that the true meaning of the documents would be clear from the outset."

Von Geusau agreed. He would work out the new arrangments with *Le Monde*. And MacEoin would deal with Robert G. Hoyt, the editor of *NCR*. He found Hoyt willing to go along with the plan, willing to credit *Le Monde* for providing the documentation. But Hoyt said he couldn't decide without consulting his staff. In effect, this most independent Catholic weekly, edited in Kansas City, Missouri, would be scooping the pope on his own reports. *NCR's* staff would take some heat on this from upholders of the status quo, much as *The New York Times* took criticism for printing the Pentagon Papers. Hoyt felt it only fair for his staff to tell him whether they were prepared to take the backlash.

Hoyt told everyone in the newsroom what he had and asked, "Do we think this is the right thing to do?" He got a unanimous yes. It would be the biggest news story of the year, of the decade, the sort of thing *NCR,* in the best muckraking American tradition, gloried in.

Under Hoyt, the *National Catholic Reporter* was the most liberating force in U.S. Catholicism, in that it gave American Catholics information hitherto denied them by their own bishops and officials in Rome. Now, people would have proof positive that authorities in the church were not only divided, but also leaning preponderantly to a new view of marriage and the family that did not condemn couples to hell for loving each other, no matter what the calendar said. It would be all the proof anyone needed that Rome was trying to promulgate "a doubtful law" as if there were no doubt.

MacEoin jetted from Rome to New York February 2 with the commission reports in his briefcase. From New York, he mailed them to Hoyt in Kansas City via certified mail. MacEoin said he could not tell Hoyt where he had obtained the reports. He didn't want credit. If publication generated any dollars, he would like the money to go to a black South African who was working his way through medical school. He assured Hoyt the documents were authentic, and when Hoyt saw them, he had no doubt. He knew MacEoin and knew he had superb connections.

Hoyt hired two U.S. priests, Larry Guillot and Phil Tompkins, who were eager to do the translations from Latin and French into English.

MacEoin's early intuitions had been correct. *Le Monde* would have been the wrong organ for this story, because, as it turned out, *Le Monde* decided to print a mere "inside dopester" piece, no texts at all, and was scheduling the story for its Saturday-Sunday edition of April 16-17, 1967. MacEoin, back in Rome, wrote Hoyt to tell him about the change of plans at *Le Monde*. He suggested that *NCR* refrain from running the complete texts or take upon itself responsibility for their authenticity.

Hoyt misunderstood. He believed MacEoin's mysterious source did not now want the reports published in full. March 24, he cabled MacEoin in somewhat of a panic:

NEED CLARIFICATION NEW APPROACH STOP SEEMS RADICALLY DIFFERENT AND REDUCES STORY VALUE 90 PERCENT STOP EVERYBODY KNOWS BASIC FACTS ALREADY STOP WHAT MADE STORY DIFFERENT WAS DOCUMENTATION STOP ALREADY HAVE MADE HEAVY INVESTMENT TRANSLATIONS AND PLANNED COMPLETE TEXTS OF MAIN THREE STOP CANNOT UNDERSTAND NEW PLAN STOP LETTER FOLLOWS

HOYT NATCATHREP

MacEoin's response took more than a week to reach Hoyt. MacEoin replied that Hoyt could print the documents in full if he wished. "Your only problem is that you are assuming the responsibility for their authenticity." If *Le Monde* wanted to change its own plans, that was beyond MacEoin's control. He had wanted to embargo publication because a prior commitment had been made to *Le Monde*. Hoyt gave a sigh of relief.

Things worked out better than Hoyt had hoped. *Le Monde* delayed its story. *NCR* came out on Saturday, April 15, and had itself a worldwide scoop. And MacEoin and von Geusau could congratulate themselves on getting worldwide coverage. Hoyt mailed a complete* set of copies to the offices of *The Tablet* on Great Peter Street in London and *The Tablet*, a growingly militant Catholic weekly that had been a presence in England since 1840, started setting the reports in type immediately.

"They just came in the mail," recalled Tom Burns, *The Tablet's* long time editor and publisher, "without a note or anything to explain. They were postmarked Kansas City, though, so I was able to guess where they had come from. I knew they were authentic. And we published them, in several installments, starting on April 22."

Monday, April 17, *The New York Times* ran the story on page one, with a full page of documentation inside. The story got a big play on the wires and the networks.

*All except for Dupuy's pastoral statement, a copy of which was later obtained (and published) by *The Tablet*.

In a letter, Hoyt told MacEoin:

> As you can imagine, it took a bit of doing . . . but everybody pulled together and we made all our deadlines. I was at my desk 36 straight hours, but, let me confess, it's the kind of thing I enjoy even while I'm suffering.
>
> I suppose it will be a long time before the consequences will be measurable. Having thought about it a long time, with all its implications, I feel our consciences can be clear. . . . It was the right thing to do, true to the nature and spirit of the church as newly revealed in Vatican II. That may sound pretentious, but I believe it.
>
> You do understand, I hope, how much we appreciate your confidence in us, your patience in the negotiations, and your understanding of our point of view about the news value involved. Thank you very much. I can hardly wait to grow old so you can tell me the rest of the story.

Hoyt added a postscript: "All the media are pressing us for information on our source, and are getting nowhere."

MacEoin wasn't so sure. Hoyt had told some reporters his source was an American freelancer in Rome. MacEoin believed that description could have led even a cretin to Gary MacEoin. There were few American freelancers in Rome to begin with. "If I were assigned the story with this data," he wrote Hoyt, "I would pay the *portiere* of each of the offices and apartment buildings of this easily countable group and, with the incoming mail, make a definite identification in a week." He told Hoyt they should exchange no further correspondence.

MacEoin was not surprised to get a call from Ellen Sullivan of *Newsweek's* Rome bureau, who had a tip that MacEoin was "the source." He had to tell her he had nothing to do with publication of the reports; if he were identified, suspicion would fall on von Geusau. MacEoin was then helping reorganize the Dutch Documentation Center for von Geusau.

But where did von Geusau get the reports? Plenty of people in the Vatican, the pope included, were ready to shake a stern finger at the insider who put these secret reports into the press pipeline. Never in their most paranoid imaginings did the pope and his staff believe anyone would leak them, much less publish them. In the first place, the Roman mind didn't think this subject was that important. (It wasn't, in much of the Latin world. In the English-speaking world, however, it was a different story.) In the second place, what commission member would want to embarrass the holy father? Were its members not loyal sons and daughters of the church?

Yes. But loyalty to the church, as newly defined by Vatican II, didn't necessarily mean loyalty to the pope or to the crowd that played on his fears in Rome. The church was now "the people of God." And whatever liberated soul gave von Geusau the reports was thinking first about the needs of the people of God.

* * *

The pope was angry. He had Cardinal Cicognani write to the commission's episcopal members: *Supremus Pastor vehementer doluit . . . quod textus documentorum editi sunt. . . .* "The Holy Father has grieved most heavily over publication of the documents. The reports, scattered so imprudently, and the inept conjectures, spread everywhere, have hardly helped bring a correct solution. The reports were supposed to remain secret."

But neither the pope nor the curia nor any local authorities would (or could) crack down on the *National Catholic Reporter* or *The Tablet* or any other news organizations that published these reports. They knew it was prudent not to try.

* * *

In the U.S., however, the very week that *NCR* published its story and the documentation on the birth control commission, 33 members of the U.S. hierarchy decided to squeeze one theologian at the Catholic University of America. These bishops, members of the university's board of trustees, had CU's rector call in Charles Curran to tell him shortly after ten in the morning Monday, April 17, that he was fired, or, more precisely, that his contract would not be renewed in August. Three witnesses heard the rector tell Father Curran this was the decision of the board, 33 cardinals, archbishops, bishops and 11 laymen, who had voted against Curran at their meeting in Chicago a week before.

"I'll have to go public with this," said Curran. He was 33, a scholar not a fighter, an assistant professor of theology. He knew his adversaries were the most powerful men in his world, the U.S. bishops who didn't want him teaching at CU because he dissented from the pope on birth control. Only now did Curran learn that, in the fall of 1966, the trustees had delegated a three-man subcommittee to report on Curran's orthodoxy. The members of this subcommittee, William McDonald, rector of CU, Philip Hannan, auxiliary bishop in Washington, and John J. Krol, archbishop of Philadelphia, never called Curran to explain himself, never called upon any members of the theological faculty to testify for him or against him. But they found Curran unacceptable and said he should be fired.[35]

Despite the power arrayed against him, Curran determined to fight, not because he enjoyed battling the bishops, but because it was necessary to maintain his integrity as a scholar. As an American college professor, he was part of a community of scholars which had long suspected Catholic scholars were only scholars after a fashion. Weren't they part of an authoritarian church which had specialized for centuries in telling people what to think, no matter what the evidence to the contrary? Therefore, didn't the headquarters of this church, the Vatican, bear more than a superficial resemblance to the Kremlin?

To Curran and many of his colleagues, the answer was no. But they had to prove it by bearing witness to the truth, no matter where it led, even if it led to battling some of their bishops. It wasn't disloyalty that sent them into battle, but loyalty to the church (and its credibility in the modern mind).

That battle, therefore, was not a face-off between bishops and theologian, for there were bishops and theologians on both sides, but between two traditions that had lived side by side for some time: a tradition of the mind on one side, a tradition of the will on the other.

The dichotomy has been expressed in different ways: reason versus faith, science versus religion, intellectualism versus voluntarism. Abstractions all, the words are an attempt to describe two epistemological currents: one group following the best of Aristotle, the realist, who said that because there are things out there, I can know them; the other group following Plato, the idealist, who said that because I know things, they are. Or, perhaps better, two habits of mind, or possibly different genetic codes: some people seek new knowledge, others would rather not know. Some are comfortable on high ground, others exchange comfort for the thrill of adventure. Some need the certainties of unequivocal understandings, others enjoy the play and byplay of analogies and ambiguities.

Those in one group tend to become priests and policemen and publishers and presidents, those in the other prophets, pitchmen, reporters and pundits. Priests put their blessings on things as they are, prophets look at things that never were and say, "Why not?"

There was a time when American priests, busy building an immigrant church, were almost invariably members of the first group. But the American church was growing up, and some of its best people, who had learned inside the institutions erected on the muscles and the tears of the builders, were secure enough to launch into the deep. Curran was such a man. He was determined to make the birth control issue carry the weight of a more important crusade, a reaching out for respectability from the seekers of his scholarly world.

This was why Curran won support from many at CU who did not necessarily agree with him on birth control. They focused on a procedural issue which, if solved, would free them to do their work, too. The theological faculty, for instance, promptly met, voted unanimously to support

Curran, and sent a telegram to each board member urging the decision on Curran be rescinded.

That evening, the theology students called their own meeting. A noisy crowd of more than 400 filled the seats and aisles of McMahon Auditorium, and cheered prominent faculty members as they entered the room. The professors came to whip up support for Curran.

Daniel Maguire told the students as much as he knew about the case, then implied something was vaguely un-American about this suppression: "If there is no room for Father Charles Curran in the Catholic University of America, then there is no room for the Catholic University *in* America." More cheers.

Sean Quinlan came to the microphone and recalled the September day in 1965 when Curran and others of his stature came to CU. "They came to a School of Theology riddled with frustration, bitterness and failure. They brought us new breath, new life, and, most of all, they brought us intelligence. And now the board would take Father Curran from us. They would destroy the school."

Robert E. Hunt said Curran was the best of America's new young theologians. If the board repudiated Curran, it was also repudiating Vatican II.

Some board members undoubtedly believed, privately, that repudiating Vatican II was a dandy idea, if that were possible; it would give everyone more peace. But that was not possible in the spring of 1967. American Catholics were beginning to understand how the reforms of Vatican II could give them new freedom and responsibility. True, those reforms were mostly words on paper. But so were the reforms written in the Magna Charta, the U.S. Constitution and the Bill of Rights. To make them a reality, people had to put shoes on them and walk them into the streets. Curran and his colleagues were doing that.

Wednesday morning, more than 2,000 rallied in front of McMahon Hall. They marched to Curley Hall and sent a two-man delegation to the rector, who thanked them for coming and said he would convey their sentiments to the board. No satisfaction there. So the group proceeded with plans for a news conference that afternoon at Caldwell Auditorium. There, Walter Schmitz, theology dean and a Curran supporter, and Eugene Burke, a Paulist, clarified things: if the board didn't act, almost 7,000 students and the faculty would hold a general strike. The faculty had just voted 400-18 in favor of it.

The board didn't act. CU went on strike. There were no classes that week at CU. But a different kind of learning went on. At a noon rally Thursday, one strike leader introduced a reporter, who read notes from his telephone interview moments earlier with Richard Cushing, cardinal-archbishop of Boston. Cushing, a CU board member, had said, "I know absolutely nothing about running a university. It makes no sense to appoint people to run a university who know nothing about it." There were tentative cheers. But what did Cushing mean? That some bishops had to learn about academic freedom: "You must teach all sides," said Cushing. "That's scholarship."

The students applauded. At least, they said, one American bishop understands. In the academic world outside CU, "Catholic University" seemed to be a contradiction in terms. Students inside CU knew it wasn't, that the canons of scholarship prevailed here as they did at Harvard. At least, they had prevailed, until the bishops started mucking about with the scholars. In a way, students and faculty had to fight the bishops, to retain the respect they were only beginning to win in the U.S. academic community.

Students walked picket lines all weekend. Saturday, they held a silent confrontation with Patrick O'Boyle, the archbishop of Washington and CU chancellor as well, who was there to dedicate a small chapel at the National Shrine of the Immaculate Conception. Sunday, Carl J. Peter, one of CU's most respected faculty members, told several thousand students in the campus mall, "The cause of truth is not served by the suppression of scientific opinion. The lot of man is not improved by removing from the scene of influence any who think and reflect and subsequently write. We stand behind Father Curran because we see at issue the right of the serious scholar to live and breathe and conduct his work freely. If his right to do so is suspended, so is ours." They marched from CU to Trinity College for a late afternoon mass, concelebrated by Curran and dozens of other priests on the faculty.

Monday, CU was still on strike. But those who gathered for another rally that afternoon were told some movement had occurred: Archbishop O'Boyle was meeting with the faculty at three o'clock. The day was dark, clouds threatened rain. But the crowd kept getting bigger. Everyone felt the issue would be resolved that afternoon. It was.

Shortly before 6 p.m., Archbishop O'Boyle appeared on the Mullen Library steps and looked out at hundreds of upturned faces. He could read the picket signs: WHEN YOU'RE OUT OF SCHMITZ, YOU'RE OUT OF GEAR. EVEN MY MOTHER IS FOR CURRAN. MORE TROUBLE FOR THE SHEPHERDS OF ISRAEL.

The sun came out from behind a cloud. Slowly and deliberately, Archbishop O'Boyle announced, "The board of trustees has voted to abrogate its decision." Huge applause. Raucous shouts. Both sides had denied birth control was the issue. But O'Boyle didn't want anyone to think that the American bishops were hereby endorsing Curran's views on certain moral questions. He added: "This decision in no way derogates from the teachings of the church by the popes and bishops on birth control." Aha. So birth control was an issue. Maybe the main issue.

No matter. CU had won a battle for academic freedom, which, in this context, would establish not only the right of a Curran to think and write about birth control in 1967, but also the rights of future Currans to think and write about nuclear war and abortion. Father Schmitz took the microphone and reported that Curran would receive a promotion to the rank of associate professor, as previously recommended by the theological faculty and the faculty senate.

Curran stepped front and center. Renewed applause from the crowd. Embraces and handshakes from those on the library steps. He went to the microphone. He did not gloat. He gave a speech rather unlike speeches students were hearing on many American campuses in 1967, more like something heard several centuries before on the campuses of the University of Paris or Louvain. On U.S. secular campuses that year, others were protesting the continued official sanction of a particular war. On this Catholic campus, students were protesting the continued university sanction of dogmatic morality in general. It was a Catholic declaration of independence, one long overdue at CU. Curran said:

Today, we have been given, today we have won not an ultimate victory but an opportunity. All of us, faculty and students alike, have been given a mandate and a charge, to continue our efforts on behalf of our university, on behalf of Catholic scholarship in America, and on behalf of theological investigation.

Curran was more prophetic than he knew. In 1968, another battle would take place in Washington over the same question, without the same happy results.

* * *

In Rome, the pope and his curia were still dancing around the birth control question. Cardinal Doepfner wrote Bishop Reuss in April 1967. He'd heard the papal nuncio in Germany had suggested to the pope and Cardinal Ottaviani that the church could effect a compromise by approving the pill: 1) to regularize the feminine cycle and 2) to ensure the natural infertility normal during lactation. These "solutions" had already been in moral textbooks since 1959. Fuchs and others on the commission had rejected them as symptomatic of the old-fashioned casuistry that had made the church a laughing stock everywhere. Doepfner said he had told the nuncio as much: "This would undoubtedly be the first step in a long chain, but it is a half solution and it will not bring the church any honor."

Doepfner told Reuss: "I fear now as before that for the moment, we are not going to get beyond half-solutions and can anticipate a trial for the faithful and their confidence in the church." July 6, he reported again to Reuss: "I fear now as before that the holy father will bring out a reaffirming document, which will, at best, furnish a microscopically small beginning for the crow bars of moral theologians."

Reuss wrote back:

Over the past few months, I have spent every free minute writing an article in which I am taking a (negative) position on the following question: should one dispute a papal decision concerning conception? This essay will appear in the July issue of *Diakonia*. It has already been translated into Italian and I will send a personal copy to the Holy Father. It is my last attempt to take a position against the proposals of Ottaviani-Colombo.

In the article in *Diakonia*, which was more like an open letter to the pope, Reuss made three major suggestions. The pope should: 1) Make future discussions on birth control public, so others capable of taking part can do so. 2) Admit frankly that the church's magisterium is not united on what is morally permissible. 3) Tell people they should be free to follow their own consciences in a matter of such clear doubt.

Several months later, Reuss would get a letter from Cardinal Ottaviani, written in Ciceronic Latin. Ottaviani pointed out that if the pope were to go against the advice of his own commission, he knew that Bishop Reuss would not uphold his own previous position, but rather give religious assent to the pope. Otherwise, Ottaviani didn't see how Reuss could be faithful to Paragraph 14 of the council's Declaration on Religious Liberty:

By the will of Christ, the Catholic church is the teacher of the truth, and its task is to announce and authentically teach the truth which is Christ, and at the same time declare and confirm on its authority the principles of the moral order which flow from human nature itself.

Touche. The declaration on religious liberty was one of the conciliar victories of the liberals, especially over Cardinal Ottaviani. For Ottaviani to use a sentence from it now, against Reuss, was an attempt by Ottaviani to have the last laugh. But, according to the council *Acta* published by the Vatican's Polyglot Press, it was one of Ottaviani's men who had had the sentence inserted in the declaration, by leave of the liberal majority, who had wanted to appease the other side. To make an authoritative point with Reuss, Ottaviani was, in effect, quoting himself.

The note infuriated Reuss. He wanted to help people. And Ottaviani was playing games with the texts of the council. Well, Reuss would not let this article in *Diakonia* be his "last attempt." He tried other ways to head off the pope. His archives are replete with copies of his correspondence in 1967 and 1968 with some of Europe's leading bishops and archbishops, who sympathized with the views of the birth control commission's majority. Included in Reuss's file: copies of letters to the pope from Cardinal Suenens and Michele Pellegrino, cardinal-archbishop of Turin, urging him not to reaffirm the traditional doctrine. The pope responded to them (as he did to Reuss) through Amleto Cicognani, with form letters in the negative.

Cardinal Cicognani wrote Cardinal Suenens on August 29 and reported that "the sovereign pontiff believes that the observations favoring a new thesis . . . do not seem sufficiently convincing." Cicognani admitted the problem was causing priests, and the pope, a good deal of anguish. He added that publication of commission reports, "which ought to have remained secret," were "a pain in the soul" to the holy father and "certainly did not contribute to a solution." Suenens sent a copy of this note to Reuss, which was a revelation to Reuss, because he had practically an identical letter from Cicognani, also dated August 29.

But if Cicognani had to write a form letter telling cardinals and bishops their arguments favoring a new thesis were not "sufficiently convincing," this would seem to indicate that other bishops* were trying to warn Paul VI. Warn him about what? Warn him not to write another *Casti Connubii*. Nevertheless, he would have one written, based on three arguments Ottaviani gave him in a 15-page paper written toward the end of 1967:[36] 1) it is not possible to contradict *Casti Connubii*, for that would undermine the doctrinal authority of the magisterium and seriously endanger the confidence of the faithful. 2) In the existing atmosphere of general eroticism, in taking an open position, one risks opening the door to a tide of hedonism. 3) If one permits the use of contraceptives for individuals, governments will be able to claim recognition of their right to state-organized family planning.

Ottaviani and his supercommission (or commissions) would go ahead now with their own encyclical. They would call it *Humanae Vitae*.

---

*Scholars will certainly find other such notes in other episcopal archives of the period. The notes were stimulated, in part, by rumors then rife about a committee of twelve working under Cardinal Ottaviani, or possibly several commissions, each working on a different part of a future papal statement. The surmise is Joseph Selling's based on a September 1983 interview with a Roman theologian who should have known. That theologian told him that after the work of the papal birth control commission was over, Ottaviani established many secret commissions, so secret that "the members of one commission did not even know about the existence of the other commissions."

Chapter Ten

It took Ottaviani's group, or groups, at least six months to draft *Humanae Vitae*. According to Jan Grootaers, a Belgian scholar who has done extensive work on this question, some who helped were: Bishop Colombo, Ermenegildo Lio, Marcelino Zalba, Jan Visser, and Josef Fuchs, all consultors to the Holy Office, and possibly Ferdinando Lambruschini and Gustave Martelet, a French Jesuit who had written some almost mystical things about marriage that had caught the eye of Pope Paul VI. Grootaers added that Fuchs had only a nominal relation to the committee and did not contribute to any of its reports.

For more than a year, during the rest of 1967 and the first half of 1968, while Vatican insiders, members of Ottaviani's commissions, were laboring over a new encyclical, outsiders continued to lobby the pope. Some thought no news from Rome was good news. Maybe the pope would say nothing and leave the matter to the prudence of each local church. Others, more naive, believed the pope was going to produce a nuanced document that would prove Rome believed in continuity through progress. Vatican II had demonstrated how easily the church could do this when it promulgated its Declaration on Religious Liberty, a statement at complete variance with Pius IX's statements in *Quantum Cura* that religious liberty was a delirium. But that question related to a real world that the Vatican had learned to live with: the pluralism of modern society.

Birth control was different. It dealt with questions about love and marriage and sex, a world that Rome had not learned to live with.

It did no good for reformers to argue for change based on new insights endorsed by a general council. Bernard Häring had proof of that. He had gotten one verbal *monitum* (or warning) from Pietro Parente, an official at the Holy Office, correcting him on a statement he had given to an Italian Catholic magazine: Häring had said that any future papal statement on marriage would have to look to the council and not to *Casti Connubii*. Wrong, said Archbishop Parente: no council document bound the pope. Later, Father Häring got a written *monitum* telling him the church's doctrine on marriage was contained in *Casti Connubii*; the council's constitution was "only pastoral." To Häring, these were ominous signs that meant forces in the curia were taking back their preconciliar power. And that members of *La Commissione di Dodici*, Ottaviani's twelve, would have their way.

On July 29, 1968, the speculation was all over. After claiming for four days that the rumors of an imminent statement on birth control were "absolutely false," Fausto Vaillanc, the Vatican's chief press officer, called a news conference to announce that the pope had just signed his long-awaited statement on birth control, an encyclical called *Humanae Vitae*, of human life.

Monsignor Vaillanc passed out copies in at least five languages. Experienced members of the Vatican Press Corps sized it up immediately as a complete repudiation by the pope of his own commission. It was addressed to all men of good will, but it propounded a particular Roman Catholic view, and, as Cardinal Doepfner had predicted, there was not even a tiny wedge in it for the crowbars of the moral theologians. George Armstrong, veteran correspondent for *The Guardian*, saw that it "upheld with no qualifications the Roman Catholic church's ban on all mechanical and chemical means of birth control." It not only ignored commission recommendations, it specifically rejected its findings, because, "above all," that commission had used criteria "at variance with the moral teachings on marriage proposed by the firm, constant teaching of the magisterium of the church."

Armstrong recognized that *Humanae Vitae* didn't bother with the substance of the pro and con arguments on birth control, but did reveal a deep and abiding mistrust of men and women and a fear of sex. The encyclical said artificial birth control would "open up a wide and easy road . . . toward conjugal infidelity and the general lowering of morality. Man, growing used to the employment of contraceptive practices, may finally lose respect for the woman and, no longer caring for her physical and psychological equilibrium, may come to the point of considering her as a mere instrument of selfish enjoyment, and no longer as his respected and beloved companion."

It was early morning in Rome, still the middle of the night in the U.S. But Jerry Miller of the Associated Press phoned his office. This was page one stuff. He got the story on the wires, instantly. A night editor in New York started phoning American members of the commission. He woke the Crowleys in Chicago, gave them the news and asked for their reactions. Patrick had no comment, but then, not knowing whether to laugh or cry, he hung up the phone and said to Patty, "Mom, just what in hell did we keep going to Rome for?"

In the crowded, chaotic *Salla Stampa* off the Via della Conciliazione, Vaillanc had a bonus for reporters. He introduced the first official commentator on *Humanae Vitae*, a commission member who had voted with the majority, but now, as one of the *Dodici*, was serving as the pope's emissary to help clarify things for the press. Ferdinando Lambruschini tried to deal immediately and honestly with everyone's question. How could the pope repudiate the reasoned arguments of his commission?

In the first place, said Monsignor Lambruschini, the commission had been divided. In the second place, the minority theologians had upheld a safer course, "the line of the preceding magisterium." In the third place, the theologians of the majority "were not unanimous in their attempt at explaining up to what point of the renewal of that magisterium its continuity would be compromised." Translation: no one was skillful enough at telling the pope how he could change the party line without confessing the church had made mistakes.

But Lambruschini wanted to zero in on the nub of everything. The pope, he said, had to give "a rigorous confirmation of traditional teaching" because he could not "undermine moral law." Hence, the meaning of the encyclical was best seen in Paragraph 14:

> Every matrimonial act must remain open to the transmission of life. To destroy even only partially the significance of intercourse and its end is contradictory to the plan of God and to his will. . . . Similarly excluded is any action, which either before, at the moment of, or after sexual intercourse, is specifically intended to prevent procreation—whether as an end or a means.[37]

This, he said, was "the center, the nucleus, the apex, the heart and the key of the encyclical." No ambiguity at all.

And no novelty either. This was the church's old act-centered approach to every sexual question. In encyclicals beginning with *Rerum Novarum* in 1891, the church had dealt with social questions based upon the entire person and the human community. Now, in dealing with sexual morality, this encyclical considered factors such as justice, responsibility and freedom of the moral agent to be virtually irrelevant. The encyclical paid some tribute to the contemporary and personalist insights of the council's document on marriage, but it did not take them seriously. It considered physical, economic, psychological and social conditions affecting responsible parenthood, then removed them as considerations germane to birth control and settled for the old biological norm, itself labeled a partial perspective earlier in the encyclical.

Lambruschini added, and repeated it twice, that *Humanae Vitae* was not an infallible statement. But the faithful were to treat it as if it were because the encyclical was at one with previous popes and the council as well, a claim which would soon be blasted by many of the learned men who had fought the battle of Vatican II. And anyone who dared to say the church was in doubt, those who taught that birth control was acceptable "must change their views and give the example by full adhesion to the teachings of the encyclical."

Lambruschini said the pope used moderate language. It *was* moderate and some apologists later noted how significant it was for Paul VI not to use the phrases "grave sin" and "mortal sin," as Pius XI had done in *Casti Connubii*. Nevertheless, said Lambruschini, the pope was laying down the law "to all bishops, priests and faithful of the church and to all men of good will, thus committing their conscience."

The last may have bothered people most. Some commentators saw this as an exercise of naked power unworthy of the church that had lately won much admiration for turning its old ministry of fear into a ministry of service. In the encyclical, the pope admitted many of the faithful wouldn't understand or agree with him on an interpretation of the natural law, but he wanted them to obey anyway. This unreasonable order had a logical result that would have an impact on the wider world: by putting papal power ahead of everything else, the pope damaged the prestige of the papal office and the moral leadership of the church.

Lambruschini knew this, but he tried to take the edge off possible criticism by telling reporters the pope's decision was "an act of great courage and an example of perfect serenity." Courage, no doubt. Some wondered about the word serenity. In October 1965, reporter Alberto Cavallari of *Corriere della Sera* had recorded the pope's lack of serenity, and that same lack of serenity must have contributed to the pope's indecisiveness for much of three years. Perhaps by July 1968 he had achieved enough serenity to sign *Humanae Vitae*. If so, he would soon lose it again when worldwide reaction reached his summer residence at Castel Gondolfo.

The Association of German Physicians said "Paul VI is completely out of touch with reality. Catholic doctors live in the world as it is and not in an ideal world longed for by the pope." Some 2,600 U.S. scientists signed an open letter to the pope, saying "the appeals for world peace and pity for the poor made by a man whose actions help to promote war and render poverty inevitable do not impress us any more." The Los Angeles Association of Laymen rejected the encyclical, suggesting the pope had "an anti-sexual bias" and may have written *Humanae Vitae* "to alleviate the anxieties he has about his own authority." They said they would develop their own informed consciences. "We will not leave the church. We will not be thrown out. We are Catholics because of our faith and our hope and our love, together, in community."

Almost two dozen theologians at the Catholic University of America, joined by 60 others from around the U.S. (more than 600 U.S. scholars would later add their names to the list of signatories), complained that the encyclical:

. . . consistently assumes that the church is identical with the hierarchical office. No real importance is afforded the witness of the life of the church in its totality. The special witness of many Catholic couples is neglected. The encyclical fails to acknowledge the witness of the separated Christian churches and ecclesial communities. It is insensitive to the witness of many men of good will. It pays insufficient attention to the ethical import of modern science.[38]

To Hans Küng, the flap over *Humanae Vitae* proved the church had to overhaul its ideas on authority, magisterium, doctrinal formulations, dogma, and particularly infallibility. Bernard Häring focused even more tightly on what he said were "the real issues," the impact of curial power and the non-collegial exercise of the teaching office.[39]

Carlo Falconi, in Rome's *Espressso*, deemed this encyclical "the first serious repudiation of Vatican II." Twenty-one of Europe's top moral theologians* who called a meeting in Amsterdam seemed to agree with him. Patrick O'Donovan said in *The Observer* of London that the encyclical proved Manichaeism in the church "far from dead." *The Economist* editorialized: "This encyclical is not the fruit of papal infallibility but of papal isolation."

Archbishop Roberts was puckish with the press. He told one reporter: "In the final analysis, the law is as strong as the power to enforce it. But the church doesn't have the power to enforce its laws in people's bedrooms." C.J. Trimbos, psychiatrist from The Netherlands, said, "The gap between teaching and practice will become even wider than it already is." John Marshall, one of the six original members of the birth control commission, was no grandstander and the very model of an English gentleman. But he felt constrained, immediately, to write a letter to *The Times* dissociating himself from the statement in the encyclical that birth control opened the road toward infidelity and a lowering of morality. *The Times* received more than one thousand letters that week on this question. But Dr. Marshall's view was an important one for the record and *The Times* printed it:

> Despite the widespread and long-standing practice of contraception, there is no scientific evidence to support this sociological assertion made in the encyclical. The assertion, moreover, casts a gratuitous slur, which I greatly regret, on the countless responsible married

*They were J.M. Aubert and C. Robert of Strasbourg, A. Auer of Tübingen, T. Beemer, P. Huizing and P. Schoonenberg of Nijmygen, F. Bockle of Bonn, W. Bulst of Darmstadt, P. Fransen, R. Gallewaerd, L. Janssens and M. DeWachter of Louvain, J. Groot, W. Klijn and F. Malmberg of Amsterdam, R. von Kessel of Utrecht, F. Klostermann of Vienna, O. Madr of Prague, E. McDonagh of Maynooth, J. Pfurtner of Fribourg and C. Sporken of Eindhoven.

people who practice contraception and whose family life is an example to all.

Some closest to the heart of the system demurred. Individual bishops had instant reactions. Cardinal Heenan wrote a pastoral letter telling his people that they must accept the pope's decision, but they could also "look forward to further pastoral guidance on the whole question. . . ." He gave some: those who had been practicing contraception should not despair and should not abstain from the sacraments. Denis Hurley, archbishop of Durban, South Africa, told his people in a front-page interview in the *Southern Cross,* a Catholic weekly in Capetown, that he believed the pope "had a right to make the decision. But I would be dishonest if I agreed with the method of consultation or the result." He said the encyclical was "the most painful experience of my life as a bishop. I have never felt so torn in half."

Gregory Baum felt torn, too. August 23, he wrote of his anguish in *Commonweal,* and asked how the church, "which, of its very nature, is universal, long-range and complex," could be delivered from the fervors of Catholic extremists on both sides of this debate. "The very nature of the crisis demands new understandings and limits for both authority and freedom within the church," he said. He added:

> It is somewhat worse than pointless, for example, for defenders of the magisterium to demand acceptance of all the conclusions of *Humanae Vitae* in the name of authority when authority, its exercise and its limits, is precisely the question, along with the question of the exercise and limits of freedom, that must now be reconsidered in the church. And it is somewhat worse than irresponsible for defenders of freedom to argue as though freedom were a value that exists within the church in splended isolation, unrelated to the nature and functions of the magisterium.

The Dutch and Belgian bishops took the advice of theologians like Baum seriously. They began meeting with leading lay men and women to prepare nuanced commentaries to help people resolve the crisis. For the first time in history, bishops and bishops' conferences everywhere felt they had to comment on a papal encyclical.

The pope hadn't expected this. Naturally enough, since it was *his* authority that was being held up for examination, he was rocked, shocked. In papal audiences at Castel Gandolfo July 31, he tried to explain.

> The knowledge of our grave responsibility cost us no small suffering. We well knew of the heated discussion in the press. The anguish of those involved in the problem touched us also. . . .

> How many times did we hesitate before the dilemma of an easy agreement with current opinion, or of a bad decision supported by

today's society, or one that would be arbitrarily too difficult for conjugal life.

It was almost as if the pope were presuming a popular decision would be a wrong decision.

Four days later, he was even more defensive. "Even if today we have to say an unwelcome word," he said, referring to *Humanae Vitae* (which certainly hadn't been designed to be so casual as "an unwelcome word" on something so fleeting as "today"), "it is not a complete treatment of marriage, the family and their moral significance. This is an immense field to which the magisterium of the church could and perhaps should return with a fuller, more organic, and more synthetic treatment."

During the next decade, Pope Paul VI would never write another encyclical. Cardinal Heenan joked about the situation in a television interview with David Frost:

Frost: I am sure there's a lot more you have to do yet. Once one is a cardinal, one day you may become pope.

Heenan: (laughing) I hope not, but, if so, I'll be very careful about writing encyclicals.

The pope had public defenders: bishops, theologians, lay people, even some of those who had helped draft *Humanae Vitae*. Gustave Martelet was one. In a long, intricate commentary in *Nouvelle Revue Theologique*, he got into deep waters with unprovable assertions that echoed Paragraph 13 of the encyclical:

Right and deep as married love's desire and capacity for total communion are, love does not fully become what it ought to become unless it allows the fruit of its intimacy to appear. Maybe this fruit will be hard to desire and even to accept. As soon as it systematically begins excluding this fruit, however, love immediately injures itself so that it leads to death—that death which is the eventual designation of every introverted eros and every couple who enjoy a life they refuse to spread.

Martelet's view might be true in some cases. But neither he nor the pope could make that judgment stand up as some kind of universal norm. That was the trouble with any moral question, particularly any having to do with love and marriage and sex. Sex was such a slippery subject. No one knew enough to pontificate about it, especially not in terms that would apply to everyone.* Sex was a great mystery. "When two beings embrace,"

---

*Martelet, appearing at a 1978 conference in Milan on the tenth anniversary of *Humanae Vitae*, told a large audience the encyclical's ban on contraception was not meant to haress individual Catholics who found themselves having to limit their families but unable to use methods allowed by the church. He called their use of contraceptives "a disorder" which was not sinful if these couples acted in good

Paul Ricoeur, the French philosopher, once noted, "they don't know what they are doing, they don't know what they want, they don't know what they are looking for, they don't know what they are finding." Men and women might discover the meaning of sex in the analysis of ancient myths, wrote Professor Ricoeur, but sex was primordial, pre-linguistic, infra-linguistic, para-linguistic, super-linguistic. "It mobilizes language, true, but it crosses, jostles, sublimates, stupefies it, pulverizes it into a murmur, an invocation. Sexuality demediatizes language; it is Eros and not Logos."[40]

But some of the pope's defenders made brave tries to explain. August 26, the U.S. bishops issued a brief pastoral letter urging priests and people to "receive with sincerity what [the pope] has taught, to study it carefully, and to form their consciences in its light." They added: "We are aware of the difficulties that this teaching lays upon so many of our conscientious married people. But we must face the reality that struggling to live out the will of God will often entail sacrifice."

John J. Wright, bishop of Pittsburgh and soon to become a curial cardinal, wasn't quite so gentle:

What Pope Paul has done, what he had to do, is recall to a generation that does not like the word the fact that sin exists; that artificial contraception is objectively sinful; that those who impose it, foster it, counsel it, whether they be governments, experts, or— God forgive them!—spiritual directors, impose, foster and counsel objective sin, just as they would if they taught racism, hatred, fraud, injustice or impiety.

Some lay commentators eager to defend the encyclical were even harsher than Bishop Wright. L. Brent Bozell, managing editor of *The National Review*, would have excommunicated those who could not agree with the pope. He said, "Those priests who refuse to accept, and faithfully carry out in their pastoral capacity, Pope Paul VI's encyclical on birth control, should leave the church." He added, quoting Canon 1325 from the Code of Canon Law, "Any person who refuses submission to an authoritative teaching by the supreme pontiff on faith or morals is a schismatic."

But the encyclical didn't go as far as the pope's defenders. *Humanae Vitae* did not speak of excommunications, nor did it even use the terms "objective sin" or "objective evil." The encyclical said contraception was "intrinsically dishonest" and "contrary to nature" but these expressions

conscience and had tried their best to follow the encyclical.

Josef Fuchs had tried to convey this idea to the cardinals and bishops during the last days of the commission meetings: "All methods of contraception contain some evil, biological, psychological, et cetera, even periodic or continued abstinence. But this evil is permitted if some proportionate good demands it."

were a far cry from the condemnations of *Casti Connubii*. As Joseph
Selling pointed out in *The Reaction to Humanae Vitae*, his monumental
doctoral dissertation at Louvain, that of all the episcopal statements
attempting to interpret the encyclical, only those of the Spanish and U.S.
bishops used the term "objective sin" or "objective evil." The French
bishops called contraception a disorder in the category of "pre-moral evil."
And the Austrian bishops wrote, ". . . if someone should err against the
teachings of the encyclical, he must not feel cut off from God's love in every
case, and may receive holy communion without first going to confession."
According to Dr. Selling, most joint bishops' statements avoided the sin
question entirely, "an indication of doubt on the part of the bishops in this
area" and an implication "that they do not accept the argumentation of the
encyclical themselves."

If this was so, little wonder. Not even the pope, and those who helped
him write *Humanae Vitae*, had seemed certain of the arguments against
contraception. When the pope addressed himself in *Humanae Vitae*
directly to priests, he said confessors should disregard the arguments pro
and con. They owed "internal and external obedience to the teaching
authority of the church. That obedience, as you know well, obliges not only
because of the reasons adduced, but rather because of the light of the Holy
Spirit which is given in a particular way to the pastors of the church in
order that they may illustrate the truth." He quickly added: "In the field of
morals as well as in that of dogma, all should attend to the magisterium of
the church, and all should speak the same language."

Not all bishops could agree. The bishops of Belgium said, "If we do not
find ourselves considering a statement which is infallible and therefore
unchangeable—generally an encyclical is not infallible, and furthermore
Humanae Vitae does not claim to be such—we are not bound to an unconditional and absolute adherence such as is demanded for a dogmatic
definition." The Belgian bishops were not alone in this interpretation.
Selling identified a dozen episcopal groups that published "mitigating"
statements, including the bishops of Austria, Canada, CELAM (the conference of bishops representing Latin America), France, Indonesia, The
Netherlands, Scandinavia, Switzerland and West Germany. Most of these
statements made some explicit or implicit reference to the encyclical's
non-infallible character.

A majority of bishops' conferences took a more rigid public stance. In a
"clear acceptance" column, Selling listed 18 national heirarchies that
included Australia and New Zealand, Poland, Portugal, Spain and Yugo-
slavia. Because of internal inconsistencies in their statements, and because
some bishops' groups made more than one statement, Selling put Brazil,
England/Wales, India, Italy and Japan in the "uncertain" column.

Wrote Selling:

The very fact that so many bishops took an active role in interpreting a papal encyclical implies that the nature of that pronouncement, if not its content, was inadequate to represent the entire teaching of the church. *Humanae Vitae* simply could not stand on its own and gain the recognition necessary to become part of what the church believes and practices. Its teaching did not represent the *sensus fidelium* and the bishops knew that it could not establish it. . . . Even those bishops who gave their complete support to *Humanae Vitae* . . . did not declare the matter closed.

A few did. Robert E. Tracy, bishop of Baton Rouge, Louisiana, said it was beside the point to plead that the pope's statement was not "infallible." It was "authoritative," therefore, "in view of Christ's mandate to Peter and his successors, the best practical guide to be followed, here and now." Bishop Tracy saw no real difference between *fallible* and *infallible*. The terms were synonymous, roughly analogous to the words *flammable* and *inflammable*. Tracy also tried to cut off an argument American priests had used for several years, that people were free to follow their own consciences when faced with a "doubtful law." Tracy said the pope did not accept this stance.

He studied it and consulted it for five years. Then, deliberately, clearly and officially, he formally rejected it. And so there is no way now for any Catholic to continue to advance such a position in his personal life, his teaching, his preaching or in the exercise of his pastoral ministry, without formally repudiating the position of the Holy Father as the supreme teacher of morals in the church.

On an informal and practical level, many Catholics dissented from the encyclical without repudiating the pope or leaving the church. Realistic lay folk too busy for philosophical or theological reflection dismissed what the pope had said on the grounds that he was old or out of touch or uninformed or all of the above. Daniel Callahan, an editor of *Commonweal*, articulated the reasons why lay people might choose to ignore *Humanae Vitae*: The magisterium had asked people to make radical sacrifices it was not prepared to make itself.

Hypocrisy is one word appropriate here [wrote Callahan]. Immorality is even better. Neither the pope nor those bishops who have supported the encyclicals have given the slightest indication that they intend to give up anything of their own security commensurate with what a poor family, trying to make do on rhythm or abstinence, would have to give up to follow their teachings.[41]

Jesuit theologian Avery Dulles may have been thinking of statements like this when he concluded in a learned paper he gave on the magisterium in 1976 that, "Many Catholics have lost all interest in official ecclesiastical statements and do not expect any light from the magisterium on their real problems."

But those who had a greater stake in the system and were saddened to see how the pope's decision had already weakened the church's credibility, were forced to analyze and criticize that decision. They did so not because they failed to recognize a need in the church for authoritative guidance. Rather, they wanted to guarantee, as one dissenting theologian put it, "continuance of the genuine enlightenment we need from the church" which had "awesome duties of arduous scholarship, of continual reassessment, of listeniing."

Their criticisms were tough. Some challenged the notion than the pope had a special handle on moral questions. Bernard Häring, who knew better than most that the pope was a (perhaps willing) captive of a narrow circle of Roman theologians, said that being consecrated bishop or anointed pope does not give a man "more insight on psychology and pedagogy of married love" than others in the church.

Robert G. Hoyt, editor of the *National Catholic Reporter*, made the same challenge, wondering in print whether the pope "had special access to the truth about human behavior." He said that the pope seemed to rely on his papal prerogative "in preference to the counsel of his own best qualified advisers, to resolve an inherently controversial issue and to impose his solution upon a divided church."

In other words [wrote Hoyt], it doesn't really matter how the debate goes, or which side seems to prevail according to the usual norms of controversy; the storekeeper is not subject to the rules.

The pope's Catholic critics are saying that this is not a sound Catholic doctrine of the papacy; it is reminiscent rather of gnosticism. Man's sexuality is indeed a mystery, but a mystery about man not about God. The papacy has not been divinely equipped to discern the answers to mysteries of this order by any magical process. Neither has it been divinely authorized to proclaim its philosophically based answers to moral questions without obligation to demonstrate their philosophical validity. If that were the case, there are other problems more urgent than contraception awaiting answers, e.g., the morality of the nuclear deterrent.*

*Hoyt wrote these words in 1968. Fifteen years later, in 1983, the U.S. bishops offered a moral judgment on the nuclear deterrent. Possibly instructed by the reception accorded *Humanae Vitae*, they did not lay down the law, or pretend to any special revelation. Rather, they called upon American Catholics to reason together with them on a difficult matter, admitting that this question, like every moral question, depends on variables that men and women can only deal with by using what Aristotle and Aquinas called human prudence, a prissy word in English, but one that means hard thinking about things to be done. Even so, some persons

What was happening? Repudiated now by the pope, the liberal wing of the church was working on something new in church history: a theology of dissent, although "theology" may be too pretentious a word to describe the common sense argument used by such as Karl Rahner in the years that followed. Father Rahner contended that if Catholics had to follow non-infallible pronouncements without question, the church could never correct its own mistakes, nor make the kinds of institutional advances demanded by a church that claims to be incarnate in history.

He implied the institutional church wasn't being true to some of its proudest history: the history of a long intellectual tradition. Sometimes the church took a long time to remember that it even had such a tradition, as in the case of Galileo, given a new "trial" by Pope John Paul II in 1982 and acquitted more than 400 years after his condemnation. But no one who knew this history and the history of the papacy should have been shocked to find that it was a band of Catholics opposed to the pope who were reasserting that tradition.

Historically, the church was proud of the advances made through its ecumenical councils, where pope, bishops and theologians reasoned together. In a council, according to the constitution *Dei Filius*, passed at Vatican I, "the sacred dogmas of religion are defined with the greatest depth, expressed with the greatest breadth. . . ."

And so now, in order to develop a reasoned dissent to *Humane Vitae*, those more open to change made a direct appeal to the authority of the Second Vatican Ecumenical Council. Pericle Felici gave them just the opening they needed. On September 7 and again on October 10, Cardinal Felici, the man who had served so faithfully as secretary general of the council, and was a member of the interlocking directorate running the Vatican, wrote two long pieces in *L'Osservatore Romano,* which traced the connections between the council's treatment of marriage and the ideas of the encyclical. According to Felici, *Humanae Vitae* was simply a restatement of the council's *Gaudium et Spes.*

Philipe Delhaye, back home in Namur, Belgium, couldn't let that go unchallenged. In a 21-page article in *Bijdragen-Tijdschrift voor Filosofe en Theologie,* Canon Delhaye presented a scholar's response, a meticulous comparison of the two documents. His conclusion: *Humanae Vitae* had reversed much of the progress made by *Gaudium et Spes.* The encyclical not only "ignored the council's broad lines of thought on marriage." It did so "in a systematic way."

Delhay's principal complaint: the council fathers had spoken of mar-

who had urged an unqualified acceptance of *Humanae Vitae's* moral guidance on birth control were the first to challenge the U.S. bishops' right to take a moral stance on the nuclear deterrent.

riage in a global sense, but the curial group who wrote *Humanae Vitae*
(led, according to Delhaye, by Bishop Colombo) kept talking about "the act
of marriage" as if there were only one, the act of intercourse. [As every
married couple knows, there are hundreds of things that married couples
do together that could be called "acts of marriage" and they span a wide
spectrum of sharing: of ideas, of feelings, of activities that contribute to the
intimacy of married life: singing, dancing, playing together with the kids,
shopping, cooking, entertaining friends, gardening, watching television,
reading in bed, lying on a beach in silence. Not acts of marriage? Most
husbands or wives would quickly recognize them as such (and as very
intimate acts, to boot) if they were to find their partners doing them
habitually with someone else.]

Delhaye, who would win appointment in 1969 to Pope Paul's International Theological Commission, a group designed "to liberate Roman
congregations from a single theological language and perspective,"
observed that *Humanae Vitae's* view of nature was old-fashioned. It was
taken from the Roman jurisconsult Ulpian who considered "nature" as a
moral instinct common to animals and humans. *Gaudium et Spes,* on the
other hand, leaned on notions first conceived by scholastics such as St.
Albert the Great, who saw an intimate connection between "nature" and
"culture." In this sense, wrote Delhaye, it is "natural" for men and women
to bring the world under their control, improve customs and institutions,
render social life more human both within the family and in the civic
community. Delhaye said Catholics delighted by this conciliar advance
were "shocked" to read an encyclical that ignored this approach.

Christians taking their cue from *Gaudium et Spes,* said Delhaye, discovered the evangelical imperatives and applied them to their own lives. In
Humanae Vitae, "only authority's point of view is considered and Catholics are asked solely to obey." And in the area of married love, Delhaye
believed the documents were eons apart:

> *Gaudium et Spes* [wrote Delhaye] described the love of a couple in
> personalist terms as a mutual giving on all levels of one's individual-
> ity: will, affectivity, sentiments, and senses. *Humanae Vitae* makes a
> hasty mention of "an attempt at communion" in order to insist on
> its objective: procreation. Vatican II had tried to rehabilitate married
> love, to show that it finds its *raison d'etre* in itself, not just on the
> erotic level, but principally as the fulfilling of one's personality.
> *Humane Vitae* returns to the Augustinian view and justifies love
> only by "finalizing" it in procreation.

* * *

During the fall of 1968, others would make their objections to the encyclical. The bishops of Belgium, West Germany and Canada did so bravely, gracefully and with respect. Some few individual bishops also screwed up their courage and put their own glosses on the encyclical, principally for the guidance of people who were depending on some authoritative voice that would allow them to consider the pope's advice, but then encourage them to act on their own "informed consciences." In the U.S., more and more pastors were quietly following the same strategy. They may have been helped in this by good press coverage of the dissent, even from some portions of the Catholic press, which had matured during the council, particularly by the *National Catholic Reporter*, whose reportage during the first half of the decade had helped thousands of American Catholics, including many priests and nuns, grow up.

Bishops and pastors who provided their own nuances did so, no doubt, because they were worried about those described by the executive board of the National Association of Laymen: "The millions of silent Catholics on whom this decision will fall as an unnecessary and harsh burden. They will obey because this is the main thrust of their religious training, to obey. They have not been allowed to reach spiritual adulthood, so they have no way to make independent judgment. For them to obey or ignore this edict would destroy the very root of their religious belief." The need to deal with *Humanae Vitae* would give these very people a good opportunity "to reach spiritual adulthood."

Interesting how the seven American lay members of the pope's birth control commission reacted. They had seen how decisions were made in Rome. That gave them a freedom they couldn't have predicted for themselves only a few years before. In late September, they took it upon themselves to meet in Washington, D.C. "It had taken us some time to arrive at our new positions," recalled John Noonan in a May 1983 interview. "We couldn't just walk away from them because of an encyclical, one we didn't agree with." Noonan and six other American members of the commission—André Hellegers, Patrick and Patty Crowley, John Cavanagh, Don Barrett and Tom Burch—called a news conference on October 1. John Noonan spoke for them all.

He said the pope's opinion was no more than his opinion, nothing infallible, and that people should form their own consciences. He complained that the pope had not listened to his own commission and had prepared his encyclical in secret and with the consultation of a dozen members of the old guard. Some day, he said, the church would repudiate *Humanae Vitae* as it already had repudiated *Mirari Vos* (1832), which condemned freedom of conscience, and *Quanta Cura* (1864), which asserted that religious liberty, even in the civil arena, was a delirium.

It was not less difficult for Noonan and his lay confreres to say such things, perhaps, than to take the criticisms and snubs that later followed.

This was true, at least, for the Crowleys. Their long time spiritual father, Reynold Hillenbrand, of Winnetka, Illinois, a fine priest whose training was pre-conciliar, refused to have anything further to do with them.

* * *

Noonan and company chose Washington, D.C., to speak their piece because they felt that Washington needed their moral support. A large number of the priests at Catholic University and in the city had joined Charles Curran in open dissent to the encyclical, a move that Patrick O'Boyle took as the ultimate disloyalty. In a September 20 pastoral letter Cardinal O'Boyle predicted that a curse from the Book of Deuteronomy would fall on those who followed their own conscience rather than divine law. He reminded his priests that Rome had spoken and called on them to "return to their senses." Those who didn't recant would find themselves out of the priesthood. O'Boyle and other U.S. prelates who served on the Catholic University's Board of Trustees had already moved to suspend 20 professors* who had helped draft the statement of July 30 dissenting from *Humanae Vitae*. But suspension was easier sought than sealed. They soon found themselves up to their armpits in a year-long, quasi-judicial inquiry, which exonerated the professors. "The professors were compelled to some kind of honest response," said the inquiry board of faculty appointed by the CU trustees. "A concerted silence would have been more truly improper." The same board chided the bishops for declarations and actions that made a mockery of academic freedom and due process at CU. (James Francis McIntyre, for instance, the cardinal-archbishop of Los Angeles, had withheld his annual heavy contribution to CU until O'Boyle quelled this theologians' revolt.)

At a June 1969 meeting in Houston the U.S. bishops accepted the findings of the inquiry board and dropped the lingering inquiries from such as O'Boyle and McIntyre about the orthodoxy of the dissenters.

It was a good lesson for many American Catholics, who had never before

---

*They were William W. Bassett, John Cavanagh (now back from Rome after his stint on the birth control commission), Christian Ceroke, Charles Curran, Leo Foley, George T. Dennis, Robert E. Hunt, Thomas Joyce, George A. Kanoti, Peter J. Kearney, Daniel Maguire, Berard L. Marthaler, Alfred McBride, Bernard J. McGinn, Roland E. Murphy, Russell Ruffino, Warren Reich, John Smolko, Paul K.K. Tong and David W. Tracy. They had asserted it was "common teaching in the church that Catholics may dissent from authoritative, non-infallible teachings of the magisterium when sufficient reasons for doing so exist." And they concluded that "spouses may responsibly decide according to their conscience that artificial contraception in some circumstances is permissible and indeed necessary to preserve and foster the values and sacredness of marriage."[42]

realized that any Catholics could dissent from an authoritative papal teaching and still be loyal to their church. The outcome forced many to reevaluate old patterns of authority in the church. Now, in the post-conciliar church, as the inquiry board put it, it was clear that "theological reflection must develop in dialogue with the entire church and with others."

Washington's parish priests didn't enjoy the same due process given their brothers at CU. Various ecclesiastical censures fell on several dozen of them. It did no good for their parishioners to protest. One group sent Cardinal O'Boyle a petition bearing 353 signatures asking him to revoke the suspension of one priest. He dismissed them as "good and simple people" who didn't know what they were asking. A larger parish sent O'Boyle the same kind of petition, this one signed by 2,276 parishioners, and they got no response at all.

Six months later a majority of these clerics had left the active priesthood. Those who remained sought legal redress through the National Federation of Priests' Councils. They got the runaround from church tribunals that claimed they had no mandate to judge a cardinal's actions. The priests' only recourse was the pope, who seemed unwilling to get involved.* On February 11, 1970, the priests appealed to Rome. They were urged to seek reconciliation with Cardinal O'Boyle. Negotiations broke down and the case went to the Sacred Congregation of the Clergy in Rome, headed by the American John J. Wright, by then a curial cardinal, where the case foundered and died.

In only one other U.S. city—Buffalo, where several priests were suspended—did the battle become so bloody. Most U.S. bishops found ways not to do public battle at all, not with their priests, not with the Catholic couples who were able to work out the conflict between "official doctrine" and their private conclusions. And life went on as ambiguously in the church as it did in every other sector of life.

In Great Britain the same pattern prevailed: wholesale dissent by many priests and strong lay opinion running against the encyclical. Some few bishops suspended a few priests who said publicly that they disagreed with *Humanae Vitae*. All but a few of them were later reinstated and most other

*Joseph Selling said the pope was unable or unwilling to come down hard on anyone who opposed *Humanae Vitae*. "In relation to earlier crises, such as that over modernism, this represents a step forward in the church. For instead of silencing the dissident voices and engaging in the politics of confrontation, members of the church have been given an opportunity for growth and learning." On the other hand, Selling also noted that *L'Osservatore Romano* ran a number of articles denouncing the dissenters (it quoted Cardinal Journet, who said that those opposing the encyclical "are those who love sin") and refused to publish anything that resembled a critical response, including the episcopal statements from Austria, Belgium, Canada, West Germany, The Netherlands and Scandinavia.

bishops followed the lead of Cardinal Heenan, who adopted a policy of peaceful coexistence. He wanted no confrontation with dissidents. "Condemnation of artifical contraception," he said, "is not the central tenet of the Catholic religion." Heenan was no doubt tiring of mucking about in hornets' nests. In a letter to *The Times,* he even proposed a moratorium on news coverage concerning the church of Rome.

May I put in a plea [wrote Heenan] for your non-Catholic readers? They must be growing very tired of the extensive coverage. . . . Every day they are told of priests who disagree with the pope, or regret their vow of chastity, of laymen who allegedly speak in the name of their enlightened brethren to express contempt for the bishops and all in authority in the church. I think that the majority of your readers would be glad of some respite. I can assure you that my community is beginning to suffer from overexposure.

Not exactly so, said one reader, C.J. Hamson, a professor at Cambridge. Professor Hamson wrote *The Times* to say that the tension in the Roman church helped illuminate a great issue, the conciliation of liberty with authority and the balance of the right of the individual with the legitimate demands of the community.

I do venture to assure you there has been no overexposure. You have caused a chink of light to penetrate into the secretive dark in which the ecclesiastical authorities have long accustomed themselves to operate. This they find, understandably enough, painful and distressing. It is, however, evidently desirable that their established practices should in this manner continue to be disturbed. Long may you continue to disturb them.

Dr. Hamson's observation demonstrated that there was even "an ecumenical boon" connected with all this dissent by loyal Catholics. Robert McAfee Brown pointed this out first in the U.S. Dr. Brown, who had been an official Presbyterian observer at the council, wrote in *Commonweal* that Protestant fears for a reunited Christendom under the pope were groundless. "Roman Catholics themselves are quite willing to disagree publicly with a papal encyclical that seems to them patently wrong. *Humanae Vitae* is thus inadvertently the greatest gift to the ecumenical scene since the election of Pope John back in 1959."

Brown admitted he was writing with tongue somewhat in cheek and that it was easier for outsiders to joke. But Brown knew others in the church were suffering.

Pope Paul VI was one. He was too forbearing to take action against the dissenters, but he couldn't help giving voice to his own anguish. On April 2, 1969, Paul VI said the dissidents were "crucifying the church." He was grieved by:

. . . the restless, critical, unruly and destructive rebellion of so many of its followers, including the most dear, priests, teachers, the lay, dedicated to the service and witness of the living Christ in the living church, against its intimate and indispensable communion, against its institutional existence, against its canon law, its tradition, its internal cohesion, against its authority, the irreplaceable principles of truth, of unity, of charity, against the very requirements of sanctity and of sacrifice.

The next day, Holy Thursday, he said the church was divided almost to the point of schism.

How can it be a church, that is, a united people, when a ferment practically of schism divides and subdivides it, breaks it into groups attached more than anything else to arbitrary and basically selfish autonomy disguised as Christian pluralism or freedom of conscience?

Others were suffering, too. This controversy would force James P. Shannon, auxiliary bishop of St. Paul-Minneapolis, out of the priesthood.[43]

After serving with distinction as president of the College of St. Thomas in St. Paul, Shannon became a bishop in 1965 just in time to participate in the last session of the council. When he returned to Minneapolis, Leo Binz, the archbishop, gave him a dream assignment: to go to the priests and people and "translate" Vatican II, which he called "the most exciting intellectual experience I ever hope to have in my adult life."

For Bishop Shannon, the council had already settled the birth control question "in favor of the couple," and he didn't mind telling this to those who flocked to hear him. Then came the shock of *Humanae Vitae*. Then, another shock, when the U.S. bishops produced a pastoral that took the Roman line. Shannon couldn't understand why the moral code had to be different in the U.S. than it was in Belgium or Canada. "That was the beginning of my trouble," Shannon recalled in a June 1982 interview.

In the summer of 1968 Shannon confided his difficulties about the encyclical to Archbishop Binz, who told him, "Once the pope has spoken, it's over. You're a bishop and you gave your word." Shannon was silent. So, too, was Binz. They had little more to say to each other. Shannon went back to his parish, St. Helena's, and, without telling his assistant priests the reason, took himself off the list of regular confessors. How, he asked himself, could he call himself a bishop, one of the pope's men, and still give people the advice he thought they needed?

Not many days passed, however, before a young woman came to the parish house who would test his resolve. It was a scene being played out in many a confessional and rectory. "I just want to tell you my situation," she said to Shannon. "I don't come from this parish, but I have some friends who know you. We're good Catholics, been Catholics all our lives. My husband didn't go to a Catholic high school, so he doesn't have as much Catholic training as I have. He's a good man and a very good husband, but we realized from the beginning that we would probably have to practice rhythm. He has an ordinary job, and he'll probably never have a better one."

This couple had an unplanned baby. And then, another one. "Bishop Shannon," she said, "I'd love to have ten. I'm the happiest mother you've ever seen. And I'm proud of my babies, and my husband loves them. But after the second baby he became apprehensive. He said, 'If this is the future for us, I can't afford this; we can barely make it now.' Something went wrong with our relationship. He became distant with me. And I became distant with him. We're both affectionate, loving people and we learned that that leads to babies.

"The reason I'm here is that yesterday was my husband's birthday. We don't have much money. We don't ever go out to dinner. But I really splurged yesterday. I didn't give the babies their naps. I fed them late, so that by the time he got home, I'd have everything nice for him. I had the babies in bed, I had candles on the table, I had a bottle of wine chilling in the refrigerator. I had the works ready for last night. And he came home, and he was so pleased, and I was doing the finishing touches at the stove and he came up behind me and he put his arms around me and he hugged me." The woman paused, then blurted out, "I, I burst into tears, and I ran into the bedroom and slammed the door and I cried myself to sleep. He ate all alone last night."

She looked up at Shannon through her tears and said, "My marriage. I don't know what's going to happen to my marriage. This is the loveliest, sweetest, gentlest man. He can't go on like this. I can't go on like this. I can't leave him. And he can't leave me. I don't know what to do. I don't know where to turn."

Shannon said, "Madam," and then rolled through his post-Vatican II speech. "I told her about the bishops there, and how the process worked, and how I voted, and how this had the endorsement of the pope. I could just see the clouds leaving her face. She had been crying profusely, of course."

The young woman said, "Would the pope agree with what you're telling me?"

Shannon said, "Madam, I have to believe he would, if he were here now. He's a pastor. He's no less a pastor than I am. He would have to say what I'm telling you, that the merciful Lord knows your situation, is with you. He knows you're not trying to cheat or outwit nature."

The woman was ecstatic. Shannon saw her to her car. She drove off. Shannon went back into the house, took off his cassock, put on his suit and drove straight to the archbishop's house. Shannon recalled that he said to Binz: "For the first time, I told a devout Catholic that it would be permissible for her to practice contraception on a regular basis, and to use something that was safe. And I came here to tell you, because I want you to hear it from me. I don't want you to hear it from a third person."

Archbishop Binz didn't know what to say. Shannon shrugged, went home, thought things over, then sat down and wrote a letter to the pope, with copies to Binz and Binz's auxiliary, Leo Byrne, and the apostolic delegate in Washington. He said he could not "in conscience give internal assent, hence much less external assent," to the papal teaching that "each and every marriage act must remain open to the transmission of life." He thought that it was impossible for many generous people to observe this rigid teaching and said he could not believe God binds people to such rigid standards. Recently, he had been "resorting to all sorts of casuistry and devious kinds of rationalization." He added: "I must now reluctantly admit that I am ashamed of the kind of advice I have given some of these good people, ashamed because it has been bad theology, bad psychology, and because it has not been an honest reflection of my own inner conviction."

Then he went to see Binz again, who was puzzled at Shannon's wanting to tell the pope. "What can the pope do for you?" asked Binz.

"I don't want to be devious," said Shannon. "I want the pope to know what I am doing. I'm trying to reconcile things. I'm trying to be faithful to the church."

Binz pointed out that his letter would be on record in the Vatican. This would not be a strong recommendation for Shannon's future in the church. Shannon ruefully agreed. Binz said he was headed toward retirement soon. He preferred that Leo Byrne, his other auxiliary, handle this case.

Bishop Byrne asked Shannon if he would talk to a theologian about his troubles, one of Byrne's choice, a theologian who was also a bishop.

Shannon said he'd be happy to do so. He ended up flying to see an American bishop who would later produce his own pastoral commentary on *Humanae Vitae,* one that put some distance between his position and the pope's. Shannon talked with this bishop for most of two days, then flew home to tell Byrne this consultor agreed with him, not with the encyclical. Byrne was scandalized. To think a bishop would disagree with the Holy Father!

For Shannon, that was it. Other bishops such as Bishop Reuss would stay and fight for their people against the impositions of the institutional church, whether that put them out of favor with Rome or not. (Reuss would continue to get threatening letters from the Holy Office on into the late 1970s for his persistent dissents to the "official doctrine.") But Shannon, more a lover than a fighter, couldn't live out of favor with his ecclesiastical superiors. He didn't see how he could remain a bishop and not teach *Humanae Vitae.*

Luigi Raimondi, the pope's chief diplomat in Washington, agreed with Shannon. If he couldn't go along with *Humanae Vitae,* the Vatican would accept his resignation. Fortunately for Shannon's peace of mind, he was given some time to think, away from his conflict situation. Invited to fill in for the spring semester as an administrator at St. John's College in Santa Fe, New Mexico, he secured the permission of Binz and Byrne to accept. At the end of that academic year he was offered the vice presidency of St. John's, and he took it. That summer he resigned the priesthood and his episcopal office and, on August 2, he married Ruth Church Wilkinson of Rochester, New York.

"I do not intend to leave the church," Shannon told the press after his marriage. "It is my spiritual home. I love it dearly."

It was a costly step for Shannon. He'd invested 23 years in the priesthood. But, under the circumstances, he felt leaving it was the only realistic thing to do. Other types might have remained in Shannon's brogans, arguing they had a duty to stay and change things.

Shannon might have, too. He was a scholar, a pastor and a warm human being, by most accounts one of the best bishops in the land. The U.S. bishops had chosen him as their press liaison officer and, in that post, in the days before the bishops' meetings were open to the media, Shannon gave honest, straightforward accounts of what went on behind closed doors. For that he won the admiration of the nation's reporters who covered the National Conference of Catholic Bishops. He might have exercised great leadership in the U.S. He could have become the cardinal-archbishop of Chicago or Washington or New York. Or the president of Notre Dame. But probably not—not with that letter to the pope in his Vatican dossier.

Such were the politics of sex and religion in the church in 1969.

* * *

Politics, however, cut both ways. John C. Ford would find many of his own colleagues in the Jesuit order unhappy enough with his performance in Rome to rob him of his expected glory. Father Ford wanted no bishopric. For Jesuits, advancement comes as it does to most scholars, through publication in the best journals, teaching in the most prestigious posts. The honor is a function of service, and the higher the service the higher the honor. And so it was a particular irony for Ford to end up as he did.

Ford had sworn that if the church changed its position on birth control he would never teach moral theology again. But *Humanae Vitae* had vindicated his position. As far as he was concerned, the church had not changed; he could return home to the New England Province of the Society of Jesus a hero. There, he would teach solid doctrine he had helped reforge under the attack of those who would destroy the authority of the pope.

Wrong. The young theologians at Weston College, where he was as-

signed to teach moral theology, were so openly scornful of Ford's performance in Rome (relayed by Jesuits there who learned what he had done) that
they refused to attend his classes. And Ford never taught moral theology
again.

Perhaps the Holy Spirit had a sense of humor. True, Ford's church (that
is, the pope and those who clung to his authority) hadn't changed. But a
new church had overtaken Ford and passed him by. The same irony prevailed in the pope's case. Ford had told the pope he must reaffirm the classic doctrine, otherwise lose his authority. Paul VI accordingly reaffirmed
the classic doctrine, and lost his authority in this arena, perhaps in others,
too. Selling summed it up:

> On the whole, the encyclical was mitigated by a significant portion of
> episcopal teaching, substantially challenged and drastically reinter-
> preted by the majority of theological commentary and simply forgot-
> ten by uncounted numbers of the faithful who ignore its existence in
> making practical moral decisions.

Chapter Eleven

If only Patrick Crowley could have told the pope what he had told his wife: that given a choice between saving the faces of dead men or helping real live people, the church had a duty to lobby for the living. The pope might have listened to such plain talk, endorsed the insight of his commission and taken his chances at finding the right way to explain how the church could suddenly admit it doubted something once so certain.

But the pope didn't. He left the impression that he could not alter papal protocols or a style of authority that survives only in such regal institutions as the International Olympic Committee. Though the doubt was certain, this lord of the church could not leave the matter in doubt. He was much like the puzzled king of Siam in the lyric by Richard Rodgers and Oscar Hammerstein:

There are times I almost think nobody's sure of what he
    absolutely knows.
Everybody find confusion in conclusion he concluded long ago.
And it's possible to learn that though a man may be in doubt of
    what he knows,
Very quickly will he fight, he'll fight,
To prove that what he does not know is so.

In doubt, this papal monarch leaned on a courtier, Father Ford, who advised him that the sexual revolution was raging out of control. Nuns and priests were leaving their vows by the thousands, generally to get married. Young people were living together without benefit of clergy. Some governments were legalizing sterilization and abortion. And the mass media, the movies most of all, were reflecting on the general breakdown. A Danish picture, "I Am Curious Yellow," then appearing all over the world, featured simulated intercourse. Against this backdrop, what was the pope to feel, other than fear, when Ford warned him that all sexual morality depended on saving the general, simple and teachable principle that sex was only and primarily for procreation? If the church denied that principle, it would open doors to all manner of evil consequences. That had to scare the bejabbers out of the pope. He took the safer course.

216

Safer meant reaffirming the old teaching and rejecting the arguments of all but seven members of the papal commission, because the majority's reasons went against "the moral teaching on marriage proposed with constant firmness by the teaching authority of the church." This logic scandalized such as William H. Shannon, a Catholic and a distinguished member of *The New York Times* editorial board, who had just written a book on the birth control debate and had more than a glimmer of what went on inside that commission. Mr. Shannon was one of many who wondered, "What was the point of bringing together several dozen consultants if their findings were to be judged *a priori* in terms of their conformity to the teachings of the past?"[44]

Others doubted the "constant firmness" of those teachings. John Noonan had shown the doctrine was subject to changes in content and style. But Noonan, relying solely on the written record, had touched only part of the truth. What about the teaching's reception among the people of God? Rosemary Haughton, a Catholic contemplative from York and the mother of ten children, pointed out how little was known about past Catholic attitudes on sex, particularly about the sexuality of ordinary married people:

> We don't know what they discussed with each other, or with intimate friends. We don't know what kinds of sexual behavior they found satisfactory. We don't know whether they accepted the dicta of theologians and bishops or whether they listened politely but, making charitable allowance for celibate ignorance, took the principles and worked out the practice for themselves. We are, in fact, in no position to form any judgment about the Christian tradition of sexuality in the church as a whole, since most of the church was illiterate. . . . All we know in most cases is the opinion of a handful of clerics, who did not always agree even with each other and were lamentably out of touch with nearly everyone else.

Despite all the doubt, the pope and his cabinet upheld the old doctrine because it was old or, as they phrased it, because it was part of the church's "ordinary magisterium." The pope had aborted the reasoned process, which he had promoted for three years, because he had a duty to maintain the authority of Peter. That did it. Once intelligent Catholics realized this was the reason for no change, they began to look on that magisterium as ordinary indeed.

After *Humanae Vitae,* practically every part of the church changed on this question, in practice or theory: theologians, married couples, particularly in the western world, priests in the confessional, even many bishops —practically everyone except the handful of clerics that surrounded the pope and those in the provinces who worshipped whatever a pope said about anything.

In 1970 Charles F. Westhoff and Larry Bumpass, Princeton sociologists, reported that two-thirds of U.S. Catholic women, and three-fourths of Catholic women younger than 30, were using birth control methods disapproved by the church, and doing so in good conscience. In 1955, only 30 percent of Catholic women younger than 30 had been using contraception, and now, according to Westhoff and Bumpass, the change was most pronounced among the most devout, those who went to communion at least once a week. The authors concluded: ". . . it seems abundantly clear that U.S. Catholics have rejected the 1968 papal encyclical's statement on birth control."[45]

U.S. Catholic clergy were changing, too. In 1969-70, the U.S. bishops commissioned a study by the priest-sociologist Andrew Greeley and his colleagues at the University of Chicago who found that fewer than one-third of American priests were going along with the strict traditional view expressed in *Humanae Vitae*; only 15 percent were willing to demand conformity of their penitents.[46]

Polling in other countries revealed the same drift through the decade. A 1979 survey of British Catholics done jointly by the Gallup organization and the University of Surrey asked for replies to the statement, "A married couple who feel that they have as many children as they want are not doing anything wrong when they use artificial methods of contraception." Seventy-four percent agreed and 13 percent disagreed. Surveys in Scotland, France, Belgium, The Netherlands and West Germany through the decade found the same prevailing trend.*

*In 1982 Penny Lernoux, prize-winning reporter for the *National Catholic Reporter* and author of an impressive book, *Cry of the People*, told me about the birth control situation in Latin America. Her report helped me see that cultural conditions have more impact on people than what churchmen say.

Ms. Lernoux wrote from Bogota: "The middle and upper classes practice birth control. I don't believe they are any more swayed by the church's position than middle-class Americans are." But the poorer classes, the majority in every Latin American country, did not practice birth control, according to Ms. Lernoux, because they did not have access to education or health facilities. They were subject to traditional superstitions ("God will punish me if I use the coil.") And they were culturally bound: "Machismo also plays an important role: many Latin American men believe that their sexuality can only be demonstrated by having large numbers of children with different women. They also feel that if their women practice birth control, they will be unfaithful."

In 1973 *Newsweek* reported that the bishops of Colombia backed their government's family planning centers and decided to approve all forms of contraception short of sterilization and abortion. But Colombia's bishops changed their minds later—and, if I could believe my own modest survey, bishops from many another Latin American nation had grave reservations about family planning. In 1982, I drew up a survey questionnaire and sent it (along with a dollar for return postage) to 100 randomly selected bishops and archbishops from Mexico to Chile. I got back

In the Vatican, it made no difference what the folk did. Officials knew they couldn't enforce their law in people's bedrooms. Laws or norms like this one were supposed to educate people. This might have been fair, had the pope's men followed through. But they didn't seem willing to use this law as an educative tool. They made no moves to find out why Catholics, including priests and even bishops, were rejecting something so solemn as an encyclical. Much less did they try to make adjustments, as good teachers often do when their students aren't getting the point. Their attitude seemed to be: "If people cannot keep the law, *beh,* God is merciful."

But what was the point of maintaining a doubtful doctrine that was honored largely in the breach? Unwittingly, Father Ford gave the game away when he said the encyclical reaffirmed "the power of the magisterium to bind consciences." For Ford, the point was not truth. It was power. The point was not to teach, but to rule.

For centuries the church had modeled itself on secular monarchies and governments, which passed laws and penalized those breaking them. To Ford, it was appropriate that the church continue to rule in this manner, no matter what John XXIII, Paul VI and the council had said about the church's new desire "not to dominate but to serve." But rule over whom? Most lay people had already gone their own way on birth control.

Some theorized that the curia was using the birth control issue as a pawn in an old clerical chess game. Object of the game: to recoup some power lost during the decentralizing moves begun by bishops at the council. After the council, in the late 1960s and 1970s, local bishops' conferences were deciding disciplinary and moral matters once settled only in Rome: whether this couple should receive a marriage annulment, whether this order of sisters could put aside traditional religious garb, whether this parish could distribute consecrated wine as well as bread in its eucharistic

---

30 completed replies and seven blank questionnaires. Twenty of those responding said they held to the strict Vatican line on birth control, but I had some reason to conclude this was more because the bishops believed their governments were pushing dumb birth control programs.

Ms. Lernoux told me the programs weren't working: "What the birth control advocates in the U.S. don't understand," she wrote, "is that you cannot put a lot of undernourished women on the pill without serious health problems." She added: "A number of agencies, including AID [the U.S. Agency for International Development], have been dumping Dalkon Shields [a form of loop or coil] down here, which are prohibited in the U.S. because of the dangerous side effects."

No wonder one of my bishop respondents wrote in the margin of his questionnaire: "All of the government programs are motivated by foreign aid, most from the U.S.A., projects to check the population growth, permitting fuller economic control over local 'prime matter' produce (very cheap) to feed the First World industries. It is scandalous!"

celebration, all disciplinary matters, or whether Catholic hospitals could allow physicians to perform surgical sterilizations, a moral question.

In making that power shift the fathers of the council, spurred on in part by Pope John XXIII, implied something had been lacking in traditional Roman approaches to every problem. Now, the theory was, Roman churchmen believed that things were getting out of hand. Not only was a sexual revolution going on, but also a general mutiny on the bark of Peter. Surely the pope would not stop those in the curia trying to take back the helm?

Whatever the motive, Rome began making orthodoxy on birth control a touchstone of loyalty to the church. In 1974, the UN's World Population Year, the Vatican Secretariat of State sent a confidential letter to the bishops' conferences, urging them to uphold publicly *Humanae Vitae*'s teachings on birth control.[47] Then the secretariat tested internal and external assent (the Latin word was *obsequium*) on members of the Vatican's Pontifical Commission on Justice and Peace who were headed for the World Population Conference in Bucharest. Some failed the test, among them Philip Land, economist and professor at the Jesuits' Gregorian University. Questioned, Father Land admitted he had reservations about *Humanae Vitae,* but would keep his private views private. The Vatican told him not to go to Bucharest and removed him from the commission.

This was a Vatican reaction, no doubt, to a quiet challenge already implied by the Society of Jesus. In December 1973 Pedro Arrupe, the Jesuit general, had called a small, private meeting at Nemi near Rome to determine possible strategies the church and the Jesuits could employ in the face of still gathering worldwide concern about population. About two dozen Jesuit scholars and a few lay experts showed up at Nemi. One wrote:

> The church should set up machinery to dialogue with the world on the process of evolving population policies. She has a duty to help people face the gravity of the population problems; should not let herself be reduced to silence by her own embarrassment on the unresolved birth control issues. . . .

But the wisest heads at Nemi* said the church would be impotent to join

---

*Including Father Land, Josef Fuchs and Richard McCormick, but not Gustave Martelet, who had the political good sense to send a paper to, but not attend, the conference. Not that Martelet was all that proud of an encyclical he was reputed to have a hand in. He later conceded the inadequacy of *Casti Connubii* and *Humanae Vitae* in these words: ". . . this vocabulary of 'intrinsically evil' used by both encyclicals to denounce in contraception something truly wrong sadly allows one to believe that this always represents in itself the most grave failure of love. This is one of the lacunae of both *Casti Connubii* and *Humanae Vitae,* that neither one nor the other sufficiently protects its readers from the awful errors of such a misunderstanding."

this dialogue until a pastoral restatement of *Humanae Vitae* could take place "at the highest level of the magisterium."

That was not to happen. The highest levels of the magisterium still had problems with sex. January 15, 1976, Paul VI gave the world a look at his own thinking by allowing the Holy Office to publish "A Declaration on Certain Questions Concerning Sexual Ethics." It was a cold treatise that drew warm reactions, pro and con, from around the Catholic world. Defenders saw it as a necessary warning about the dangers of the sexual revolution. But, to Bernard Häring, the document was the most logical, systematic presentation of rigorism ever attempted. German theologians meeting in Tübingen said this declaration made it clear that the church was "not an intellectually and ethically livable place."

It was especially unlivable for theologians who had dared think new thoughts on matters sexual. A few of them, Gregory Baum, the Augustinian from Toronto, Charles Davis, the *peritus* to the English hierarchy, and Raymond Sigmond, a member of the papal birth control commission, left the priesthood. Other, such as Leo Josef Suenens, limped to their corners of the world and licked their wounds, hardly to be heard from again on anything that would threaten the status quo in Rome.

In 1969, in the aftermath of *Humane Vitae*, Cardinal Suenens suggested in a celebrated interview with an editor of the French journal *Informations Catholique Internationales*[48] that the pope should have dealt with birth control in a more collegial way. For this, Paul VI is supposed to have asked Suenens for his resignation. Suenens refused. They say he told the pope, "It doesn't matter. You have me whipped in any event." He did not 'scape whipping because he had fingered Rome's sore spot: papal authority.

* * *

Pope John XXIII had started taking first steps to give up old understandings of papal primacy. "I'm not infallible, you know," he used to say with a twinkling smile. And he did not act as if he were, which set a style that gave the pope and the church more credibility than ever in its history. Soon, many of the church's best theologians were rejecting infallibility out of hand or redefining it in ways that made it mean far less than the pope's courtiers would have liked to think.

But Paul VI found John XXIII's legacy difficult to live. He tended to operate, toward the end of his reign, more in the manner of Giovanni Maria Mastai-Ferretti, who in 1854 became Pope Pius IX and king of a temporal domain, the Papal States. In 1869, this pope rammed through*

---

*The most enduring image from the history of that council is a picture, described by August Bernhard Hasler in *How the Pope Became Infallible*, of the Greek the first Vatican Council a declaration of papal infallibility that has been used once since then, to express the church's belief in the Assumption of the Blessed Virgin Mary, body and soul, into heaven.

Most church historians agree: Pius IX felt a conciliar definition of infallibility would assert his kingly power in face of the on-marching forces of the *Risorgimento* and help maintain his control over a tightly organized church.

Hans Küng has written books on this question, and, for doing so, he has been told by Rome he can no longer teach "as a Catholic theologian." His writings show that papal primacy and papal infallibility, while old, are hardly of the essence of the faith; the notions began when the Gregorian popes in the eleventh century established a monarchic system throughout Christendom. Their actions were based on forged documents and power plays hardly in keeping with the scriptural and ecumenical tradition of the church during its first thousand years. The Isidorian Decretals, 115 forged documents purporting to represent the most important papers of the earliest bishops of Rome, from Clement onward, created the spurious impression that the early church had already been ruled by papal decrees from Rome. Father Küng, leaning on impeccable scholarship, tells how the decretals were used:

> In the second half of the eleventh century, Gregory VII relied on these and similar statments for his monarchical conception of the church, which in fact represented a new church constitution; then in the first half of the thirteenth century Gratian, founder of the science of canon law, produced his law book, which was basic for all later times—including the 1918 Code of Canon Law—and in which 324 passages from popes of the first four centuries are cited, 313 of them proved forgeries. From now on Matthew 16:18 is used in Rome precisely in this monarchic-absolutist sense with reference to the Roman church and the Roman pontiff, with all the juridical consequences which the great papal legislators of the twelfth and thirteenth centuries were able to deduce from this primacy and able to establish in a highly practical way with the aid of papal synods, papal legates and the mendicant orders. . . .

Melkite Patriarch Gregor Yussef, called on the carpet by the pope for opposing the definition of infallibility: "When Yussef kissed the foot of Pius IX in the traditional fashion, the pope place his foot on the patriarch's head (some said his neck) after the manner of a pagan conqueror, and said, 'Gregor, you hard head you.' Then he rubbed his foot about on the patriarch's head awhile longer. After Pius had died, the Holy Synod of the Greek-Melkite church filed two separate reports of this event in Rome in order to block the pope's canonization."

Even Thomas Aquinas was hoodwinked. He incorporated this politico-juridical development of the thirteenth century into the dogmatic system. Bolstering his argument with quotations from the forged documents, Aquinas proved that the Roman pontiff is the first and greatest bishop, that the same pontiff presides over the whole church, that he has the fullness of power in the church, that in the same power conferred by Christ on Peter the Roman pontiff is the successor of Peter and decides "what belongs to faith." Pope Boniface VIII, who reigned from 1294 to 1303, liked this. In the Bull *Unam Sanctam*, he declared subjection to the Roman pontiff "necessary for salvation."

Almost 600 years later, in 1870, Pius IX tightened the lid on papal primacy by getting his definition of papal infallibility passed by the bishops of Vatican I (though some fled the city rather than sign the constitution *Aeternus Pastor*). The definition didn't help him keep his real estate. Leaders of the *Risorgimento* seized central Italy, leaving the pope an enclave of 60 acres on the unfashionable side of the Tiber. But the definition did help him save his ancient authority, as an abstraction at least. The popes used this abstraction to give an aura to every papal decision from then on, and, by extension, to every curial decision as well.

Thus began a new kind of power for the pope and his cabinet. Standing in the symbolic glow of infallibility, they could make rules for the world, demand obedience from a half billion Catholics, and get it. After a century of this tightening control, Peter Nichols, long time correspondent in Rome for *The Times* of London, observed that this implosion of authority looked "more like a psychosis than a vision of church government." In the 1950s, the American Management Institute gave the Vatican its highest marks for having arranged this system just so. Multinational corporations could well emulate this model of power.

Pope Paul VI was supposed to give this up? Some reformers at Vatican II thought he should. Küng, a council *peritus*, and others, including many thoughtful cardinals, urged this abdication, a trading of one kind of power for another, a power that would be exercised by the pope in collaboration with the world's bishops. They did so not because God pre-ordained either mode, but because shared power was more in accord with the signs of the times. Pope John XXIII gave that biblical expression, the signs of the times, a new currency: God revealed himself through history. Church leaders had only to step out of their ecclesiastical ghettos to see the world was changing, because the people were changing. People didn't look kindly on monarchies, but on democracies. A sign of the times? Pope John thought so, and said so in his encyclical *Pacem In Terris*.

But birth control became the best sociological measure of the changing times. In 1983, Andrew Greeley reported:

The rank and file of Roman Catholicism in much of the North

Atlantic world is in quiet but effective revolt. It will neither leave the church nor accept the validity and legitimacy of ecclesiastical authority. . . .

There can be no solution at all until the pope and the bishops realize they no longer have the power of physical or moral coercion nor the power of sacred persuasiveness. Both the pope and the bishops must be able to say to themselves, "People are simply not going to do what we tell them merely because we tell them, probably not ever again."

Pope Paul VI knew this, intuitively, at least. After *Humanae Vitae*, he never wrote another encyclical. His successor, John Paul II, has been bolder, but he has given no more indication than Paul that he lives in a world conditioned by history. He cites cultural norms, especially old rules on sexual behavior, as if they were direct revelations from God.

The tragedy of all this is clear enough. Because people see the pope so often wrong in this moral area, they have a hard time listening to him on other, more pressing moral issues. He is all parade, drawing huge crowds wherever he goes, and no circus. People flock around, listening selectively, but they do the pope no favor: the hugeness of the crowds helps him cling to the illusion that he has as much power everywhere as he does in Poland. Now and then, this pope gets a dose of reality. On May 18, 1981, almost 80 percent of the Italian voters spurned the urging of the pope and their own bishops to vote against an anti-abortion referendum ordered up by the Vatican.

A priest from Milan, reflecting on that vote, told me the next day, "This proves that the church in Italy ought to reexamine itself. It doesn't have the power it claimed over the people. Even good Catholics I know voted against that law. The pope? Never have the newspapers and the television played up a pope like they have this one. And yet, what results does he get? None. What real evangelism is he accomplishing?"

This priest picked up a copy of that day's *Corriere della Sera* and showed me a headline quoting the pope's cry when he was taken to the penthouse of the Gemelli, the hospital where he was being treated after being gunned down a week earlier in St. Peter's Square: I LOVE IT! FROM HERE, I CAN SEE ST. PETER'S! "Here is a man," the priest said, "who loves power."

Either that, I said to him, or maybe adulation. He nodded. The pope's outburst may have implied neither, but we were both thinking of those spectacles in Mexico City and Dublin, Manhattan and Rio where John Paul II was mobbed by millions. The man was exhausting himself and his aides with a travel schedule that would kill four Beatles and two Lyndon Johnsons. He waved, he smiled, he sang, he kissed the tarmac of airports all over the world, he donned feathered headdresses, he kissed babies. He seemed to be running for president of the world. Whatever he was up to, it seemed more like an end in itself than a way of commending Christ in the twentieth century.

* * *

It could have been easy for John Paul, and good for the world, if he had followed the Second Vatican Council's lead when it applied faith and tradition to the problems of modern times. The council fathers produced not mere documents, but a new style of dealing with the world.

Christians would be incarnate in history, not above it. Mass would no longer be in a dead language, Latin, but in English, Urdu and Japanese. This shocked some Catholics. Church historians told them not to worry: the church had been changing things for centuries. From the beginning of its existence, its members tried to puzzle out the meaning in their daily lives of the fact that God had entered human history. Historians reminded everyone of the story told in the fifteenth chapter of the Acts of the Apostles. With astounding success, Paul, Barnabas and other disciples had carried the Good News of Christ to the Gentiles. But their confreres who had been of the Pharisees' sect and still thought of themselves as Jews said that Paul and Barnabas had to make their converts undergo circumcision and observe the Jewish law. Others insisted Jesus had freed them from the Judaism that had made it virtue to walk 39 steps on the Sabbath and vice to walk one more.

There was a good deal of contention over this. From the beginning, it was not always clear what was essential (and in a pilgrim church that may never be altogether clear). But the presbyters and apostles set a new course. Peter took the lead. He said they had a mandate to bring the Good News to the Gentiles, they did so, and God had given the Gentiles the Holy Spirit "just as he did to us." He added: "Why then do you now try to test God by putting on the neck of the disciples a yoke which neither our fathers nor we have been able to bear?"

Peter's yoke was a chain of legalisms tied to a particular place, time and culture that had little or nothing to do with what many claimed was the essence of Jesus' message: love one another.

A majority agreed with Peter. They decided Christianity differed radically from Judaism, and the difference had to do with the primacy of love over law. Christ had come to liberate people from, among other things, the excessive formalism of the Jewish law and inspire a new covenant of love and freedom.

The church of Jerusalem sent Paul and Barnabas back to the Gentiles with two other leaders, Judas and Silas, bearing a letter that attempted to outline what was and what was not essential to their faith. This was good marketing. The faith caught on. The successors of the apostles carried the Good News to other peoples in other languages and cultures (where the non-essential trappings of their Jewish past would have made the message impossible to understand). And so, the church grew in many cultures.

But the simpler the message, the easier it is to forget: nineteen centuries later, the church was still dealing with problems raised by Peter and the others in what some later called the First Council of Jerusalem. Some fathers of the Second Vatican Council thought the Latin mass was essential. A preponderant majority, those who had the same missionary instincts as Peter, decided it was not. The first mass wasn't in Latin. It was in Aramaic. After weeks of debate, the fathers voted for change.

Once the dam broke, some positions fixed for four centuries were swept away. The fathers of the council discussed and promulgated changes in polity, in practice, even in doctrine. They said they wanted to reverse centuries of too much Romanism so that the church could serve the whole world, differently in different places, for the world was not of a piece.

As Karl Rahner pointed out, this was the first council in history where the church's universality moved from theory to practice. Surrounded as they were by the church's bewildering diversity as reflected in their episcopal brethren from Kingston to Kuala Lumpur, the council fathers worked out a new theory of missionary activity. Henceforth, the church would try not to promulgate the gospel with an overlay of European language and culture. Rather, the people of God would try to make the gospel relevant in every culture. The fathers called this "enculturation," a way Christians could imitate their God who had become man.

The notion won ready acceptance from an overwhelming majority of council fathers, who saw the most immediate application of the idea in the liturgy: if dancing and drums were part of the African soul, why not a Missa Luba, with dancing and drums? Africans, among others, reacted with glee. A new vitality took hold throughout the continent. The church there started to "Africanize" itself, in its spirituality, its liturgy, its theology, its ministry.

But Karol Wojtyla, one of the bishops who voted for enculturation at Vatican II, changed his mind. In May 1980, as Pope John Paul II, he visited Africa and made clear he had an administrator's second thoughts: how could he keep these people from going too far, keep them "in line"? As Erving Goffman noted in his sociological classic, *Asylums*, this is the kind of question asked by administrators in every total institution, where rules are generally made to benefit the keepers rather than the kept.

In Zaire, to the disappointment of many of that country's 66 bishops and 15 million Catholics, the pope refused to attend a mass with dancing and drums, and tried to put the brakes on other adaptations under way. Peter Hebblethwaite, Vatican correspondent for the *National Catholic*

Reporter and perhaps the most well-informed reporter in Rome for the past decade, was following the papal party. He paraphrased what the pope said:

The dangers of Africanization were particularly apparent in worship. There should be a "substantial unity with the Roman rite."

Theology, said the pope, should not be merely a confrontation between the Gospel message and the local culture: it could not, without grave loss, ignore the cultures in which it has been historically expressed (European cultures). There is only one Gospel and one theology.

This was an incredible statement. During the church's long history, there had been one faith, but many theologies, from Augustine to Aquinas, from John of the Cross to John Courtney Murray. If this pope believed that there was only one theology, then he had just made theology into catechesis. He would be ventriloquist, theologians would become dummies. John Paul II, like Paul VI, seemed to accept uncritically what was handed to him: an absolutism few others, in or out of the church, were willing to buy. But the African trip made it clear: If Wojtyla was pope, he would be dictator, too. It was a Polish seminarian's dream come true.

Those who read press accounts of the pope's remarks said he had repealed Vatican II. And there didn't seem to be any misunderstanding. As his remarks to young married couples in Kinshasa indicated, he believed that if he let Africans Africanize their mass, soon they would try to Africanize their marriage customs, too. Would the church in Africa become so African as to allow trial marriage and polygamy? The pope knew some were suggesting that. More of Hebblethwaite's report:

The same principle was applied to marriage customs. In an address to young couples in Kinshasa, the capital of Zaire, John Paul went back to the first chapters of Genesis to show that monogamous marriage was a Semitic idea (not "European"). Africans were perfectly capable of it, and standards must not be lowered. Being a Christian means being converted.

It was a stern lecture, as though John Paul had come to Africa to retrieve a situation that was in danger of getting out of hand.

But this pope's intentions and the faith of the church did not necessarily converge. Six months later, bishops came to Rome from all over the world to participate in a general synod. There, about 40 African bishops suggested the church ought to bless African marriage customs; in Africa, they said, a marriage unfolds progressively and is not sealed until after the birth of the first child. They had heard the pope in Africa. But at the synod in Rome, they disagreed with him.

Chapter Twelve

The tale of the synod further explains the politics of sex and religion. In the fall of 1980, Pope John Paul II opened a general synod of bishops to discuss "The Role of the Family in the Modern World." To many of the 161 bishops elected to the synod by their peers, this was an opportunity. They knew *Humanae Vitae* was official doctrine. But maybe they could deal with the question anew. They realized many of the faithful had come to terms with birth control in a moral sense. But church leaders hadn't agreed on a rationale. Insofar as they hadn't, they had lost much of their authority on other moral questions as well, at a time the world needed good leadership more than ever.

Some saw the synod as a way they could help Rome take a more credible position, for the good of the church, and the globe, which seemed to be stumbling toward nuclear war. At the council, the moral authority of the world's bishops helped make the church less triumphal, more humble. Perhaps the bishops could prevail once more over those in Rome who wanted to keep things on the old, imperial, take-it-or-leave-it basis.

As it turned out, this view was too optimistic. The bishops tried their best to open some doors. But the pope and his men locked them again. This pope took the power of the keys all too literally.

The history of four previous synods since the council should have told the bishops a synod wasn't a council. A four-year council had a more leisurely pace than a four-week synod, which seemed more amenable to curial manipulation. One of Pope Paul VI's post-conciliar synods had put the lid on discussions raging in the church over clerical celibacy. And Pope John Paul II had used an extraordinary synod, attended only by himself and the Dutch bishops, to put the screws on creative movements (which the curia called heresy) in The Netherlands.

But the Vatican had created the impression it wanted an open synod. It had sent a position paper on the family to all the bishops, who were requested to consult with a wide spectrum of their priests and others, especially lay people. Many episcopal conferences took this document seriously. In May, Derek Worlock, archbishop of Liverpool, brought together 10,000 Catholics for a National Pastoral Congress in Liverpool that won extraordinary respect throughout England. "The presence of the Holy Spirit has been sensed by all of us, and in a quite remarkable way," said George Basil Hume, the Benedictine cardinal-archbishop of Westminster.[49]

What was so remarkable? *The Tablet* said it was impressed with the democratic give and take among bishops, clergy, religious and laity, who called for "a fundamental re-examination of the church's teaching on marriage, on sexuality and on contraception." *The Tablet* editorialized: "The call for change or development—to our minds the words in this context are virtually synonymous—has the support of practically the whole assembly."

The bishops of Indonesia, South Africa, France and Belgium had similar consultations with their people. They, too, were preparing for an open synod in Rome—and, again, some new statement on birth control.

So, too, were the U.S. bishops. Their four elected delegates* had presided over a nationwide consultation by mail, then met for four days in June at the University of Notre Dame.

By and large, the bishops were not surprised by some lay reactions to the Vatican position paper. They themselves tended to agree that the draft document was difficult to read and unlikely to appeal to its ultimate audience. Apparently, it also took an unrealistic view of family life, one that did not much accord with the experience of many married Catholics in the U.S.

According to a summary report of lay reactions, some respondents thought the document reflected a clerical view of marriage as inferior to the celibate religious life. One respondent felt that document's authors saw sex as suspect or immoral. Some objected to an obvious effort to endorse "Natural Family Planning."

Other objections: there was too much focus on the nuclear family, not enough on differing styles and types of family life. The document did not speak of birth control nor of the changing roles of men as well as of women. Some said the document tended to equate marriage and sex. One group said in the joint statement: " 'Unbridled disordered passion' is not the problem of Catholic married couples. It is how to make sexuality and conjugal love redemptive and sanctifying." Another commented: "There are probably more marriage breakups from the lack of sexual intimacy than from the abuse of it." Another said, "Such heavy stress on procreation and so little on love."

---

*John Quinn, archbishop of San Francisco, president of the National Conference of Catholic Bishops, Joseph Bernardin, archbishop of Cincinnati (later cardinal-archbishop of Chicago), Robert Sanchez, archbishop of Santa Fe, and J. Francis Stafford, auxiliary bishop of Baltimore.[50]

The U.S. and Canadian bishops decided to share ideas on the upcoming synod. And so, for the first time, the Canadian bishops* joined the Americans at Notre Dame. The meetings were closed, but the people there were open to the kinds of new ideas endorsed by the council, open to facts about family life in America as revealed by studies of the National Opinion Research Center done under the general guidance of Andrew Greeley.

Bishop Stafford, who handled the logistics for this meeting, brought others to Notre Dame: Richard McCormick and John Connery, Jesuits who held slightly differing opinions on key questions dealing with birth control, Dolores Leckey, executive secretary of the U.S. bishops' committee on the laity, Margaret Farley, a Sister of Mercy then studying social ethics at Yale, and, unofficially, Father Greeley. Whatever influence these men and women had on the delegates, Archbishop Quinn went to Rome prepared to ask, in the name of all the American bishops, for a wholesale re-evaluation of birth control.

This plan was hopeful. But it was also a bit naive—and the American bishops should have known. Pope John Paul II was not ready to re-evaluate anything. Nor would he let others try. He had tipped his hand in several ways before the synod began. A year earlier, in Chicago, he had harangued the American bishops on birth control, quoting their 1968 pastoral at them, as if to say, "Here's your own doctrine, when are you going to start insisting on it?" And, without getting much advice from local bishops, he chose fifteen married couples to attend the synod, which was closed to the public, as auditors. Everyone chosen was a follower of John Billings, promoter of the Billings method of natural family planning. Billings himself was there. So was a Chilean mother of 17 children. The pope hailed her as a heroine.

Some believed the pope was rigging the evidence for the synod. John F.X. Harriott, lead editorial writer for *The Tablet*, wrote an angry column about it:

> I do not believe the synod fathers wanted to hear only from married couples who have no doubts about *Humanae Vitae*. I do not believe they want any kind of doctored evidence. I do not believe they wish to lend themselves to any kind of manipulation.

Perhaps they did not wish it. But they were manipulated before, during and after the synod. And by the pope, not the curia, as Father Harriott had suggested.

He manipulated the bishops before the synod by delivering a year-long diatribe on sex. Since September 5, 1979, John Paul II had been present-

*G. Emmett Carter, cardinal-archbishop of Ontario, Joseph MacNeil, archbishop of Edmonton, president of the Canadian bishops, Henri Legare, archbishop of Grouard-McLennan, and Robert Lebel, bishop of Valleyfield, Quebec. `

ing his own special views on human sexuality, weekly lectures during his Wednesday audiences. These lectures, which would continue to be dutifully reported each week in much of the Catholic press, demonstrated a papal obsession with sex. The pope's slant was the bias of a cleric, a celibate and a Pole with old world (if not pre-Christian) ideas about "the roles" of husbands and wives.

But he saved his most bizarre ideas for the synod. At his weekly general audience in St. Peter's Square October 8, he told some 10,000 persons that husbands who look at their wives "with concupiscence" would commit adultery in the heart.

Sensational for the pope to come up with this. He was commenting on Christ's sermon on the mount, but the interpretation was from a pagan philosopher, Seneca, the stoic, who wrote in the first century: "A wise man ought to love his wife with judgment, not affection. Let him control his impulses and not be borne headlong into copulation. Nothing is fouler than to love a wife like an adulteress." In his book on contraception John Noonan had cited this passage, which survives only in the writings of St. Jerome, as an example of the stoic literary tradition in the thinking of early church fathers. Taking "concupiscence" to mean natural desire, commentators had a field day with it, and eventually, on November 5, the pope made a clarifying retraction. "Not all eros falls under Christ's condemnation of concupiscence," he said to another general audience of 7,000 visitors.

But the pope's sport with the words *eros* and *concupiscence* was only a sideshow to the synod's drama, a fairly subtle one, with principals on both sides strenuously denying a power struggle. But struggle there was, the same back and forth that went on at the council, among some of the same actors and over the same issues: love versus law, freedom versus tyranny, being "an acting person"—the words were much loved by Cardinal Wojtyla before he became pope—versus being an obedient child of the church. The difference: this synod didn't have a Pope John XXIII in his apartment silently cheering on the forces of change.

This synod met under the watchful, deadpan gaze of John Paul II, who wanted no change.[51] Many of the 161 elected bishops did. In general, they wanted the church to proclaim a new, updated, positive theology of sexuality and to teach values instead of precepts. More concretely, they wanted to take a new look at the church's ban on contraception, and to bring divorced and remarried Catholics back to communion. But they were quickly squelched by some of the 20 Curial cardinals there, and by many of the 24 at-large bishops named by the pope, including Terence Cooke, cardinal-archbishop of New York.

On September 29, at the beginning of the synod, Archbishop Quinn gave an intervention on behalf of the U.S. bishops that might have won him accolades at Vatican II. Instead, within 24 hours, he was stuttering an apology and insisting he hadn't "challenged" the pope over *Humanae Vitae*. No. In fact, he had gone obsequiously overboard by asserting, "There is no doubt that the teaching of *Humanae Vitae* on contraception is authentic teaching of the magisterium of the church," something then challenged by many theologians. But then he asked that the church set up a post-synodal commission "including theologians who support the church's teaching and those who do not . . . to express themselves with candor concerning the problems they encounter with the content and style of this teaching."

This might put the church back where it was during the 1960s when Paul VI's birth control commission was raising expectations. If Quinn wasn't issuing a challenge, he was doing almost everything but. Quinn said he accepted the teaching "as it has been enunciated by Pope Paul VI in the encyclical letter *Humanae Vitae* and by Pope John Paul II in his address to the bishops of the United States in October 1979." But he asked whether only three options were available: silence, repetition of magisterial teaching or dissent? He ventured the opinion that another course was open—one Pope Paul VI suggested, two weeks after the publication of *Humanae Vitae*, when he said the encyclical:

> . . . clarifies a fundamental chapter in the personal, married, family and social life of man, but it is not a complete treatment regarding man in this sphere of marriage, of the family and of moral probity. This is an immense field to which the magisterium of the church could and perhaps should return with a fuller, more organic and more synthetic exposition.

Quinn suggested that the time for that new study was now. He noted that many men and women of good will did not accept the "intrinsic evil of each and every use of contraception." He quoted a recent Princeton study reporting that 76.5 percent of U.S. Catholic women were practicing birth control, 94 percent of them using methods condemned by the encyclical and that only 29 percent of U.S. clergy believed contraception was immoral, reflecting a conviction found among "theologians and pastors whose learning, faith, discretion and dedication to the church are beyond doubt." These authorities did not believe that contraception was good, desirable or morally indifferent. Their problem, said Quinn, was in the teaching recognized by the code words *quilibet actus*—that every marriage act must be open to the transmission of life.

Quinn argued that the church could not dismiss this fact, and pointed out that the church "has always recognized the principle and fact of doctrinal development." He cited examples indicating that by development he meant change: Vatican II had reversed previous papal teachings on biblical studies and religious liberty. Even on birth control, he said, change had already taken place:

> The fact that in practice, the widespread nonobservance of the teaching is coupled with widespread reception of the eucharist and that in the realm of theory a notable body of theological opinion reinforces dissenting practice, means that the moral issue as such has been resolved by many.

The problem then was not moral but "ecclesiological." Quinn might have used the term "political," for he worried about the eroding power of the magisterium. Quinn called this "a major challenge" for the synod. And it couldn't be met "without treating the doctrine of contraception *in se.*" He said the synod could not repeat past formulas or ignore dissent. He proposed that delegates promote three things: 1) a new context for the teaching that would elaborate the church's views on the responsible transmission of life and articulate its comprehensive teaching on human sexuality, 2) formal dialogue among Catholic theologians throughout the world on the problems raised by dissent from *Humanae Vitae,* and 3) careful attention to the process used in writing magisterial documents. In effect, he was proposing that a teaching document really teach:

> . . . it will not be sufficient to publish magisterial documents which are correct and precise from a doctrinal and theological point of view alone. Today these kinds of documents are widely publicized and are no longer read only by bishops, priests or specialists. They are summarized or highlighted and appear in major newspapers all over the world, often distorted and not infrequently appearing ridiculous in this distorted version.

Quinn called for an international staff skilled in the art of journalism to help write magisterial documents "in a language which would be directly comprehensible to moderately educated people in today's world."

He was not alone in such a call. On the same day, Cardinal Hume told the synod about those folk in England and Wales who could not accept *Humanae Vitae.* "It cannot just be said that these persons have failed to overcome their human frailty and weakness. Indeed, such persons are often good, conscientious and faithful sons and daughters of the church. They just cannot accept that the use of artificial means of contraception in some circumstances is 'intrinsically wrong' as this matter has been generally understood." And, he said, their views represented for the church a genuine *fons theologiae,* a fact for theologians to theologize about.

Cardinal Carter of Toronto, echoing Hume, noted that many eminent theologians and Catholic couples had moved beyond *Humanae Vitae.* He suggested this was a way the Holy Spirit was speaking to the whole church and an expression of the *sensus fidelium.* He concluded that "the magisterium must take account of this phenomenon or run the risk of speaking in a vacuum."

And what was the synod's reaction to all this? Almost nil. Quinn's concrete proposals sank with hardly a trace. No one took up Hume's request for a formula that would solve matters, though some few voices in the wilderness would try. Denis Hurley, archbishop of Durban, South Africa, focused attention again on that difficult phrase "intrinsically evil," applied to contraception, but not to killing. In Archbishop Hurley's intervention, mysteriously suppressed by L'Osservatore Romano (but reprinted almost a month later by The Tablet), he said that he found it difficult to explain to his people:

> . . . that the act of artificially limiting the exercise of one faculty of life is intrinsically evil, while the act of exterminating life itself is not, for in certain circumstances a person may kill, as in self-defense or in a so-called just war. An argument from natural law which is difficult to follow produces a grave obligation. This makes us fall back on the argument from authority. This is the very thing that . . . cannot be done without detracting from the value of the teaching.[52]

Hurley's views contrasted with those of many at the synod who had seen which way the papal wind was blowing by watching Quinn recant. Insiders say Quinn got the word the pope was unhappy, but they can only speculate on how. Was it sufficient for Quinn to hear Pericle Felici, one of the top curial cardinals, dismiss Quinn's intervention with this terse comment next day in the synod hall: "There is no need of rediscussing Humanae Vitae, no need to pay attention to statistics, because statistics don't signify anything"? Or did he need to hear two other big guns—Joseph Hoffner, cardinal-archbishop of Cologne, speaking for the Germans, and Carlo Martini, cardinal-archbishop of Milan, speaking for the Italians—who also denounced "counting heads" as a way of discovering the sensus fidelium?

Emmett Carter, who was close to the U.S. delegation, said in a private interview in 1984 that he doubted that anyone had put pressure on Quinn. He said Quinn was the first one at the synod to discuss anything reportable. "The press put the spotlight on Quinn," said Cardinal Carter. "It was too glaring. And therefore, it was a false light. He had to move out of that light."

Quinn made haste at a news conference on September 30 to take back what he'd said the day before. He did so by repudiating press accounts of his speech as "clearly incorrect." Peter Hebblethwaite bought this calumny against the press. He said Quinn's paper "fell into the hands of a certain news agency which reduced it to a lone-line summary: ARCHBISHOP QUINN CHALLENGES POPE OVER HUMANAE VITAE IN SYNOD."

He had no option [wrote Hebblethwaite] but to issue a *dementi*
the next day in which he reaffirmed his support for *Humanae Vitae*.
But by saying this he seemed to be withdrawing also the other valuable suggestions that he had made and to be minimizing the very real
problems to which he had drawn attention. Thus a single asinine
journalist may be said to have wrecked the synod.

Wrong. If Hebblethwaite was referring to the Associated Press, that
agency's report was rather complete. *The New York Times* carried the AP
story at the top of page one and it wasn't a "lone-line summary," it ran 17
column inches. As befitting its roles as a newspaper of record, *The Times*
also printed 16 column inches of excerpts from Quinn's speech, which
demonstrated to readers that the AP reporter had gotten it exactly right.
No "single asinine reporter . . . wrecked the synod." If anyone wrecked
Hebblethwaite's synod, the pope did, and those bishops who decided to
stick with *Humanae Vitae*.

After Quinn's widely publicized "clarification," one bishop after another got up in the synod to say the teaching of *Humanae Vitae* was certainly correct. Contraception was intrinsically evil. But the church should
take a "pastoral approach." Married couples who couldn't follow the teaching would be told to be patient with themselves and work toward "the
ideal" presented in the official teaching. Many bishops referred to "the law
of gradualness." Father Martelet, who had always seen the encyclical as
presenting an ideal, certainly nothing with the force of positive law, had
been writing in this vein for some time.*

Americans may have had a hard time understanding "the law of gradualness." Laws are to help people, not hurt them, and if they are observed
mostly in the breach (as they were during Prohibition) they are repealed.

---

*Those from a Latin tradition probably understood. But did the rest of the
world?

Thomas Reese, an American Jesuit reporting on the synod for *America,* put it in
context for his U.S. readers:

> The Italian bishops take it for granted that men and women are sinners,
> nonobservers of the law. For them it is more important that the church hold
> firm to an ideal law than that the law be adapted so that it is easier to ob-
> serve.

> Many people pointed out to me that Italian law forbids two people riding
> on a motorbike but that every motorbike made in Italy has a seat for two per-
> sons. The only time I saw the law enforced was when a young police officer
> stopped two pretty girls on a motorbike. They knew, he knew and the crowd
> that gathered knew that the law was the least of his reasons for stopping
> them. Americans, on the other hand, get nervous when laws are not ob-
> served. . . .

These interventions changed the synod's course. The bishops didn't look at contraception *in se,* as Quinn had suggested, they put the issue back in the realm of agreeing or not with the pope. The bishops were making an effort to save the pope's authority but, to those who had an Anglo-Saxon view of law, they lost it again in that very process.

James Tunstead Burtchaell, an American theologian from Notre Dame, read press accounts of the synod, then wrote a U.S. bishop in Rome to tell him how they were losing credibility:

Either Paul VI was right when he taught that every single act of contraception was morally evil, or he was mistaken. If he was right, then the only helpful pastoral attitude toward contraception is to repeat, in season and out of season, that it is destructive. If he was mistaken, then the only pastoral attitude we can adopt is to admit the mistake and revise the teaching. What would be very harmful to the magisterium would be to repeat that he was right but say that it doesn't matter very much. That makes morality a matter of bad feelings between humans and their God, rather than one of substantial welfare and relationships.

What does make morality? The old Baltimore Catechism approach leaned on Roman handbooks full of explicit guidelines, written out of a legalistic mentality that told people how far they could go before crossing the line between venial and mortal sin. But a new Catholic view was emerging. In 1978, Archbishop Hurley tried to sum it up in *The Tablet*:

. . . in complex human situations there can be a conflict of moral values in which the choice must be left to the conscience of the individual. The important thing in this regard is that moral values that can come into conflict must be thoroughly weighed to ensure that the more important ones receive the respect that is their due. . . .

For several decades Catholic moral theologians had been trying to work out principles that could help people weigh the values and disvalues in any conflict situation. Their discussions went on and on; the literature they produced was enormous. Had the bishops reported these dicussions to the people at large, they could have served those confronted with daily conflict situations. The synod did not do that.

Some fathers suggested this approach. Hubert Ernst, bishop of Breda in The Netherlands, pointed out that the church's teaching on social ethics sticks to general principles and leaves application to individual conscience. Why, he asked, should the church's teaching on sexual ethics descend to so many specifics? Why not let people work out the implications for themselves?

Hebblethwaite reported that a number of French bishops echoed Ernst's idea. And Godfried Daneels, successor to Cardinal Suenens in

Malines-Brussels, said the church should emphasize values, not rules. These interventions seemed an intelligent way to proceed. Surely the church, being universal, wouldn't want to "solve" every local problem with a single, univocal solution?

None of these interventions seemed to matter. Paul VI may have wanted honest advice from previous synods. John Paul II didn't want to encourage what Quinn called "a completely honest examination of the serious problems which fidelity to the teaching of the church creates for individuals, for pastors and for the world." This pope wanted a celebration of unity on a subject that had long divided the church and confused the faithful. The debate was over, as the synod would demonstrate.

At an "academic session" October 10, five physicians proclaimed the virtue and efficacy of "natural methods of birth control." And Father Martelet, one of the authors of *Humanae Vitae,* told the synod that *Humanae Vitae* had been amply vindicated. Hebblethwaite wrote:

> All the synodal sideshows—the so-called "academic session" on 10 October, the renewal of marriage vows in St. Peter's Square on "World Family Day" on 12 October, the session devoted to "witnesses" that same evening—were designed to demonstrate that the church was united on these most contentious issues. So it was not surprising that Pope John Paul, at the Angelus on the day after the synod had ended and slipped into history, should say that "the synod has shown the unity which exists among the world's bishops." That, after all, was its purpose.

But at what cost? During the synod John Paul II commemorated the anniversary of Albert Einstein's birth by announcing a process was underway to rehabilitate Galileo and rescind his conviction as a heretic. At the same time he was screwing down the lid on efforts to apply reason once more in the battle over birth control. During the council, 16 years before, Cardinal Suenens had pleaded that the church "avoid another Galileo case. One is enough for the church."

Joseph Selling guessed Pope John Paul could agree with this sentiment only if it was modified to read "One Galileo case at a time."

Nothing could help Dr. Selling prove the pope was leading the church into another Galileo case any more than the Quinn affair. By the end of the synod, Quinn was making no sense at all. At the final press conference sponsored by the U.S. bishops on October 23, he said the synod, which had thrown out everything he had proposed, had been "magnificent." Furthermore, he explained why a doctrine that was not received in 1968 should be welcomed on its reassertion in 1980. His reasons: because contraception had not reduced the number of abortions and because divorce statistics had risen. As a result of these bitter experiences, he said, more people were ready to accept the church's teaching.

Not proven. On the contrary, blocs of bishops at the synod were ready to re-evaluate not only the church's teaching on birth control but also the long standing condemnation of Catholics who had divorced and remarried. Among the Greek Orthodox, some bishops pointed out, those living in second marriages are not denied the sacraments; they are even allowed the sacraments when attending Roman Catholic liturgies. Archbishop Worlock reported Catholic couples in second marriages "long for the restoration of full eucharistic communion with the church and its Lord," and asked, "Is this spirit of repentance and desire for sacramental strength to be forever frustrated?"

Though seven out of eleven synod subcommittees agreed with Worlock, the synod's final answer to his question was yes because it was the pope's answer as he ended the synod October 25.

That answer made page one of *The New York Times*:

POPE ENDS SYNOD,
    DEFINES STRICT RULE
    FOR THE REMARRIED
        Asserts Such Divorced Catholics
        May Receive Communion Only
        if They Abstain from Sex

The headline said it all. The pope made no mention that many bishops had proposed the church at least study this question further. Selling's comment on the pope's decision was refreshing. He called the suggested "brother-sister" arrangement an abomination.

> Once another relationship has been entered into, fostered, lived, even made "fruitful," and the cares and burdens of living out that relationship have been taken on as a commitment, who really cares whether or not such a couple is having a sexual relationship? Healthy married people, and those who have come to terms with their own sexuality, certainly do not mind. It is time that we liberate ourselves from the notion that one's sexual behavior is the final criterion of a moral life. If remarried persons can in fact be welcomed back into the community, if they can be allowed to fully participate in the life of the church, why must they be barred from receiving the eucharist simply because they wish their lives to be complete, including acts which are "noble and worthy"?[53]

According to *The Tablet*, the rest of the pope's concluding remarks did "little more than echo what were foregone conclusions virtually imposed on a so-called consultative body." But the pope made one other specific comment on the synod's work. He said, "the law of gradualness . . . cannot be the same as gradualness of the law, as if there were various grades or forms of commandment for different men and circumstances in the divine law."

Here, the pope was denying in so many words exactly what some fathers of the synod were trying to tell him: the church was not a monolith; that in moral matters dealing with such an intimate and intricate institution as the family, the pope could not expect the whole world to follow a formulation of the divine law that had been written from some very special perspectives—and by a tiny group of celibate clerics who were more eager to preserve what they perceived as traditional doctrine than inclined to plumb the depths of God's intentions for humankind.

The Canadian bishops were unhappy with the way things had gone. Cardinal Carter said the synod was "disappointing for those of us who lived through the council. The synod is the child of the council, and we were looking for a continuation of collegiality." The Canadians were so miffed they produced their own statement. "The church," they said, "is not concentrated in the bishops, but is indeed fulfilled in all of us and particularly in all our families." They were convinced that "solutions to many of the problems we face will be found only when family members accept the ministry of bringing the Good News to their own situations."

So this was a family problem that families should attempt to solve. Two American journalists had already said as much when they satirized the pope's widely published condemnation of husbands who look on their wives with concupiscence. Art Buchwald, the syndicated columnist, confessed that he had concupiscence for his wife, not just a little, but a lot. Excerpts:

> I can't look at her without having this instinctive urge to do something about it. I know it diminishes the richness of our marriage, and can cause great problems in our interpersonal relations, but I can't help myself. What makes it worse is that she has concupiscence, too. . . . We were just getting to accept our lust when Pope John Paul came out with his strong statement. Then the roof fell in. I was reading the newspaper when my wife walked into the bedroom in her silk negligee.
> "Any news?" she asked.
> "Nothing much," I said, trying not to look at her.
> She put on a Henry Mancini record.
> "Okay," I said, "knock it off."
> "What did I do wrong?"
> "Nothing, but we can't practice concupiscence any more. It lowers the dignity of our marriage and brings out the worst in us."
> She started to cry. "Is there somebody else?"
> "If you must know, there is," I said.

"Who is it?"

"Pope John Paul. And don't ask me to go into the sordid details."

Paul Conrad, the prize-winning cartoonist from *The Los Angeles Times*, made the same statement with one picture, no words: a drawing of the pope stretched out in bed between a startled couple.

Footnotes

In general, I have tried to give my sources in the text itself (unless that inhibited the narrative flow). It must be clear to readers that I have reconstructed the history of the Pontifical Commission for the Study of Population, the Family and Birth from the commission's records themselves. I found these unavailable at the Vatican, but discovered other copies elsewhere: in the Crowley Collection at the Archives of the University of Notre Dame, in the personal papers of John T. Noonan in Berkeley, California, and in the personal archives of Bishop Josef Maria Reuss in Mainz, West Germany. Bishop Reuss' papers were in remarkable order, tied with heavy cord and sealed with wax seals. I may have been the first scholar to see them.

I am indebted to Canon Pierre de Locht of Brussels for setting down many of his recollections on the commission's work in a diary, parts of which he reprinted in *Les Couples et l'Eglise* (Paris: Editions du Centurion, 1979), which he generously gave me permission to use. To gain further perspectives on the work of the commission, I had extended interviews with some of its members: notably, Cardinal Suenens, Patty Crowley, John T. Noonan, Bishop Reuss, de Locht, Dr. John Marshall, Thomas K. Burch, Giacomo Perico, Alfons Auer and Bernard Häring.

For those readers who want more:

Introduction

1. The best histories of the Second Vatican Ecumenical Council available in English are (in alphabetical order): Rock Caporale, *Vatican II: Last of the Councils* (Baltimore: Helicon, 1964); Yves Congar, *Report from Rome* (Montreal: Palm, 1963 and 1964); Robert Blair Kaiser, *Pope, Council and World* (New York: Macmillan, 1963); Michael Novak, *The Open Church* (New York: Macmillan, 1964); Xavier Rynne, *Letters from Vatican City, The Second Session, The Third Session, The Fourth Session* (New York: Farrar, Straus, 1963, 1964, 1965, 1966); Edward Schillebeeckx, *The Real Achievement of Vatican II* (New York: Herder and Herder, 1967); and Ralph Wiltgen, *The Rhine Flows into the Tiber* (New York: Hawthorn, 1967).

The best commentary is a five-volume series under the general editorship of Herbert Vorgrimler published by the international editorial consortium called *Concilium*. The U.S. edition was published as *Commentary on the Documents of Vatican II* (New York: Herder and Herder, 1968).

Readers will find a short, readable and very well-annotated history of the development of Catholic doctrine by the Dutch Dominican Mark Schoof, *A Survey of Catholic Theology, 1830-1970* (New York: Paulist Newman Press, 1970).

241

Interest in George Tyrrell has been enkindled by several recent studies: Ellen Leonard, *George Tyrrell and the Catholic Tradition* (London: Darton, Longman and Todd, 1983), David G. Schultenover, *George Tyrrell: In Search of Catholicism* (London: Patmos Press, 1981) and David F. Wells, *The Prophetic Theology of George Tyrrell* (London Scholars PUS, 1982). Also: *Letters from a 'Modernist': The Letters of George Tyrrell to Wilfred Ward (1893-1908)*, Mary Jo Weaver (ed.) (London: Patmos Press, 1981).

2. Patrick Boyle, a Jesuit theologian from Loyola University of Chicago, detailed the entire history of the "no small matter" doctrine in his 1983 doctoral dissertation at Marquette University, "*Parvitas Materiae in Sexto* in Contemporary Catholic Thought."

3. Yves Congar has written a history of the development of the term "magisterium": "*Pour une histoire semantique de term 'magisterium'*" and "*Bref historique des formes du 'magistere' et du ses relations avec les docteurs*," both in *Revue des sciences philosophiques et theologiques* 60 (1976).

4. Msgr. Kelly's book was called *The Battle for the American Church* (New York: Doubleday, 1981).

5. Cf. Charles A. Buswell, bishop of Pueblo, Colorado, "Dissent is not Disloyalty," *Commonweal* 89 (1968).

Hans Küng described "the paradigm shift" in a December 1983 interview with Patricia Lefebvre in *The National Catholic Reporter*. John Cogley did his "Poems on Postcards" for *America* during the council years, 1963-1965.

6. Cardinal Suenens used the nautical metaphor in a letter written in advance to the people of Great Britain before a visit there in 1970. It was printed in *The Tablet*, 3 October 1970.

7. Quotes from the 1980 synod came from *Origins*, published by the U.S. Catholic Conference in the fall of 1980.

Gabriel Daly quotes from *The Tablet*, 25 April 1981.

8. Bishop Mugavero's letter was printed in *Catholic Mind* 74, no. 1303 (May 1976), Father McCormick's comments in his *Notes on Moral Theology* (Washington: University Press of America), p. 679.

9. Quotes from Michel Foucault come from *The History of Sexuality, Volume I: An Introduction* (New York: Vintage Books, 1980).

Chapter One

10. Bishop Bekkers' remarks were printed in *Herder Correspondence*, October 1963.

11. My own 40,000-word file for *Time* helped me recall my 1964 interviews in The Netherlands, Belgium and France.

Chapter Two

12. Msgr. Sheridan's column appeared in the 17 April 1964 issue of *The Tidings*.

13. St. John-Stevas did a book on this: *The Agonizing Choice: Birth Control, Religion and the Law* (London: Eyre and Spottiswoode, 1971).

14. Accounts of the events at Notre Dame were published as *Conference on the Problem of Population* (Chicago: University of Notre Dame Press, 1964, 1965).

15. The Buelenses statement appeared in *The Tablet*, 24 October 1964, pp. 1212-13.

Chapter Three

16. Häring's remarks appeared in *Commentary on the Documents of Vatican II,* Vorgrimler (ed.) (New York: Herder and Herder, 1968).

17. See also John N. Kotre, *Simple Gifts: The Lives of Pat and Patty Crowley* (New York: Andrews & McMeel, 1979).

18. My information about the flap over the NCCM affair came from interviews during 1982 and 1983 with John Walsh, John Leo and Martin Work, and from documentation supplied by Walsh and Leo.

Chapter Four

19. Readers can follow Noonan's entire argument in *Contraception: A History of Its Treatment by the Catholic Theologians and Canonists* (Cambridge: Harvard Univ. Press, 1965).

Chapter Five

20. Information on *The Green Book* came from Bishop Reuss' archives at Mainz. The story about Paul VI's trying to short-circuit everything with a simple *allocutio* in September 1965 came from separate interviews with Canon Victor Heylen and Father Arthur McCormack.

21. A report on Father Häring's sermon appeared in the *National Catholic Reporter,* 7 September 1965.

22. Davis himself gave me a copy of the paper he read to the English bishops.

23. Details from Cavallari's book, *The Changing Vatican* (New York: Doubleday, 1967).

Chapter Six

24. I found documentation on Ford's moves toward Vagnozzi, Ottaviani and Paul VI in an archive on *Schema* 13 in the library at *La Civiltà Cattolica* in Rome.

25. Accounts by Xavier Rynne in *The Fourth Session*; by St. John-Stevas in *The Agonizing Choice* (both cited above). Grootaers' report appeared in his essay "Trois Lectures," reprinted in H. & L. Buelens-Gijsen and Jan Grootaers, *Mariage Catholique et contraception* (Paris: E. de l'Epi, 1968). Ambrogio Valsecchi's report came from his *Controversy* (Washington: Corpus Books, 1968).

26. Details on the extra-conciliar meeting in the Reuss archives at Mainz.

27. Leo Josef Suenens, *Love and Control* (London: Burns & Oates, 1961).

Chapter Seven

28. Ford's report printed in *The Tablet,* 29 March 1967, pp. 478-85.

29. Majority theologians' rebuttal in *The Tablet,* 6 May 1967, pp. 510-13.

Chapter Eight

30. See the treatment of *malum physicum* and pre-moral evil in Joseph Selling, *The Reaction to Humanae Vitae* (Ann Arbor: University Microfilms, 1979), pp. 776 ff.

Chapter Nine

31. Conference papers were published in James T. McHugh (ed.), *Marriage in the Light of Vatican II* (Washington, D.C.: United States Catholic Conference, Family Life Bureau, 1968).

32. Bruce Stewart's letter appeared in *The Tablet,* 19 November 1966, p. 1309.

33. Perico's article appeared in *La Civiltà Cattolica,* 19 November 1966.

34. The story of "The Big Leak" came from interviews with Gary MacEoin and an oral history with Robert G. Hoyt on file at the Archives of the University of

Notre Dame. All four reports were reprinted in Hoyt's *The Birth Control Debate* (Kansas City: The National Catholic Reporter Press, 1968).

35. Story of the Curran affair at CU: from interviews with some of the principals and from the notes and papers of Father Curran.

36. I found Cardinal Ottaviani's 15-page paper in the Reuss archives in Mainz. They were also summarized in Selling, *The Reaction to Humanae Vitae,* cited above, p. 149.

37. Msgr. Lambruschini's news conference documented in *Catholic Mind* 66 (1969), n. 1225, pp. 49-57, and in *The Tablet,* 14 September 1968, p. 924.

38. Statement of the 21 theologians reported in Selling, p. 161.

Chapter Ten

39. Reactions to *Humanae Vitae* quoted here came from news files, from two books, F.V. Joannes, *The Bitter Pill* (Philadelphia: Pilgrim Press, 1970); Robert G. Hoyt, cited above, and from Joseph Selling's doctoral dissertation at Louvain, *The Reaction to Humanae Vitae,* also cited above.

40. Ricoeur's comments in "Wonder, Eroticism and Enigma," *Cross Currents,* Spring 1964, pp. 140-141.

41. Callahan's remarks in "An Alternative Proposal," *Commonweal,* 23 August 1968.

42. The CU affair was well chronicled in two books: Charles E. Curran and Robert E. Hunt, *Dissent in and for the Church,* and John F. Hunt and Terrence R. Connelly, *The Responsibility of Dissent: The Church and Academic Freedom* (both New York: Sheed and Ward, 1969).

43. Bishop Shannon himself told me his own story in a long dinner interview in Minneapolis, early June, 1982.

Chapter Eleven

44. William Shannon, *The Lively Debate* (New York: Sheed and Ward, 1970). Curiously, Shannon took the trouble to get a *Nihil Obstat* and an *Imprimatur* for this work. Rosemary Haughton quote from "Toward a Christian Theory of Sexuality," *Cross Currents,* Fall 1968, p. 289.

45. Final report by Westhoff and Bumpass published in *Science* 179 (1973), pp. 41-44.

46. Greeley's study reported in part in his *The American Catholic: A Social Portrait* (New York: Basic Books, 1977).

47. Cardinal Cicognani's confidential letter reported in a three-part series in *The Tablet,* "The Vatican and World Population: Note to Episcopal Conferences I-III," 16-30 March 1974.

48. Suenens' remarks appeared in "L'unité de l'eglise dans la logique de Vatican II: Le Cardinal Suenens repond aux questions de Jose de Broucher," *Informations Catholiques Internationales,* 15 May 1969.

49. The Küng material comes from his *Infallible? An Inquiry* (New York: Doubleday, 1971).

50. Notes on the pre-synod meetings of the U.S. and Canadian bishops are on file at the University of Notre Dame Archives.

51. I reconstructed the meetings of the 1980 synod through *Origins,* published by the U.S. Catholic Conference in Washington, D.C., news accounts in *The Tablet, The National Catholic Reporter, The National Catholic Register, The Wanderer*

and from the definitive work by Jan Grootaers and Joseph Selling, *The 1980 Synod of Bishops "On the Role of the Family"* (Leuven: University Press, 1983).

52. Archbishop Hurley's remarks finally made print in *The Tablet,* 8 November 1980, p. 1106.

53. Selling's remarks appeared in "Gedachten bij de Synode over huwelijk en gesin 1980," *Sacerdos* 48 (Maart 1981), n. 3, pp. 291-305.

Appendix A

Members of the Pontifical Commission on Population, Family and Birth
The Most Rev. Leo Binz, archbishop of St. Paul, Minnesota
The Most Rev. Joseph Reuss, auxiliary bishop of Mainz, Germany
Canon Paul Anciaux, professor of the major seminary of Malines, Belgium
Rev. Alfons Auer, professor of theology, Würzburg, Germany
Dr. Donald Barrett, professor of sociology, University of Notre Dame, Indiana
Dr. J.R. Bertolus, psychoanalyst, Paris, France
Dr. Thomas Burch, population expert, Georgetown University, Washington, D.C.
Dr. John R. Cavanagh, psychiatrist, professor, Catholic University of America, Washington, D.C.
Dr. Colin Clark, economist, professor, Oxford University, England
Prof. Bernardo Colombo, professor, Venice and Padua, Italy
Dr. Mercedes B. Concepcion, demographer, professor, University of the Philippines, Manila
Mr. and Mrs. Patrick Crowley, Christian Family Movement, Chicago, Illinois
Canon Philippe Delhaye, Catholic theological faculty, University of Lille, France
Dr. Michael Dembélé, director of the Ministry of Planning, Dakar, Senegal
Dr. Manuel Diegues, Rio de Janeiro, Brazil
Dr. Anthony Feanny, Kingston, Jamaica
Dr. Jacques Férin, gynecologist, professor, University of Louvain, Belgium
Rev. John C. Ford, S.J., Catholic University of America, Washington, D.C.
Rev. Joseph Fuchs, S.J., Gregorian University, Rome, Italy
Dr. Marcel Gaudefroy, gynecologist, Lille, France
Rev. Tullo Goffi, seminary professor, Brescia, Italy
Prof. Albert Görres, professor of medicine and psychology, Frankfurt, Germany
Rev. Bernard Häring, C.SS.R., moral theologian, Rome, Italy
Dr. André E. Hellegers, gynecologist, Johns Hopkins University, Baltimore, Maryland
Msgr. George A. Kelly, director of the Family Life Bureau, New York, New York
Mrs. J.F. Kulanday, Public Health Department, New Delhi, India
Rev. Michel Labourdette, O.P., theologian, Toulouse, France
Msgr. Ferdinando Lambruschini, theologian, University of the Lateran, Rome, Italy
Rev. Louis Lebret, O.P., sociologist, Paris, France

Msgr. G. Lemaitre, president of the Pontifical Academy of Sciences, Louvain, Belgium

Rev. Stanislas de Lestapis, S.J., theologian, Paris, France

Canon Pierre de Locht, National Center of Family Pastoral Work, Brussels, Belgium

Prof. Juan Jose Lopez-Ibor, psychiatrist, University of Madrid, Spain

Msgr. Jean Margeot, vicar-general of the diocese of Port Louis, Mauritius

Dr. John Marshall, neurologist, University of London, England

Prof. A. Mattelart, sociologist, Catholic University of Santiago, Chile

Prof. André van Melsen, philosopher of science, Nijmegen, Holland

Rev. Clement Mertens, S.J., population expert, Eegenhoven, Belgium

Prof. Jacques Mertens de Wilmars, economist, Louvain, Belgium

Dr. Henri Moins, Tunis, Tunisia

Dr. Paul Moriguchi, Tokyo, Japan

Rev. Giacomo Perico, S.J., theologian, University of Milan, Italy

Dr. and Mrs. Laurent Potvin, Ottawa, Ontario

Dr. R. Rabary, Tananarive, Madagascar

Dr. J. Razafinbahiny, sociologist, Madagascar

Dr. and Mrs. Henri Rendu, Paris, France

Rev. Henri de Riedmatten, O.P., Geneva and Fribourg, Switzerland

Dr. Pierre Van Rossum, Brussels, Belgium

Mr. John C. Ryan, demographer, Bangalore, India

Rev. J. Sasaki, demographer, University of Eichi, Osaka, Japan

Rev. Raymond Sigmond, O.P., Institute of Social Studies, *Angelicum*, Rome, Italy

Dr. Marcel Thibault, director of the Center of Zoological Research, Paris, France

Rev. Jan Visser, C.SS.R., theologian, Lateran University, Rome, Italy

Prof. Francesco Vito, rector of the University of the Sacred Heart, Milan, Italy

Rev. Marcelino Zalba, S.J., theologian, Gregorian University, Rome, Italy

Consultant: Dr. John T. Noonan, University of Notre Dame, Indiana

Appendix B

Commission Final Report

The pastoral constitution on the Church in the modern world *(Gaudium et Spes)* has not explained the question of responsible parenthood under all its aspects. To those problems as yet unresolved, a response is to be given in what follows. This response, however, can only be understood if it is grasped in an integrated way within the universal concept of salvation history.

In creating the world, God gave man the power and the duty to form the world in spirit and freedom and, through his creative capacity, to actuate his own personal nature. In his Word, God himself, as the first efficient cause of the whole evolution of the world and of man, is present and active in history. The story of God and of man, therefore, should be seen as a shared work. And it should be seen that man's tremendous progress in control of matter by technical means, and the universal and total "intercommunication" that has been achieved, correspond perfectly to the divine decrees (cf. *Gaudium et Spes* [*GS*], I, c. 3).

In the fullness of time, the Word of the eternal Father entered into history and took his place within it, so that by his work humanity and the world might become sharers in salvation. After his ascension to the Father, the Lord continues to accomplish his work through the church. As God became man, so his church is really incarnate in the world. But because the world, to which the church ought to represent the mystery of Christ, always undergoes changes, the church itself necessarily and continually is in pilgrimage. Its essence and fundamental structures remain immutable always; and yet no one can say of the church that at any time it is sufficiently understood or bounded by definition (cf. Paul VI *Ecclesiam Suam* and in his opening speech to the second session of Vatican Council II).

The church was constituted in the course of time by Christ, its principle of origin is the Word of creation and salvation. For this reason the church draws understanding of its own mystery not only from the past, but standing in the present time and looking to the future, assumes within itself the whole progress of the human race. The church is always being made more sure of this. What John XXIII wished to express by the word "aggiornamento," Paul VI took up, using the phrase "dialogue with the world," and in his encyclical *Ecclesiam Suam* has the following: "The world cannot be saved from the outside. As the Word of God became man, so must a man to a certain degree identify with the forms of life of those to whom he wishes to bring the message of Christ. Without invoking privileges, which would

248

but widen the separation, without employing unintelligible terminology, he must share the common way of life—provided that it is human and honorable—especially of the most humble, if he wishes to be listened to and understood" (par. 87).

In response to the many problems posed by the changes occurring today in almost every field, the church in Vatican Council II has entered into the way of dialogue. "The church guards the heritage of God's Word and draws from it religious and moral principles, without always having at hand the solution to particular problems. She desires thereby to add the light of revealed truth to mankind's store of experience, so that the path which humanity has taken in recent times will not be a dark one" (GS, I, c. 3, § 33).

In its fulfillment of its mission the church must propose obligatory norms of human and Christian life from the deposit of faith in an open dialogue with the world. But since moral obligations can never be detailed in all their concrete particularities, the personal responsiblity of each individual must always be called into play. This is even clearer today because of the complexity of modern life: the concrete moral norms to be followed must not be pushed to an extreme.

In the present study, dealing with problems relating to responsible parenthood, the Holy Father through his willingness to enter into dialogue has given it an importance unprecedented in history. After several years of study, a commission of experts called together by him, made up for the most part of laymen from various fields of competency, has prepared material for him, which was lastly examined by a special group of bishops.

PART 1: FUNDAMENTAL PRINCIPLES
Chapter 1: The Fundamental Values of Marriage

"The well-being of the individual person and of human and Christian society is intimately linked with the healthy condition of that community produced by marriage and the family. Hence Christians and all men who hold this community in high esteem sincerely rejoice in the various ways by which men today find help in fostering this community of love and perfecting its life, and by which spouses and parents are assisted in their lofty calling. Those who rejoice in such aid look for additional benefits from them and labour to bring them about." (GS, II, c. 1, § 47).

Over the course of centuries the church, with the authority conferred it by Christ our Lord, has constantly protected the dignity and essential values of this institution whose author is God himself, who had made man to his image and raised him to share in his love. It has always taught this to its faithful and to all men. In our day it again intends to propose to those many families who are seeking a right way how they are able, in the conditions of our times, to live and develop fully the higher gifts of this community.

A couple (*unio conjugum*) ought to be considered above all a community of persons which has in itself the beginning of new human life. Therefore those things which strengthen and make more profound the union of persons within this community must never be separated from the procreative finality which specifies the conjugal community. Pius XI, in *Casti Connubii* already, referring to the tradition expressed in the Roman Catechism, said: "This mutual inward molding of a husband and wife, this determined effort to perfect each other, can in a very real sense be said to be the chief reason and purpose of matrimony, provided matrimony be looked at not in the restricted sense as instituted for the conception and education of the child, but more widely as the blending of life as a whole and the mutual interchange and sharing thereof" (AAS., XXII, 1930, page 547).

But conjugal love, without which marriage would not be a true union of persons, is not exhausted in the simple mutual giving in which one party seeks only the other. Married people know well that they are only able to perfect each other and establish a true community if their love does not end in a merely egotistic union but according to the condition of each is made truly fruitful in the creation of new life. Nor on the other hand can the procreation and education of a child be considered a truly human fruitfulness unless it is the result of a love existing in a family community. Conjugal love and fecundity are in no way opposed, but complement one another in such a way that they constitute an almost indivisible unity.

Unfolding the natural and divine law, the church urges all men to be true dispensers of the divine gifts, to act in conformity with their own personal nature and to shape their married life according to the dictates of the natural and divine law. God created man male and female so that, joined together in the bonds of love, they might perfect one another through a mutual, corporal and spiritual giving and that they might carefully prepare their children, the fruit of this love, for a truly human life. Let them regard one another always as persons and not as mere objects. Therefore everything should be done in marriage so that the goods conferred on this institution can be attained as perfectly as possible and so that fidelity and moral rightness can be served.

Chapter II: Responsible Parenthood and the Regulation of Conception

To cultivate and realize all the essential values of marriage, married people should become ever more deeply aware of the profundity of their vocation and the breadth of their responsibilities. In this spirit and with this awareness let married people seek how they might better be "co-operators with the love of God and Creator and be, so to speak, the interpreters of that love" for the task of procreation and education (GS, II, c. 1, § 50).

1. *Responsible parenthood* (that is, generous and prudent parenthood) is a fundamental requirement of a married couple's true mission. Illumined by faith, the spouses understand the scope of their whole task; helped by divine grace, they try to fulfill it as a true service, carried out in the name of God and Christ, oriented to the temporal and eternal good of men. To save, protect and promote the good of the offspring, and thus of the family community and of human society, the married couple will take care to consider all values and seek to realize them harmoniously in the best way they can, with proper reverence towards each other as persons and according to the concrete circumstances of their life. They will make a judgment in conscience before God about the number of children to have and educate according to the objective criteria indicated by Vatican Council II (GS, II, c. 1, § 50 and c. 5, § 80).

This responsible, generous and prudent parenthood always carries with it new demands. In today's situations, both because of new difficulties and because of new possibilities for the education of children, couples are hardly able to meet such demands unless with generosity and sincere deliberation.

With a view to the education of children, let couples more and more build the community of their whole life on a true and magnanimous love, under the guidance of the spirit of Christ (I Cor. 12, 31-13, 13). For this stable community between man and woman shaped by conjugal love, is the true foundation of human fruitfulness. This community between married people through which an individual finds himself by opening himself to another, constitutes the optimum situation in which children can be educated in an integrated way. Through developing their communion and intimacy in all its aspects, a married couple is able to provide that environment of love, mutual understanding and humble acceptance which is the necessary condition of authentic human education and maturation.

Responsible parenthood—through which married persons intend to observe and cultivate the essential values of matrimony with a view to the good of persons (the good of the child to be educated, of the couples themselves and of the whole of human society)—is one of the conditions and expressions of a true conjugal chastity. For genuine love, rooted in faith, hope and charity, ought to inform the whole life and every action of a couple. By the strength of this chastity the couple tend to the actuation of that true love precisely inasmuch as it is conjugal and fruitful. They accept generously and prudently their task with all its values, combining them in the best way possible according to the particular circumstances of their life and in spite of difficulties.

Married people know well that very often they are invited to abstain, and sometimes not just for a brief time, because of the habitual conditions of their life, for example, the good of one of the spouses (physical or psychic well-being), or because of what are called professional necessities. This abstinence a chaste couple know and accept as a condition of progress into a deeper mutual love, fully conscious that the grace of Christ will sustain and strengthen them for this.

Seeing their vocation in all its depth and breadth and accepting it, the couple follows Christ and tries to imitate Him in a true evangelical spirit (Mt. 5, 1-12). Comforted by the spirit of Christ according to the inner man and rooted in faith and charity (Eph. 3, 16-17), they try to build up a total life community, "bearing with one another charitably, in complete selflessness, gentleness and patience" (Eph. 4, 2-3, cf. Col. 3, 12-17). They will have the peace of Christ in their hearts and give thanks to God the Father as his holy and elected sons.

A couple then is able to ask and expect that they will be helped by all in such a way that they are progressively able to approach more and more responsible parenthood. They need the help of all in order to fulfill their responsibilities with full liberty and in the most favorable material, psychological, cultural and spiritual conditions. By the development of the family, then, the whole society is built up with regard to the good of all men in the whole world.

2. The *regulation of conception* appears necessary for many couples who wish to achieve a responsible, open and reasonable parenthood in today's circumstances. If they are to observe and cultivate all the essential values of marriage, married people need decent and human means for the regulation of conception. They should be able to expect the collaboration of all, especially from men of learning and science, in order that they have at their disposal means agreeable and worthy of man in the fulfilling of his responsible parenthood.

It is proper to man, created in the image of God, to use what is given in physical nature in a way that he may develop it to its full significance with a view to the good of the whole person. This is the cultural mission which the Creator has commissioned to men, whom he had made his co-operators. According to the exigencies of human nature and with the progress of the sciences, men should discover means more and more apt and adequate so that the "ministry which must be fulfilled in a manner which is worthy of man" (GS, II, c. 1, § 51) can be fulfilled by married people.

This intervention of man in physiological processes, an intervention ordained to the essential values of marriage and first of all to the good of children, is to be judged according to the fundamental principles and objective criteria of morality, which will be treated below (in Chap. 4).

"Marriage and conjugal love are by their nature ordained towards the begetting and educating of children" (GS II, c. 1, § 50). A right ordering toward the good of the child within the conjugal and familial community pertains to the essence of human sexuality. Therefore the morality of sexual acts between married people takes its meaning first of all and specifically from the ordering of their actions in a fruitful married life, that is one which is practised with responsible generous and prudent parenthood. It does not then depend upon the direct fecundity of each and every particular act. Moreover, the morality of every marital act depends upon the requirements of mutual love in all its aspects. In a word, the morality of sexual actions is thus to be judged by the true exigencies of the nature of human sexuality, whose meaning is maintained and promoted especially by conjugal chastity, as we have said previously.

More and more clearly, for a conscience correctly formed, a willingness to raise a family with full acceptance of the various human and Christian responsibilities is altogether distinguished from a mentality and way of married life which in its totality is egotistically and irrationally opposed to fruitfulness. This truly "contraceptive" mentality and practice has been condemned by the traditional doctrine of the Church and will always be condemned as gravely sinful.

Chapter III: On the Continuity of Doctrine and Its Deeper Understanding

The tradition of the Church which is concerned with the morality of conjugal relations began with the beginning of the Church. It should be observed, however, that the tradition developed in the argument and conflict with heretics such as the Gnostics, the Manichaeans and later the Cathari, all of whom condemned procreation or the transmission of life as something evil, and nonetheless indulged in moral vices. Consequently this tradition always, albeit with various words, intended to protect two fundamental values: the good of procreation and the rectitude of marital intercourse. Moreover, the Church always taught another truth equally fundamental, although hidden in a mystery, namely original sin. This had wounded man in his various faculties, including sexuality. Man could only be healed of this wound by the grace of a Saviour. This is one of the reasons why Christ took marriage and raised it to a sacrament of the New Law.

It is not surprising that in the course of centuries this tradition was always interpreted in expressions and formulas proper to the times and that the words with which is was expressed and the reasons on which it was based were changed by knowledge which is now obsolete. Nor was there maintained always a right equilibrium of all the elements. Some authors even used expressions which depreciated the matrimonial state. But what is of real importance is that the same values were again and again reaffirmed. Consequently, an egotistical, hedonistic and contraceptive way which turns the practice of married life in an arbitrary fashion from its ordination to a human, generous and prudent fecundity is always against the nature of man and can never be justified.

The large amount of knowledge and facts which throw light on today's world suggest that it is not to contradict the genuine sense of this tradition and the purpose of the previous doctrinal condemnations if we speak of the regulation of conception by using means, human and decent, ordered to favoring fecundity in the totality of married life and toward the realization of the authentic values of a fruitful matrimonial community.

The reasons in favor of this affirmation are of several kinds: social changes in matrimony and the family, especially in the role of the woman; lowering of the infant mortality rate; new bodies of knowledge in biology, psychology, sexuality and demography; a changed estimation of the value and meaning of human sexuality and of conjugal relations; most of all, a better grasp of the duty of man to humanize and to bring to greater perfection for the life of man what is given in nature. Then must be considered the sense of the faithful: according to it, condemnation of a couple to a long and often heroic abstinence as the means to regulate conception, cannot be founded on the truth.

A further step in the doctrinal evolution, which it seems now should be developed, is founded less on these facts than on a better, deeper and more correct understanding of conjugal life and of the conjugal act when these other changes occur. The doctrine on marriage and its essential values remains the same and whole, but it is now applied differently out of a deeper understanding.

This maturation has been prepared and has already begun. The magisterium itself is in evolution. Leo XIII spoke less explicitly in his encyclical *Arcanum* than did Pius XI in his wonderful doctrinal synthesis of *Casti Connubii* of 1930 which gave a fresh start to so many beginnings in a living conjugal spirituality. He proclaimed, using the very words of the Roman Catechism, the importance, in a true sense the primary importance, of true conjugal love for the community of matrimony. The notion of responsible parenthood which is implied in the notion of a prudent and generous regulation of conception advanced in Vatican Council II, had already been prepared by Pius XII. The acceptance of a lawful application of the calculated sterile periods of the woman—that the application is legitimate presupposes right motives—makes a separation between the sexual act which is explicitly intended and its reproductive effect which is intentionally excluded.

The tradition has always rejected seeking this separation with a contraceptive intention for motives spoiled by egoism and hedonism, and such seeking can never be admitted. The true opposition is not sought between some material conformity to the physiological processes of nature and some artificial intervention. For it is natural to man to put under human control what is given by physical nature. The opposition is really to be sought between one way of acting which is contraceptive and opposed to a prudent and generous fruitfulness, and another way which is in an ordered relationship to responsible fruitfulness and which has a concern for education and all the essential, human and Christian values.

In such a conception the substance of tradition stands in continuity and is respected. The new elements which today are discerned in tradition under the influence of new knowledge and facts were found in it before; they were undifferentiated but not denied; so that the problem in today's terms is new and has not been proposed before in this way. In light of the new data these elements are being explained and made more precise. The moral obligation of following fundamental norms and fostering all the essential values in a balanced fashion is strengthened not weakened. The virtue of chastity by which a couple positively regulates the practice of sexual relations is all the more demanded. The criteria of morality, therefore, which are human and Christian, demand and at the same time foster a spirituality which is more profound in married life, with faith, hope and charity informed according to the spirit of the Gospel.

Chapter IV: The Objective Criterion of Morality

The question comes up which many men rightly think to be of great importance, at least practically: what are the objective criteria by which to choose a method of reconciling the needs of marital life with a right ordering of this life to fruitfulness in the procreation and education of offspring?

It is obvious that the method is not to be left to purely arbitrary decision.

1. In resolving the similar problem of responsible parenthood and the appropriate determination of the size of the family, Vatican Council II has shown the way. The objective criteria are the various values and needs duly and harmoniously evaluated. These objective criteria are to be applied by the couples, acting from a rightly formed conscience and according to their concrete situation. In the words of the Council: "Thus they will fulfill their task with human and Christian responsibility. With docile reverence towards God, they will come to the right decision by common counsel and effort. They will thoughtfully take into account both their own welfare and that of their children, those already born and those which may be foreseen. For this accounting they will reckon with both the material and spiritual conditions of the times as well as of their state in life. Finally they will consult the interests of the family community, of temporal society, and of the Church herself. . . . But in their manner of acting, spouses should be aware that they cannot proceed arbitrarily. They must always be governed according to a conscience dutifully conformed to the Divine Law itself, and should be submissive toward the Church's teaching office, which authentically interprets that law in the light of the gospel" (GS II, c. 1 § 50; cf. c. 5, § 87).

In other questions of conjugal life, one should proceed in the same way. There are various objective criteria which are concretely applied by couples themselves acting with a rightly formed conscience. All, for example, know that the objective criteria prohibit that the intimate acts of conjugal life, even if carried out in a way which could be called "natural," be practiced if there is a loss of physical or psychic health or if there is neglect of the personal dignity of the spouses or if they are carried out in an egotistic or hedonistic way. These objective criteria are the couples', to be applied by them to their concrete situation, avoiding pure arbitrariness in forming their judgment. It is impossible to determine exhaustively by a general judgment and ahead of time for each individual case what these objective criteria will demand in the concrete situation of a couple.

2. Likewise, there are objective criteria as to the means to be chosen for responsibly determining the size of the family: if they are rightly applied, the couples themselves will find and determine the way of proceeding.

In grave language, Vatican Council II has reaffirmed that abortion is altogether to be excluded from the means of responsibly preventing birth. Indeed, abortion is not a method of preventing conception but of eliminating offspring already conceived. This affirmation about acts which do not spare an offspring already conceived is to be repeated in regard to those interventions as to which there is serious grounds to suspect that they are abortive.

Sterilization, since it is a drastic and irreversible intervention in a matter of great importance, is generally to be excluded as a means of reponsibly avoiding conception.

Moreover, the natural law and reason illuminated by Christian faith dictate that a couple proceed in choosing means not arbitrarily but according to objective criteria. These objective criteria for the right choice of methods are the conditions for keeping and fostering the essential values of marriage as a community of fruitful love. If these criteria are observed, then a right ordering of the human act according to its object, end and circumstances is maintained.

Among these criteria, this must be put first: the action must correspond to the nature of the person and of his acts so that the whole meaning of the mutual giving and of human procreation is kept in a context of true love (cf. GS, II, c. 1, § 51). *Secondly,* the means which are chosen should have effectiveness proportionate to the degree of right or necessity of averting a new conception temporarily or permanently. *Thirdly,* every method of preventing conception—not excluding either periodic or absolute abstinence—carries with it some negative element of physical evil which the couple more or less seriously feels. This negative element or physical evil can arise under different aspects: account must be taken of the biological, hygienic and psychological aspects, and personal dignity of the spouses, and the possibility of expressing sufficiently and aptly the interpersonal relation or conjugal love. The means to be chosen, where several are possible, is that which carries with it the least possible negative element, according to the concrete situation of the couple. *Fourthly,* then, in choosing concretely among means, much depends on what means may be available in a certain region or at a certain time or for a certain couple; and this may depend on the economic situation.

Therefore not arbitrarily, but as the law of nature and of God commands, let couples form a judgment which is objectively founded, with all the criteria considered. This they may do without major difficulty, and with peace of mind, if they take common and prudent counsel before God. They should, however, to the extent possible, be instructed about the criteria by competent persons and be educated as to the right application of the criteria. Well instructed and prudently educated as Christians, they will prudently and serenely decide what is truly for the good of the couple and of the children, and does not neglect their own personal Christian perfection, and is, therefore, what God revealing himself through the natural law and Christian revelation, sets before them to do.

PART II: PASTORAL NECESSITIES
Chapter I: The Task and Fundamental Conditions of Educational Renewal

Sometimes when a new aspect of human life obtains a special place in the area of man's responsibility, a task of educational renewal is imposed in a seriously binding way.

In order that spouses may take up the duty of responsible parenthood, they must grasp, more than in the past, the meaning of fruitfulness and experience a desire for it. In order that they may give to married life its unitive value, and do so in service of its procreative function, they must develop an increasingly purer respect for their mutual needs, the sense of community and the acceptance of their common Christian vocation.

It will not be a surprise that this conviction of a greater responsibility will come about as the effect and crown of a gradual development of the meaning of marriage and conjugal spirituality. For several generations, in an always increasing number, couples have sought to live their proper married vocation in a more profound and more conscientious way. The doctrine of the magisterium and especially the encyclical *Casti Connubii* notably contributed and strengthened this formation of conscience by giving to it its full meaning.

The more urgent the appeal is made to observe mutual love and charity in every expression of married life, the more urgent is the necessity of forming consciences, of educating spouses to a sense of responsibility and of awakening a right sense of values. This new step in the development of conjugal life cannot bear all its fruits, unless it is accompanied by an immense educational activity. No one will regret that these new demands stirred by the Holy Spirit call the entire human race to this profound moral maturity.

Couples who might think they find in the doctrine, as it has just been proposed, an open door to laxism or easy solutions make a grave mistake, of which they will be the first victims. The conscientious decision to be made by spouses about the number of children is not a matter of small importance. On the contrary, it imposes a more conscientious fulfilling of their vocation to fruitfulness in the consideration of a whole complex of values which are involved here. The same is true of the responsibility of the spouses for the development of their common life in such a way that it will be a source of continual progress and perfection.

The God who created male and female, in order that they might be two in one flesh, in order that they might bring the world under their control, in order that they might increase and multiply (Gen. 1-2), is the God who has elevated their union to the dignity of a sacrament and so disposed that in this world it is a special sign of His own love for His people. He Himself will gird the spouses with His strength, His light, His love and His joy in the strength of the spirit of Christ. Who then would doubt that couples, all couples, will not be able to respond to the demands of their vocation?

Chapter II: Further Consideration;
Application of the Doctrine of Matrimony to Different Parts of the World

1. It seems very necessary to establish some pontifical institute or secretariat for the study of the sciences connected with married life. In this commission there could be continual collaboration in open dialogue among experts competent in various areas. The aim of this institute (or secretariat) would be, among other duties, to carry further the research and reflection begun by the commission. The various studies which the commission has already done could be made public. It would be in a special way for this institute to study how the doctrine of matrimony should be applied to different parts of the world and to contribute to the formation of priests and married couples dedicated to the family apostolate by sending experts to them (cf. GS II, c. 1, § 52).

2. Universal principles and the essential values of matrimony and married life

become actual in ways which partially differ according to different cultures and different mentalities. Consequently there is a special task for episcopal conferences to institute organizations for investigation and dialogue between families, between representatives of the different sciences and pastors of souls. They would also have the task of judging which may be in practice the more apt pastoral means in each region to promote the health formation of consciences and education to a sense of responsibility.

Episcopal conferences should be particularly concerned that priests and married lay persons be adequately formed in a more spiritual and moral understanding of Christian matrimony. Thus they will be prepared to extend pastoral action to the renewal of families in the spirit of "aggiornamento" initiated by the constitution on the church in the modern world.

Under their guidance there should also be action to start in each region the genuine fostering of all families in a context of social evolution which should be truly human. The fostering of the role of woman is of special importance here.

There are many reforms and initiatives which are needed to open the way to decent and joyful living for all families. Together with all men of goodwill, Christians must approach this great work of human development, without which the elevation of families can never become actual. Christianity does not teach some ideal for a small number of elect, but the vocation of all to the essential values of human life. It cannot be that anyone would wish to elevate his own family without at the same time actively dedicating himself to opening a way for similar elevation for all families in all parts of the world.

Chapter III: Demographic Fact and Policy

The increase of inhabitants cannot in any way be said to be something evil or calamitous for the human race. As children are "the most excellent gift of matrimony" (GS II, c. 1, § 50) and the object of the loving care of the parents, which demands from them many sacrifices, so the great number of men pertaining to a certain nation and constituting the whole human race spread over the globe is the foundation of all social sharing and cultural progress. Thus there should be afforded to it all those things which according to social justice are due to men as persons.

The church is not ignorant of the immense difficulties and profound transformations which have arisen from the conditions of contemporary life throughout the world and especially in certain regions where there has been a rapid rise in population. That is why she again and again raises her voice to urge various nations and the whole human family to help one another in truly human progress, united in true solidarity and excluding every intention of domination. Then they might avoid all those things both in the political and in the social order which restrict or dissipate in an egotistical way the full utilization of the goods of the earth which are destined for all men.

The church, by her doctrine and by her supernatural aids, intends to help all families so that they might find the right way in undertaking their generous and prudent responsibility. Governments which have the care of the common good should look with great concern on subhuman conditions of families and "beware of solutions contradicting the moral law, solutions which have been promoted publicly or privately, and sometimes actually imposed" (Constitution on the Church in the Modern World, II, c. 5, § 87). These solutions have contradicted the moral law in particular by propagating abortion or sterilization. Political demography can be called human only if the rights of parents with regard to the procreation and education of children are respected and conditions of life are fostered with all vigor so that parents are enabled to exercise their responsibilities before God and society.

Chapter IV: The Inauguration and Further Development
of Means for Education of Couples and Youth

1. Couples are burdened by multiple responsibilities throughout the whole of life; they seek light and aid. With the favor of God there will develop in many regions what has already been initated often by the married couples themselves, to sustain families in their building and continual development.

Maximum help is to be given to parents in their educational task. They strongly desire to provide the best for their children. The more parents are conscious of their office of fruitfulness, which is extended over the whole time in which the education of their children is accomplished, so much the more do they seek a way of acquiring better preparation to carry out this responsibility. Moreover, in exercising this educational office, the spouses mature more deeply in it themselves, create a unity, become rich in love and apply themselves with the high task of giving themselves with united energies to the high task of giving life and education.

2. The building up of the conjugal and family community does not happen without thought. Therefore it is fitting everywhere to set up and work out many better means of remote and immediate preparation of youth for marriage. This requires the collaboration of everyone. Married people who are already well educated will have a great and indispensable part in this work. In these tasks of providing help to spouses and to the young who are preparing to build and develop a conjugal and family community, priests and religious will cooperate closely with the families. Without this cooperation, in which each one has his own indispensable part, there will never be apt methods of education to those responsibilities of the vocation which places the sacrament in clear light so that its full and profound meaning shines forth.

The church, which holds the deposit of the Gospel, has to bring this noble message to all men in the entire world. This announcing of the Gospel, grounded in love, illumines every aspect of married and family life. Every aspect, every task and responsibility of the conjugal and family community shines with a clear light, in love toward one's neighbor—a love which is rich with human values and is formed by the divine interpersonal love of Father, Son and Holy Spirit. May the spirit of Christ's love more and more penetrate families everywhere so that together with John, the beloved disciple of Jesus, married couples, parents and children may always understand more deeply the wonderful relation between love of God and love of one another (1 John 4, 7-5, 4).

The Tablet
April 22, 1967

Pastoral Approaches

Appendix C

Today, as throughout the course of her history, the church wishes to remain the institution divinely established to lead men to their salvation in Jesus Christ, through the different states of life to which they have been called. Of these, marriage is the one to which the greater part of mankind is destined, and in which it lives. It is the church's task to defend and promote the holiness of this state in fidelity to the principles of the Gospel.

No one can be ignorant of the guidance she has lavished on all, emphasizing the greatness of the institution of marriage which is, on earth, a sign of that other fruitful union sealed on the cross between Christ and the church (cf. Ephesians 5:25-32). No one can fail to be aware of her efforts to make this doctrine inform her way of life, efforts which give rise to institutions appropriate to the needs of the times, so as to help humanity toward the evangelical ideal of the Christian family.

Without going back beyond more recent times, we can recall that Leo XIII, anxious to demonstrate the Christian teaching to the modern world in a positive way, published his encyclical on marriage, *Arcanum*. A few decades later, faced with a world in which the stability and unity of the family were being threatened by various forms of legislation, in which formerly prosperous nations seemed to be losing their grip and sliding toward death, Pius XI forcefully recalled the great benefits of marriage understood in a Christian way: children, conjugal fidelity, the holiness of the sacrament.

Pius XII not only upheld the whole of this teaching, particularly during the war years which caused such suffering to families, frequently endangering their very existence, but in certain documents he showed the deepening of the doctrine that had come about in the meantime and clarified the various ends of the marriage union.

A New Situation

All this teaching, it must be stressed with joy, has, in many countries, produced lay and Christian family movements which have contributed very powerfully to a deeper understanding of marriage and the demands of the marriage union. It has also stimulated pastors and laymen, theologians, doctors and psychologists to undertake a more rigorous investigation of the conditions and difficulties involved in a more exact and generous observance of the laws that must govern the family and of the meaning and value of human sexuality. At the same time, the conscience of married couples has been faced with a different situation: no longer the threat of

259

nations slowly disappearing through a lack of generosity toward life, but the difficulties provided both by the accelerated pace of human development and by other important factors, such as people's increased mobility in search of work to support themselves, the massive concentration of populations in towns where the living space vital to families is more strictly limited or, finally, the social advancement of women.

It was this development of reflection and of experience of family life lived most generously by an ever-increasing number of Christian couples, and also livelier appreciation of the dignity of the human person, of the sense of his free and personal responsibility for carrying out God's plan for humanity, that led the Fathers of the Council to reaffirm strongly the stability and holiness of the family institution, based on the God-willed love of two people for each other, two peope who have decided to become one flesh for the sake of the life-work ordained for them and entrusted to them by the Creator—the exercise of a joint, responsible and generous parenthood.

Through all these teachings and all this rich experience of the faithful, the church remains faithfully attached to the divine imperatives of the unity, stability and fecundity of marriage: "Be faithful, multiply and fill the earth" (Genesis 1:28; 9:1); "they shall be two in one flesh" (Matthew 19:6). She remains attached also to other related commandments: the solemn task of bringing up children (cf. Ephesians 6:4), (Timothy 2:15) and man's urge to dominate creation according to God's plan (cf. Genesis 2:24).

Responsibilities of Marriage

So faithful believers, nourished by the Holy Spirit (cf. *Lumen Gentium* § 12), have been led to find all the riches of the church's teaching, and all its implications, in the experience of their married life. They have come to realize that human acts are charged with multiple responsibilities; the *magisterium* listens to the expression of these, clarifies it, controls it and authenticates it, so that it can bear it in mind when pronouncing on the morality of these acts. Today's needs invite us to give particular emphasis to this aspect. Today, thanks to the progress made in reflection on the subject, and without in any way detracting from the importance of procreation, which, allied to true love, is one of the ends of marriage, we have a clearer view of the multiple responsibilities of married couples: towards each other, first, so that they can live a love that leads them to unity; towards their children, whose development and education—more and more demanding—they must assure; then towards the institution of marriage, whose stability (cf. I Cor. 7:10-11) and unity they are to maintain through the quality of their love and respect for each other's dignity (cf. I Pet. 3:1-7); and finally towards society, since the family is its basic unit.

All this creates a complex of obligations which, far from eliminating duties, invites one to take account of them so that they can all be undertaken together as far as is humanly possible, with due respect for their hierarchy and relative importance. So the church, particularly through the teaching of Pius XII, has come to realize more fully that marriage has another meaning and another end besides that of procreation alone, even though it remains wholly and definitely ordered to procreation, though not always immediately.

What has been condemned in the past and remains so today is the unjustified refusal of life, arbitrary human intervention for the sake of moments of egotistic pleasure; in short, the rejection of procreation as a specific task of marriage. In the past, the church could not speak other than she did, because the problem of birth control did not confront human consciousness in the same way. Today, having clearly recognized the legitimacy and even the duty of regulating births, she recognizes too that human intervention in the process of the marriage act for reasons drawn from the finality of marriage itself should not always be excluded, provided that the criteria of morality are always safeguarded.

If an arbitrarily contraceptive mentality is to be condemned, as has always been the church's view, an intervention to regulate conception in a spirit of true, reasonable and generous charity (cf. Matt. 7:12; John 13:34-5; 15:12-17; Rom. 13:8-10) does not deserve to be, because if it were, other goods of marriage might be endangered. So what is always to be condemned is not the regulation of conception, but an egotistic married life, refusing a creative opening-out of the family circle, and so refusing a truly human—and therefore truly Christian—married love. This is the anti-conception that is against the Christian ideal of marriage.

As for the means that husband and wife can legitimately employ, it is their task to decide these together, without drifting into arbitrary decisions, but always taking account of the objective criteria of morality. These criteria are in the first place those that relate to the totality of married life and sexuality.

Sexuality in marriage must be a unifying force. Husband and wife have to solder their community more and more strongly together, as this engages them as complete people.

This community is entirely creative; furthermore, it is in the tasks they undertake together, and particularly in bringing children into the world and educating them, that husband and wife together come to effect that deep exchange and communion of love that belong to the state of marriage.

Love and Control

The act of love, like all expressions of intimacy between them, needs to be humanized, progressively refined. The physical expressions of love will enrich their love for each other, but it will grow through abstention too, when this better fits the wishes or needs of one or the other.

Continence is one of the indispensable forms of married love. If it is freely accepted, it will help to prevent intimate life together from becoming stale, and help to protect its quality and meaning. There is an ascesis in this, whose rule, at once supple and very demanding, will be the human quality and growth of their love.

So the means chosen should be suitable for exercising a healthy and responsible parenthood, in the light of certain guiding principles: beside being effective, they should have regard for the health of the parents and their eventual offspring; they should not violate respect for the personal dignity of either husband or wife, who must never be treated as objects—this applies to women, who are still kept in a state unworthy of them in many countries, as much as to men; they should pay attention to any possible psychic consequences they might entail, depending on the person and circumstances; and finally they should not hinder the power of expression of an increasingly close union between two persons.

None of this in any way implies that it can be legitimate for anyone to attack already existing human life, even in the first moments of its existence. The church has always condemned abortion as a particularly vile form of murder in that it destroys a helpless and innocent human being.

This renewed formulation of conjugal morality might lead some people to believe that they have been wrong to act as they did in the past, since the rules to which they submitted faithfully have now had to evolve. This immediate reaction, however understandable, would not be correct since the views we hold now are not a turning back on traditional values but a deepening of them. And this new stage is only possible today thanks to the sacrifices and faithfulness of those who have gone before us. If the church seems to them to have taken a long time to express what she thinks now, to act on this deepening of values and on the factors that our age has produced for her to reflect on, they should recognize that because of the importance of the subject in question, the church owed it to her children not to make a pronouncement except with extreme and wise caution. And let not legitimate modifications be taken as casting doubt on the meaning and value of different attitudes in the past. It will always remain true that for Christians procreation confers the dignity of cooperating with God the creator, and that children will always be a great good and a joyful responsibility: husbands and wives will only be convinced that they should deprive themselves of them with the greatest sorrow.

The whole of this developed doctrine can only appear to those who reflect on it as an enrichment, in full continuity with the deep, but more rigorous, moral orientations of the past. Its proclamation in a renewed formulation is not giving way in any sense to laxity. It is not an invitation to the faithful to let themselves go on a quest for exclusively selfish pleasure; on the contrary, it is an invitation calling married couples to a truer, more complete love, in which each should be able to forget himself, or herself, to go out to meet the other, so that together they find a joint will to responsible and generous parenthood. The church is calling them to a deeper understanding of their love, to a more conscious self-mastery in the service of the life ministry that God has entrusted to them.

The church knows from experience how difficult it is for human beings, wounded as they are by sin, to love truly. She knows that selfishness watches from deep inside them, spying on the impulse to love which God, who is Love (I John 4:8-16), has placed in mankind, created in his image. But she also knows that Christ is present in the People of God through his Spirit, particularly in the sacraments which the church dispenses.

She also knows that any just point of view, like any indisputable right, can lead to abuses on the part of those who start from bad intentions. This is why she is convinced that only an enlightened and thorough process of education can instill the Christian ideal of the family into men's minds. So she invites all her children to promote an immense effort to form men's minds and hearts, so as to allow everyone to discipline the God-given force of sexuality so that it will serve in the accomplishment of his life's work. Those intending to marry should also receive a clearer, more delicate and more generous preparation for their family vocation; and, finally, those already married should be helped to overcome their difficulties, to live in a harmony of love, service to each other and to the children they have called into life. Obviously, looking back at those Christian families who have already contributed so much to a better understanding of the family, the church must make a special appeal to them still to intensify this educational effort.

Priests and married couples are called to a close collaboration in this education in responsibilty and all the values of marriage. Through this collaboration, in a climate of respect for the specific tasks and gifts of each, mutual knowledge and respect will grow.

The church also knows that frequently the generous will of parents comes up against difficulties of a physical, psychological or material nature. So she must invite all those who work in professions devoted to the improvement of physical or mental health to participate in this work of helping young people and married couples. And she must also renew her insistent and repeated appeals for more generous mutual aid and more equitable social and economic justice, not only among members of the same nation but also between nations, to make excessive differences in living conditions disappear as soon as possible, so that all families can develop, not of course in wealth, but in the relative well-being that virtue requires.

So, in response to the questioning of her children, and beyond them, of the whole world, this is the beautiful but demanding teaching worthy of a humanity redeemed by the blood of Christ, all of whose members are called on to form the family of God, that the church proposes to the people of today. Through this teaching, today as in the past, the church, protected from error in proclaiming the values whose essence has been confided to her through the word of her well-beloved Head, wishes to promote the Christian advancement of the family.

The Tablet
September 21, 1968